TO SING

IN ENGLISH

TO SING

IN ENGLISH

A GUIDE TO IMPROVED DICTION

Dorothy Uris

BOOSEY AND HAWKES · NEW YORK AND LONDON · 1971

III

Library of Congress Number: 79-17264
© Copyright 1971 by Boosey & Hawkes, Inc.

IV

To Lotte Leonard

THE MANY TO THANK

It all began with Lotte Leonard, fine teacher, superb artist, and endearing woman to whom this work is dedicated. Dismayed by her pupils' delivery in English, she sought my advice as speech consultant, baiting the trap by inviting me *just* to listen. This I did and discovered the not uncommon phenomenon of well-trained American voices singing a puzzling mixture of mannerisms and localisms. "What's going on?" I asked. Madame Leonard replied firmly, "You tell me!"

And so I've been at it ever since—researching, proselytizing, writing, and teaching speech and diction for singers at the Mannes College of Music and the Manhattan School of Music, coaching for opera companies including the Metropolitan and the Santa Fe, and working privately with many singers.

Though more often like an obstacle race, teaching sung English has brought many joys. It has expanded the scope of my life's work by adding music to what had been until then merely words. To correct a lisp gladdens a therapist's heart while to improve diction in song enchants her ear as well.

Now to do the impossible and single out a few of the many to whom I owe so much. It was Donald Engle's enthusiasm as director of the Rockefeller Fund for Music that made research possible for the book and therefore the book itself. In the manuscript's preparation first Hilda Fuhrman and later Claire Kire rendered immeasurable assistance as did Arnold Freed who readied the copious song materials for publication.

My students were the guinea pigs in the laboratory of my classrooms where much of TO SING IN ENGLISH was tested before it was finally recorded here. If I managed to convey, perhaps even to quicken in these young voice majors, a passion for our magnificent and musical language, then some portion of the debt their teacher owes has been repaid. One of them wrote me recently, "There is something so beautiful in being able to communicate with familiar sounds."

Last, but always to be remembered, are six gifted former pupils, singers, and an accompanist who were all music research assistants on the book at different times: Gwendolin Sims, Joan Lindstrom, Maryanne King, Linda Poston Smith, Barbara Railo, and Mara Waldman. When one of them would leave to pursue graduate study or a career, another would step in until this final song excerpt, paraphrased from Charles Ives, was inserted at the end of the last page.

to   live   and   SING! _____

In English, of course,

DOROTHY URIS

ILLUSTRATIONS

ACKNOWLEDGMENTS

I am grateful to the following composers and publishers for permission to reprint excerpts from their copyrighted works:

BARAB, SEYMOUR

Songs of Perfect Propriety. Copyright 1959 by Boosey & Hawkes, Inc.

BARBER, SAMUEL

from *Collected Songs:*
"I Hear an Army." Copyright 1939 by G. Schirmer, Inc. "Rain Has Fallen." Copyright 1939 by G. Schirmer, Inc. "The Daisies." Copyright 1936, 1942 by G. Schirmer, Inc. "Nocturne," Copyright 1941 by G. Schirmer, Inc. "A Nun Takes the Veil." Copyright 1941 by G. Schirmer, Inc. "Sure on this Shining Night." Copyright 1941 by G. Schirmer, Inc. "St. Ita's Vision." Copyright 1954 by G. Schirmer, Inc.
from *Vanessa:* "Must the Winter Come so Soon?" © Copyright 1958 by G. Schirmer, Inc.
Knoxville, Summer of 1915. Copyright 1949 by G. Schirmer, Inc.

BERG, ALBAN

from *Wozzeck:* "Why Hangs Your Fine Black Hair." Copyright 1926 by Universal Edition. English translation Copyright 1955 by Alfred A. Kalmus.

BERNSTEIN, LEONARD

from *West Side Story:* "I Feel Pretty" and "Maria." © 1957 by Leonard Bernstein and Stephen Sondheim.

BLITZSTEIN, MARC

Regina. Copyright 1953, 1954 by Marc Blitzstein. Used by permission of Chappell & Co., Ltd.

BRITTEN, BENJAMIN

from *A Ceremony of Carols:* "In Freezing Winter Night." Copyright 1943 by Boosey & Co., Ltd. Renewed 1970.
from *Peter Grimes:* "Peter's Dream." Copyright 1945 by Boosey & Hawkes, Ltd.
Rape of Lucretia. Copyright 1946 by Boosey & Hawkes, Ltd.
The Turn of the Screw. Copyright 1955 by Hawkes & Son (London) Ltd.
War Requiem. Copyright 1962 by Boosey & Hawkes Music Publishers, Ltd.

COPLAND, AARON

from *Twelve Poems of Emily Dickinson:* "Going To Heaven!," "Sleep Is Supposed To Be," "When They Come Back," and "Dear March, Come in." Copyright 1951 by Aaron Copland. Sole Publisher: Boosey & Hawkes, Inc.

DELLO JOIO, NORMAN

from *Three Songs of Adieu:* "Farewell." Copyright 1962 by Edward B. Marks Music Corporation.
A Christmas Carol. © Copyright 1962 by Edward B. Marks Music Corporation.

D'HARDELOT, GUY

Because. Copyright 1902 by Chappell & Co., Ltd.

DOUGHERTY, CELIUS

Listen! The Wind. Copyright 1958 by Boosey & Hawkes, Inc.

FLAGELLO, NICOLAS

Softly Sweet in Lydian Measures. "By permission of the composer, Nicolas Flagello."

FLOYD, CARLISLE

Susannah. © Copyright 1957 by Boosey & Hawkes, Inc.

FREED, ARNOLD

Sea Change. "By permission of the composer, Arnold Freed."

HAGEMAN, RICHARD

When I Am Dead, My Dearest. Copyright 1940 by Galaxy Music Corporation.

HINDEMITH, PAUL

To Music, To Becalm His Fever. © Copyright 1946 by B. Schott's Söhne, Mainz, Germany.
The Wild Flowers Song. © Copyright 1945 by B. Schott's Söhne, Mainz, Germany.

HOIBY, LEE

The Tides of Sleep. © Copyright 1967 by Boosey & Hawkes, Inc.

HOVANESS, ALAN

from *New Vistas in Song:* "O Lady Moon." © Copyright 1964 by Edward B. Marks Music Corporation.

IVES, CHARLES

from *Sacred Songs, 1958* and *Thirteen Songs:* "Abide With Me." © Copyright 1958 by Peer International Corporation.
from *Fourteen Songs:* "Eyes So Dark." Copyright 1955 Peer International Corporation.
from *Ten Songs:* "Memories." Copyright 1953 by Peer International Corporation.
Walking. Copyright 1939 by Arrow Music Press, Inc. Renewed 1967. Copyright and Renewal Assigned to Associated Music Publishers, Inc., New York.

CONTENTS

/ē/	[i]	b*eat*	84	/ûr/	[ɝ]	b*ir*d	120
/ĭ/	[ɪ]	b*i*t	87	/ər/	[ə]	b*other*	124
/ā/	[eɪ]	b*ai*t	90	/ōō/	[u]	f*oo*l	128
/ĕ/	[ɛ]	b*e*t	94	/ū/	[ju]	f*ue*l	128
/ă/	[æ]	b*a*t	99	/o̽o̽/	[ʊ]	f*u*ll	134
/ī/	[aɪ]	b*i*te	103	/ō/	[oʊ]	f*oa*l	138
/ä/	[a]	b*ar*d	107	/ô/	[ɔ]	f*a*ll	142
/ŭ/	[ʌ]	b*u*tt	110	/oi/	[ɔɪ]	f*oi*l	145
/ə/	[ə]	*a*bout	113	/ou/	[aʊ]	f*ou*l	148

CHAPTER SIX. INVITATION TO A DICTION CLASS, 261

APPENDICES

TO SING

IN ENGLISH

Foreword
(and backward)

"...Like so many foreign-born singers and unlike so many American ones, he set an example of clear diction that was almost startling in its purity...." "...Between excessive volume in the orchestra and slip-shod diction on the stage — at least the action made sense if the words did not...." "...He sings English with uncommon clarity and makes it sound like the language as it is spoken...." "...Taking the cast as a whole, perhaps two words in ten could be understood...." "...Her group of American songs could scarcely have had a more persuasive interpreter — her enunciation was impeccable..." "...Miss X might have been singing in the original Russian — somebody should start giving courses in enunciation; otherwise why bother with translations...?" "...Since this music was written against the word, the conductor could hardly help obscuring the text...." "...To achieve a complete fusion of word and music he sings through the bar line and into the phrase. The words and musical meaning and not the bar, condition his singing...."

From this sampling of typical reviews, it appears certain that the performance of sung English is uneven at best. Too often sadly inadequate diction deprives the many devotees of vocal music of the meaning within the English texts which they have come to hear.

The following observations have been gathered during the years of playing a double role as teacher and defender of the faith in the language. Teaching English as a communicative force in song has entailed constant wrestling with obstacles encountered in schools, colleges, and professional companies. These obstacles continue to thwart the development of well-sung English as part of American musical culture.

THE SILENT ESTABLISHMENT

Opera inevitably steals the limelight as the most prominent and glamorous form of vocal music. But resplendent productions that enchant the eye and ear expose lackluster diction in all languages of the repertoire. The leading opera companies entrenched in a few major cities, catering as they do to international stars who spell box office, seldom perform works in English. In the occasional native or translated work, the English diction remains somewhat below the conservatory level (with some wonderful exceptions). The average translation may provoke more criticism than lyricism, but why blame the underpaid librettist while huge sums are lavished on sets?

Little responsibility is assumed by the higher echelons for fostering high goals in diction. On the contrary, the powers-that-be deny their role as leaders. They insist it would be an insult to suggest to an artist that his lines for an English role need sharpening! Should we assume that the outraged star at Lincoln Center would go on strike, stalk out of the Met, and head across the river to the Brooklyn Academy of Music? No conscientious artist would refuse to bolster his role *if* standards were set at the top (as they are in other countries). Indeed, foreign stars who gratefully accept such help often turn out to be the only intelligible ones in the cast, as the critics note the following morning.

In the smaller cities the resident opera companies who perform more frequently in English* still lack diction of prestige quality and

*In major opera companies in the United States and Canada, in the 1968-69 season, 9 out of 29 productions were presented in English. In professional and semi-professional companies, 55 out of 84 productions (including concert versions) were in English; in summer festivals, 14 out of 24. As to the prolific college opera workshops, the Central Opera Service reports a considerable portion of yearly programs devoted to English performance. Two outstanding examples are the University of Texas Opera Workshop, in Austin, directed by Walter Ducloux, and the Eastman School in Rochester.

4

exert little influence. Summer opera organizations that mount lively and more avant-garde productions can spend little time on improving pronunciation in the few weeks' rehearsal time allotted each presentation. Those performers who already have lucid enunciation stand out, while others continue to lag behind. And so national standards of sung English are little affected.*

Opera workshops in the college music departments, where works in English, translated or original, are a regular feature, proliferate throughout the country. Still we find English diction usually taught in a package along with Italian, French, and German — all in two semesters.

PASSIVE AUDIENCES AND PERMISSIVE CRITICS

American audiences appear to take for granted that the pleasing sounds directed toward them in operas, recitals, and oratorios need convey little meaning. Apparently, non-communication in English has become accepted as a permanent national disability.

Patrons of the musical theater would make for the exits were stage performers to assail them with distorted vowels, gaps for consonants, and scrambled word rhythms. A flick of the switch would silence such performance on television.

The reviewers, in judging sung English have seemingly arrived at a formula: 75% clarity receives general praise, 40% no comment, and 10% infrequent scolding. These critical percentages, though convenient perhaps, do not stimulate the raising of standards so urgently needed. Besides, critical disapproval most often lands on the performer, rarely on those in authority who, at the very least, should share the blame.

TATTERED CONCEPTS

The unsingability of English. What other tongue which great poesy and music have found supreme expression requires such constant defense! One can understand the foreigner's resistance to a second language and culture. But what about the inverted snobbism of natives steeped in the same old-world tradition? For these, "Ich liebe dich" is rhapsodic, but "I love you" strictly pedestrian! People are moved to tears when

*The weak status of sung English generally should be viewed in the light of the financial insecurity besetting the whole field of vocal music. These dollar doldrums restrict entrepreneurs, creators (composers, set designers, etc.), and educators, who must depend on erratic subsidy by private donors and foundations since substantial government support seems remote. Funds that have to be dispensed so frugally leave precious little for the study of diction.

Manon bids adieu to her "petite table," but "goodbye, my little table" causes the opera buff acute anguish. Upon such nonsense do myths flourish.

The world role of the United States in the past half century has strengthened the position of American English. Its cultural force in literature, music, and the arts parallels this role with continuing impact — a development apparently overlooked by esthetic judgments impaled upon the past. If the art of song in its varied forms is to expand, or even survive, we may be certain that it will move forward with English as an internationally sung language.

The stigma of impurity. The "pure" vowel has become part of the dogma of the singing profession. It is claimed that English vowels (somewhat like original sin) are naturally impure, and that foreign substitutes must take their place. We need a new affirmative definition of purity: a vowel (*even* a diphthong) faithfully and resonantly reproduced in the country of its origin.

Ugly sounds. Singers can handle the derogated diphthongs naturally enough when not confused by the outworn theory of two-vowel execution. The detractors of sung English also focus on two simple vowels and one consonant. The *a* in *cat*, dubbed "the bad vowel," is second in disrepute only to "the dull vowel" in *love*. As for the *r*, it appears that this consonant when unflipped and untrilled is reserved mainly for folk singers.

A moribund diction. *Pronunciation for Singers,** a text published in 1877, contains all the essentials of the same pronunciation still favored by die-hards after almost one hundred years! A live language is in constant flux (only a dead one remains fixed like a fly in amber). This multi-media century has evolved a speech standard flexible and adaptable to singing (see pp. 12-14).

The affectation pervading performances of English song springs from indulging in stilted effects that are too far removed from the identifiable forms of good American speech. Caught in a kind of split-diction personality, singers lean toward such substitutes often to cover

---

*A textbook by Alexander J. Ellis, printed by J. Curwen & Sons Ltd., in London, remains a remarkable compilation of professional advice to the singer, much still valid. The style of diction, however, is no longer suitable for performers today.

their own inadequate speech. The custom of judging American English negatively on the basis of poorly spoken (and obviously unsingable) models leads inevitably to making a permanent fixture of this "superior" diction.

Tone and articulation — irreconcilable? Singers who have been persuaded to believe they must choose between distinctness of articulation and quality of musical tone live in fear that recognizable vowels and, especially, consonants will undermine their vocal security. For the sake of tonal build-up, skillful use of the articulators, the other half of their instrument, suffers neglect.

If one singer can make himself understood, then why is this not the norm for the whole cast, or for other performers in recital or oratorio? Superb voices that fill an opera house can be intelligible whether tenor or baritone, soprano or mezzo.* For sopranos, vocal display minus language has become a convention which, along with other quasi-myths, needs toppling.

FRAGMENTED TEACHING

Current diction courses (including English when it is given) place entirely too much emphasis on severing sounds from the body of language. Drilling isolated vowels and consonants and even individual words has only limited value unless the pieces are linked to form the flow of song. In addition, to make sense in English, the singer must understand its structure (the sense stress).

As for speech education, the main diet of courses in public speaking in the colleges has proved of little benefit to American voice and speech. The tonally deficient localisms and slack pronunciation are passed over in favor of preparing prescribed outlines for speeches made in classrooms. And so students who "took speech" leave school, their careless habits intact.

The speech and drama department is at the opposite end of the campus, sometimes literally and nearly always figuratively, from the voice and music department. If the music experts would "walk across the green" to collaborate with their speech colleagues, and vice versa,

---

*Ferdinand Hiller, composer, 1811-85, wrote of Rubini, the great tenor, "...the sonority and overpowering beauty of his high notes combined with unerring precision in attack, thrilled all hearts. In dexterity of execution he excelled the most famous instrumentalists. Further, he had the most distinct pronunciation." (From *The Encyclopaedia Britannica*, 1953 edition, "Rubini."

7

such exchange of skills would revitalize both fields. Who knows — we might then have more song in speech, and more speech in song.

PLEASE — NO JURISDICTIONAL DISPUTES

No diction coach in his right mind would seek entanglement in the ramifications and subtleties of voice culture, or intrude in an area where other professional skills operate. Voice training belongs properly in the domain of the singer and his voice teacher, and we leave to them (with considerable relief and gratitude) the responsibility for promoting high vocal standards in the performance of English song.

We have observed that different and equally prized methods of voice development work toward the same goal of maintaining a high level of vocal quality in a so-called line of tone into which a language can be molded. Accuracy in that language, its vowels and consonants, based on speech science and adapted to song is the complementary goal of the specialists in pronunciation.

OUR SOMETIMES FRIEND, THE COMPOSER

Composers, dead and alive, have created works of superb support for the sounds, structure, and stresses of the mother tongue. This despite English poetry which, for all its richness and power, does not easily yield to the disciplines of another art. Music as well follows its own laws, imposing its own disciplines and metrics on the composer. But since we sit in the performer's corner and share with him his concern for the sung word, let us point out some musical impediments to intelligibility.

A composer who turns a deaf ear to the prosodic demands of English in favor of musical invention, generally burdens the performer with a text so awkwardly set that even the best will and skill could not possibly transmit its content. Or crucial words may be swamped by a wall of sound that none but the bravest voices dare surmount.

A composer lost in his own creativity may forget that the people in the back rows have no typewritten sheets of text to enlighten them. If he works with the voice and not against it, he will find means to set essential words lucidly, leaving more dispensable ones for the complex effects. However, in an unresolvable conflict between music and text, music must assuredly win. All the more reason then why writers for the voice, including lyricists, librettists, and translators, require a firmer understanding of the basic elements and intonation of English. For them, as for the singer, instinct is not enough.

8

SINGING IN CHORUS — EFFECT OR COMMUNICATION?

One can sense the dedication to form and content of the director when beautifully blended voices match lucid language. Clarity of text has always enhanced choral art.* With certain types of contrapuntal music the words must lose to over-all design, but even then the repetition written into the musical structure and careful articulation permit vital phrases to penetrate the tapestry of sound. However perfectionist in nuance, sonority, and rhythm, a conductor who omits language values offers his audience only half an experience. As for choruses in opera, another convention has grown around the idea that these are really not expected to be understood at all.

Group performers tend to exhibit all the diction habits of the soloist — multiplied. The many voices magnify the twin errors of over-accentuation and under-articulation. In fact, exaggerated stress on weak syllables has grown into a choral cliché; countrywide we pick up *angel, caress, silence,* and **de**votion. As for final consonants, they disappear altogether in fade-out effects.

American joy in singing is expressed in the choral groups, choirs, societies, and glee clubs of fifty states. It would seem that speaking voices burdened by work-a-day pressures take wing in singing.

The multiple required subjects for music majors who become teachers leave little room for the study of choral skills, including good diction. Yet group singing is an important and popular feature of school curricula from classroom activity to auditoriums, and from all-city choruses to state-wide performance. What an opportunity group singing provides to develop, beginning with the lower grades, a distinct, unlabored pronunciation! First taught in song, spilling over into speech at an early age, this grass-roots American English would sprout into a lasting blend of attractive tone and clear articulation.

Much of the material to be covered in subsequent pages can be applied with advantage to the delivery of choral texts. This study of the sounds, shapes, and rhythms of the language serves the needs of soloist or ensemble.

DIVIDED WE FAIL

A small army of aides is enlisted in the development and maintenance of a singer's career: voice teacher (closest, most influential), coach, accompanist, conductor, stage director, and instructors in acting, body work, and languages (with English generally in last place). The educa-

*A listing of suggested choral recordings can be found in the Appendix, p. 295.

tion of a singer is thus a division of labor; unfortunately, the principals involved often reveal a division of interest. Instead, all hands should join, reaching toward a totality of artistic excellence. The student (and the artist too) hurries from one to another of these aides, each enclosed in his private studio. Rarely do we have a meeting of minds and purpose among the mentors who lay claim to a part of the performer's creative life.

What is the be-all and end-all of the art of song but to transport sounds of living emotion to attending ears? To communicate these unified themes of music and words in English, an area of neglect and uncertain standards, may well require an act of faith. The diction teacher is too often a lonely champion of sung English. But even the collective efforts of all teachers with their specialized skills would come to naught without the leaders who wield power in the field of music. It is at the top where the obligation belongs to initiate reforms and to set priorities and standards for the native language.

The artist, whose singular gift provides the most personal musical instrument for transmitting the text, also takes the bravos and blame onstage. His delivery in English needs bolstering by unanimous cooperation of all the experts (not just the diction coach).

The audience, no longer passive, experiences a deeply felt rapport with the artist who crowns his vocal magic with meaningful words in a language common to both. When text matches music in communication, everybody wins — poet, composer, instrumentalist, conductor, performer, and their listeners.

THE TIME IS NOW

Please let us abstain from the endless debate of whether vocal literature should be performed in the original or in translation. We cannot direct our concern to *opera in English*, but to the *English in opera*, and in art songs, oratorio, or in any other form that unites music and words. Dealing with English *as of now*, teachers continue to cultivate its clarity and artistry in all song material that students and performers must learn.

CHAPTER ONE

THE RANGE OF DICTION

"If you wish to sing beautifully — and you all do — you must love music; and the nearer you get to music the more you will love it. If you wish to sing your native language beautifully — and you should — you must love your native language; and the nearer you get to it the more you will love it..."

Nellie Melba

From the text of a lecture on English diction delivered at the Guildhall School of Music, London, about 1913.

IN THE BEGINNING, THE SPOKEN WORD

English vocal literature, whether original or translated,* old or new, calls for pronunciation firmly rooted in the spoken language. Divorced from life patterns, the sung language becomes an artificial *singer's diction,* a lifeless substitute weakening the bonds of communication between artist and audience. The many performers who resist this outmoded form turn instead toward contemporary usage to reinforce their rapport with those out front.

So-called Standard Speech, a British derivative originally fostered in New England by Ivy League colleges, was long ago rejected by the rest of the country. Yet this style still persists in an "elocution dialect"

---

*The need for better translations has long agitated singer and teacher alike. Nonetheless, the singer should not be deterred from performing all works in English with maximum clarity.

foisted upon actors and singers in and out of school. In addition, too many American singers have fallen into the habit of performing their native language with foreign accents. Sometimes German or French, but mainly Italian vowels have been grafted onto English song. These non-English vowels, as well as foreign *r's* that are flipped or trilled before vowels and removed altogether after them, produce a spurious diction that supposedly passes for style and elegance. Indeed, a good deal of singing in English is a mishmash of accents and distortions resembling no known dialect heard anywhere on earth except on concert and opera stages.

A LIVING LANGUAGE

It becomes essential to choose a lifelike pronunciation in keeping with the growing emphasis on realistic portrayal of roles in opera and on song delivery free of unnatural gesture and stilted diction. Just as good American speech invigorates the playing of Shakespeare in this country, so it breathes new life into songs, operas, oratorios, and choral works. American English, alive and well in the United States, long ago came of age as a spoken, written, and *sung* language. The quality of its intrinsic sounds can be as beautiful and effective as any English anywhere.

The *Académie Française* wields authority over French; the Italians and Germans have similar quasi-governmental bodies to preside over correct usage; but there exists no English counterpart here or abroad. The King's English, which once held sway in England, has given way to a variety of regional patterns, and we can attest that the President's English certainly never ruled the American electorate! In the absence of any constituted authority, we must base ourselves on those forms of the spoken language cultivated by representative speakers.

In order to conform to today's realities, not yesterday's traditions, the delivery of poetry and drama in English texts demands diction which can fulfill the following criteria:

1. Pronunciation readily grasped by American audiences. The best authorities for cultivated usage generally are the professional speakers who use the language sensitively and well, such as national television and radio announcers and commentators, actors, and especially actors in musical theater. (The performing style of many singers of popular music* also displays clear and careful articulation of the lyrics.)

*Other vocalists, however, equally numerous, feature a contrary style of slack, sloughed off words, all but obscured in the blaring beat.

All these have developed an American standard that has proven itself across the land in interaction with audiences, who do not themselves necessarily speak it. With similarities much greater than differences, the speech patterns of this standard exemplify a truly composite style. The pronunciation does not arise from the preferences and prejudices of any particular group, but from the challenge of meeting the needs of communication in an electronic age.

That small miracle, the home video cassette combining the sound of stereo with the picture of television may finally put an end to artificial or unintelligible English. The home audience would not long tolerate a singer on the intimate screen gesturing and mouthing words they cannot understand.

2. A style unobtrusive and free from regionalism and affectation. Authorities have traditionally marked three major speech areas in the United States, including the diverse minor subdivisions: Eastern, Southern and, spreading over the rest of the country to the Pacific, General American. The speech of this vast expanse (two-thirds of the population), while exerting predominant influence on the way Americans speak, is itself modified by the patterns of the other areas. Apparently, regional dialects that endured into the jet age now seem destined to merge with one another. In any case, this fluid national distillation, a viable speech with few obtrusive features from any one section, provides the contemporary basis for singing the language.

3. American pronunciation that is consistent with high standards of voice production. Singers need not look any further for a suitable diction — they need only explore the hidden treasure in native vowels and consonants and their sonorous combinations. These native sounds and shapes call for the same care automatically devoted to foreign languages of the vocal repertoire. By forming a precise image of an accurate vowel and then skillfully adjusting the sound to the enlarged resonating system of the singing voice, performers are able to elevate speech to song. American English becomes a cultivated style entirely congenial to the esthetics of song when high standards of voice production are joined to high standards of speech.

4. Diction appropriate for performing the texts of vocal literature. Poetry, from which most texts derive, is best spoken with lack of pretension, in a simple and unaffected manner. Achieving all they can of

13

naturalness, performers convey the poetic meaning of texts, enunciated in song larger than life with the reinforcement of lifelike sounds.

With an American model as the norm, dialectical touches add reality to the portrayal of roles and enrich songs with color and character.* All dialect can be beautifully sung and faithfully rendered in the interest of truthful projection.

Thus we have at hand a speech model that meets the criteria for an appropriate diction: an American style that is readily understandable, free of conspicuous localisms, adaptable to the high standards of vocalism, and responsive to the range of emotion and drama in text and music written for the voice.†

DICTION, AN UMBRELLA WORD

Hallowed by time and dictionary, the primary definition of diction concerns the choice of words, the clearness or effectiveness of wording, written or spoken, and secondarily, the *distinctness* of speech. The world of song, however, has taken the term diction for its own. In *Webster's Third New International Dictionary, Unabridged,* the singer's definition receives official sanction: "pronunciation and enunciation of words in singing."

Diction embraces *pronunciation, enunciation,* and *articulation,* three terms which have grown somewhat fuzzy in recent usage and now tend to be interchangeable as, for example, *"articulate:* to *pronounce* distinctly and carefully: *enunciate" (American Heritage Dictionary of the English Language).* To delineate the boundaries for the study of sung English, a review of more precise meaning for these terms would be useful.

Articulation refers more specifically to the adjustment and movements of speech organs (the articulators: tongue, lips, teeth) involved in the formation of a sound, especially a consonant. *Enunciation* emphasizes clarity in pronouncing words resulting in ease of perception by the listener. *Pronunciation,* in a comprehensive definition. *(American College Dictionary,* Random House, 1966) is "the act or result of producing the sounds of speech, including articulation, vowel formation, accent, inflection and intonation, often with reference to the correctness or acceptability of the speech sounds."

Thus it is clear that enunciation and pronunciation would be impossible without articulation. The meaning of words, spoken and sung,

*See The Diction of Dialects, Appendix, pp. 289-93.

†See list of suggested recordings of American English pronunciation, pp. 294-96.

depends primarily on *pronunciation* since this term embraces the accent or stress on word and syllable essential to language.

We must set under the umbrella term *diction* a final component, the lyric linkage of sounds, syllables, and words in the flow of song. The definition of *linkage,* "the manner or style of being fitted together or united" *(Webster's),* is quite apt in describing the process which leads to the *legato* essential to singing any language. Thus diction is the sum of articulation plus enunciation plus pronunciation plus stress plus linkage plus legato. But the term diction is qualitatively greater than the sum of its parts; the concept of the whole, transcending the parts, engenders the fusion of words and music in the art of singing.

A LEARNED SKILL

The notion still persists that performers who speak English can also sing it — a notion dispelled daily by the reactions of listeners and critics and the experiences of singers themselves. Few workers in the theater would assume that an actor with talent for naturalistic playing could step into Shakespearian and classical roles without speech training.

The cogent reasons that we cannot expect automatic transfer from speech to song begin with the nature of music itself, its designs of rhythm and pitch which words must accommodate. The prolongation of speech sounds in singing imposes constant problems of adjustment. The negligence of everyday patterns further widens the gap between speech and song, as do teachers who exalt tone as an end in itself. All these factors and more make clear that serious and specialized study of sung English must be a part of total training of the voice — a tone-producing *and* word-producing instrument at one and the same time.

STUDY SPEECH FIRST?

Obviously a well-spoken singer can more readily adapt the spoken sound to song than one who has no clear impression of the accurate sound in the first place, and it would be of immeasurable help if all singers had initial training in speech. But to insist that good speech habits be acquired in advance is a perfectionist and impractical attitude that runs counter to the reality of pressured schedules and expensive training. Besides, Americans as a people generally sing better than they speak. With the aid of good voice production, some singers can uplift in song the sounds they downgrade in daily talk. While correction can take place on the musical level, such accidental results cannot be considered dependable. The way to security in the delivery of English texts is through the specialized study of the language as sung.

In this manual for singers, the spoken sounds of good usage provide the solid basis for singing the sixteen vowels and twenty-five consonants of American English. The speech-to-song process in the Study Plan, useful to actors as well, offers ample practice material for speech improvement.

"TO SING IN ENGLISH" (THE WORKING PLAN)

The coming chapters encompass English diction in all its aspects as applied to singing. As we launch the discussion let us dispel the expectation that a studious breakdown of the language into vowels and consonants will automatically produce clear and intelligible words. This fragmented approach, with only limited value at best, has the effect of disenchanting singers who seek guidance in performing their own language. The over-all structure should be inspected before it comes apart brick by brick. And so, postponing until Chapter IV, the study of the English system of sounds, we begin with a fresh look at two fundamental features of the language which contribute materially to communication of song or speech: the intrinsic stress patterns of English and the lyric linkage of its sounds.

Study of the language's basic elements (Chapters IV and V) begins, as may be expected, with the vowels, the universal instruments of vocal training. Because this is not a book on voice production, the main focus is directed at acquiring accurate vowels as intelligible conveyors of meaning. The delivery of readily recognized vowels and consonants, to which country-wide audiences are attuned, reinforces the trained tone by investing sung sounds with communicative power.

THOSE UNIQUE ENGLISH RHYTHMS

The words we speak carry within them the innate rhythms of our native tongue; as we sing, however, music interposes rhythms of its own. The tendency of the score (and the singer) to obscure and flatten the built-in beat of the language endangers the clarity of the text. Music presents a constant challenge to the weak and strong stress patterns of English words and syllables which together communicate as importantly as the sounds of the words themselves.

Singers need to discover, rather than simply take for granted, the nature of these contrasts that make sense of the text at the listening end. They need to develop extra-sensitivity, a bodily response to the language's rhythms. The knowledgeable performer can then make good use of techniques as he strives to preserve the word structure within the musical framework.

ENGLISH AND LEGATO

The erratic patterns of daily speech should not deter singers from discovering the grace with which English can lend itself to the uninterrupted flow of song. Although the achievement of legato in English song is not an easy matter, it is nonetheless imperative. Singers may master the stress patterns of English along with its isolated sounds, but unless they have developed the skill of linking these sounds in smooth sequence, they will not succeed in performing the language clearly.

Overly precise advice, "be sure to pronounce all the *letters*" (sic), makes us less intelligible, not more. Dependent on visual patterns, many of us tend to hesitate at change points between words, having grown eye-minded probably from those early years when small fingers moved from word to word learning to read. While singing word by word reveals some of this "small-finger" carry-over from childhood, disjointed diction must be blamed on inept delivery, particularly the unlyrical use of consonants to break the legato. *Until a musical rest brings a pause, no sound in English need interrupt the vocal line.* The end product of lucid vowels and consonants firmly linked within and between words that are underscored with intrinsic English rhythms is American *bel canto*.

VOWELS FROM SPEECH TO SONG

The sixteen vowels in standard American usage are analyzed individually in Chapter IV, each vowel following the same study plan. The predominant point is the adjustment of the accurate vowel or phoneme to the singing voice — the reproduction of the sound in song determining its fidelity to the spoken form as identified by the listener.

The target vowel is examined first: its production according to established speech methods and what pitfalls to avoid, especially current localisms distorting the sound and rendering it unsingable. Then, to bridge speech gradually to song, there is practice in speaking the target vowel in the context of a short poetry selection and then singing it in an improvised musical fragment. Finally, a musical excerpt from vocal literature provides practice in matching the accurate vowel to its setting.

CONSONANTS FROM SPEECH TO SONG

The genius of a language is reflected in its speech sounds. The vowels and consonants of English, "its extraordinary imaginative and musical mixtures of sounds,"* mutually enhance each other to the great advantage of song. As interdependent elements, they together fashion the patterns of sound waves conveyed on outgoing breath to the ear of the listener. Without consonants song becomes mere vocal display.

Consonants are studied in Chapter V in a planned sequence relevant to singing the language rather than in a conventional speech procedure. The order of study is based on the relative sonority of English consonants, the inherent quality of their varied sounds. The most sonorous, those with vowel-like quality and the all-tone consonants, head the progression of twenty-five, with the least sonorous, the breath called *h,* at the end. In this way, singers are alerted to become more conscious of the spectrum of consonant color from resonance to voicelessness, both in the execution of the individual consonant and in its acoustic effect.

The Study Plan presents consonants in seven groups that are related in production and share characteristic sound. Poetry selections for the groups and individual consonants contribute speech practice. While vowels allow for some latitude in production, consonants require precise articulation, and mastery of all twenty-five calls for exacting care. Chapter V includes for each one explicit instructions for correct execution and desired acoustic result; the building of kinesthetic sensation reactive to specific movements of the articulators; diagnoses and remedies for common faults as spoken and sung; and finally, how to sing and link the consonant in dexterous and economical movement.

Lastly, in musical excerpts, combinations with vowels, or consonant clusters are by a unique method, extracted, practiced in isolation, and then replaced in the phrase.

THE TEXT FROM SPEECH TO SONG

The key question of how best to study a text cannot be answered arbitrarily. Some singers favor learning the music first, others choose

*This phrase is quoted from the famed musical *My Fair Lady* based on the play *Pygmalion* by George Bernard Shaw. The passage reads: "The majesty and grandeur of the English language is the greatest possession we have. The noblest sentiments that ever flowed in the hearts of man are contained in its extraordinary imaginative and musical mixtures of sounds." Copyright by Alan Jay Lerner and Frederick Loewe, 1956.

the words, and no one teacher can dictate the absolutely "right" way to prepare a text for performance. Diction teachers would naturally start with the "script," and experience has repeatedly proved the advantages of their position.

The final chapter demonstrates such an approach in studying the texts of major parts of two songs (including accompaniment). In an open session of a diction class a step-by-step method, from speech to song, is examined in lively discussion with invited guests. Various opinions on how to work on a text are exchanged with others from the field of vocal music: voice teacher, conductor, composer, choral director, and professional performers.

Studying the text as demonstrated prepares the groundwork for interpretation, the personal art of the performer. A lifelike diction assures him of greater empathy in performance and rapport with his audience. The indigenous sounds of English which he elevates to song evoke in him sensory and emotional responses that perforce affect his performance just as the very notes in a selection inspire in the instrumentalist interpretative reaction. Song, a form of communication unlike any other, binds sender and receiver in a reciprocal exchange of feeling and pleasure from which meaningful language can never be absent.

CHAPTER TWO

STRUCTURE, SENSE,
AND STRESS

Section I: How to Sing Sense in English

INDISPENSABLE INGREDIENTS

English as sung suffers from the general neglect of those intrinsic stress features of the language — *sense stress* and *syllable stress* (or accent) — which convey the basic verbal meaning of the text.

Sense stress is defined as the prominence of those words of a phrase or sentence to which proportionate attention of the hearer is directed, thus revealing the relation of the ideas.* The strong word-types of English receive more attention, and hence greater stress, than the weak word-types, which supply mainly the conventional links of sentence structure.

If these essential stress ingredients are lacking, singers may pronounce every vowel and consonant yet not make the words clear, or even project each word and yet not make sense in English.

*This definition has been excerpted and abridged by the author from *A Guide to Pronunciation*, in *Webster's New International Dictionary, Second Edition.*

NOT GRAMMAR!

Correct speech cadence does indeed spring from English grammar — the syntax (the way words are put together) and the syllables (the way words are divided). We respond automatically in our daily talk to what can be called grammatical signals. But a singer needs a *conscious* grasp of English structure to understand *how* the listener receives lyric messages from him, the sender.

While this discussion may begin to sound more or less familiar, vague memories of grammatical rules do not suffice to counter the problems in singing the language. Singers need system, not guesswork; they need a coherent approach, organized specifically for the study of English texts.

THE BUILT-IN BEAT

English, a *stress* language, is more strongly accented than other languages of the vocal repertoire. Its special genius lies in vivid contrasts of *strong* and *weak word-types* and word segments or *syllables*. These unique speech rhythms of *stress* and *unstress* are vital for transmitting signals of meaning to the audience.

To demonstrate how stress patterns convey the basic meaning of lines of poetry, we use these markings: / for the strong beat signals and ⌣ for the weak beat signals.

Observe how marking reveals the over-all sense stress of these lines.

Music that gentlier on the spirit lies,
Than tir'd eyelids upon tir'd eyes;

Alfred Lord Tennyson

The tendency of musical patterns to obscure English stress patterns constantly presents singers with verbal hurdles to surmount. Seduced by the score, too many respond by flattening the obligatory contrasts of the language. This brief refresher course in structure and stress is designed to fortify performers when they "face the music."

STRESS AND INTERPRETATION

"I'm going for a walk." When this statement is made casually, the words *going* and *walk* receive natural stress and all other words remain unstressed. But remarks with special emphases, such as "**I** am going for a walk" or "I **am** going for a walk," depend upon individual interpretation. *Stress* refers to the normal or structural prominence given a word within a phrase, or a syllable within a word. *Emphasis* is the special prominence given to a word by the judgment of the interpreter.

Sense stress, unchanging, belongs to every expression of thought in words; interpretation, varying greatly, expresses the thought and emotion of the individual. Inherent stress patterns of the language give the sense of the text — nothing more — and open the way to interpretation.

A ready knowledge of where accents fall heightens the performer's awareness of meaning and inspires him to seek further in the text for deeper content. When singers fail as interpreters, they do so mainly through neglect of the underlying stress structure and word rhythms of English.

Bates   Ward: America, The Beautiful

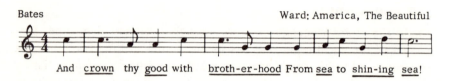

And crown thy good with broth-er-hood From sea to shin-ing sea!

Note that the *sense stress* is borne out by the underlined strong word-types in this excerpt.

THE TELEGRAM TEST

"Since I have developed severe laryngitis, I find I must cancel my appearance at the recital this Thursday evening." It is unlikely that anyone (even the very rich) would send such a wire. Instead, the message would probably read: "HAVE LARYNGITIS CANNOT SING THURSDAY."

When sending a telegram, we have little difficulty selecting key words to convey our message. Inevitably, the choice is from the four strong word-types of English, *nouns, active verbs, adjectives,* and *adverbs.* Expense restricts the use of small words that merely connect essential ones. So with singing. Featuring indispensable words in the text, and underplaying all others, saves the expenditure of energy and delivers the meaning.

Apply the telegram test:

Howe   Battle Hymn Of The Republic

Mine   eyes have seen the glo-ry of the com-ing of the Lord;

Message: EYES SEEN GLORY COMING LORD. These essential words do the job. When strong words stand out in relief from weak ones, the "wire" comes in clearly at the receiving end. (Of course, with a well-known song, listeners fill in what they miss. Do performers realize how much help comes from out front?)

> WAR ENDS
> SIGNALS HEARD FROM MARS
> THOUSANDS JAM BEACHES
> SENATE IN UPROAR

Experts who compose headlines also single out the most telling words to fit limited space. For the most telling effect in song, every line can likewise be scanned for essentials.

LEAD THROUGH STRENGTH

In every given phrase or sentence — spoken or sung — we find words from the four main categories: *nouns*, *verbs*, *adjectives*, and *adverbs*. Communication would collapse if we did not mutually respond to the stimuli triggered by these dominant words.

In order to turn dead grammar into live language, let us briefly review these conventional grammatical terms, beginning with the two most important parts of speech: *nouns,* designating things or persons; *active verbs,* describing the action that sets the phrase in motion.

Now for a look beneath the labels: In the phrases "Birds fly" and "Fly birds," the *thing*, "birds" (the noun), is first a subject and then an object, while in both the *action* is "fly" (the verb).

The significant combination in any language of the thing plus the action meets the minimum requirement for making sense in spoken communication. Since no other word is *absolutely* essential, the performer above all should hold firm in an English phrase to the *thing* plus the *action*.

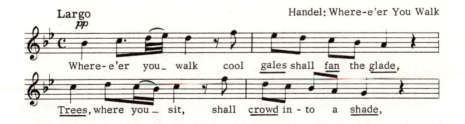

Largo
pp
Handel: Where-e'er You Walk

Where-e'er you_ walk cool gales shall fan the glade,

Trees, where you _ sit, shall crowd in - to a shade,

For such musical excerpts, the *nouns*, subject or object, and *active verbs* (the things plus the actions) are underlined. When these two strong word-types are properly stressed, the main meaning of any phrase becomes clear. (Note: the dependent adverbial clauses are left unmarked.)

In this second excerpt, the *things* plus the *actions* are again underscored (all nouns and active verbs).

Shakespeare   William Schuman: Orpheus With His Lute

PLUS TWO EQUALS FOUR

Adjectives and *adverbs,* the other two strong word-types of English, serve to vary the meanings of nouns and verbs. In "Small birds fly swiftly" essential information has been added to "Birds fly." But even with these expressive additions, if *birds* fades out the phrase has been decapitated, if *fly* does, the action is severed. While singers have the interpretive option of emphasizing strongly *small* or *swiftly,* or both, *birds* and *fly* will still dominate structurally.

The churmy girl smiled tintily.

Though these are nonsense words, we know by their position and form in the sentence that *churmy* must be an adjective describing the noun *girl,* and that *tintily* is an adverb connecting with the verb *smiled.* These modifiers, adjectives and adverbs, easily identifiable as to function, can be either single words or phrases (groups of words).

The girl with the churm smiled at him tintily.

Here, the "with" phrase has the same import as a single adjective, and the "at" phrase the same as an adverb.

By investing language with essential meaning, adjectives and adverbs maintain positions of strength in sung poetry and prose. Strong word-types, they receive inherent sense stress, with the interpreter contributing such added intensity as the text may inspire.

THE VITAL CONNECTION

Modification is a structure of connection consisting of two parts, the "head" and the modifier. In song, the "head" often appears a distance from the modifying word or phrase. The score tends to further obscure these movable modifiers. In order to sing sense, performers must determine which modifier applies to which "head," and attempt firmly to link the two.

American: Black Is The Color Of My True Love's Hair

Slow, in recitative manner

Black, black, black   is   the   col - or   of   my true love's   hair;

This familiar phrase illustrates a frequent inversion of position. The three *black*'s, obviously adjectives despite their appearance at the beginning of the line, connect with *color* which in turn connects with the adjectival phrase *of my true love's hair*. Singers will take off energetically, placing major stress on the *black*'s, minor stress on *color*, and least of all on *hair* at the end of the line. Standing the sentence on its feet, "The color of my true love's hair is black" might make a balladeer shudder, but it does clarify the structure. So hang on to *hair!*

And what about *love's* hair? Is *love's* an adjective or what? The label matters not, the function does: *love's* modifies *hair*. This simple example in a folk song prepares the way for the more complex in vocal literature.

Ives   Ives: Eyes So Dark

Take __   now   with thy   som - bre   mag - ic __

from __   my   sight __   this   world   a - way

Begin by righting the inverted phrase: "Now take this world away from my sight with thy sombre magic." In this more logical arrangement we can readily find the link between the "head" (what is being modified) and the modifier (what does the describing). Thus, we discover the active verb *take* is the "head" connecting with *away from my sight* and *with thy sombre magic.* To make sense of the phrase, the singer must keep the links clear.

THE OVERWHELMING MODIFIER

Watch the tendency to blow up modifiers and downgrade subjects and objects. In this example the adjectives *delightful* and *ravished* all but obscure the noun *sight* placed on descending notes in the weakest part of the measure.

Rule: Scan the phrase, spot *nouns* and *verbs,* then attach modifiers.

THE SINKING LAST WORD

A key word, one of the big four (like *sight* above) often shows up at the end of a line. English structure typically relegates one of the strong word-types to this final position, where singers, instead of sustaining, tend to slacken support. Since audiences listen for this end-of-sentence pattern as part of English word order, how frustrating when the last word sinks into obscurity!

Despite the generous note value on the words *us* and *warn,* both in the final position on the low note are in danger of being lost without the most careful enunciation and strong support.

Bad habits (all reversible) contribute to this falling-off of energy when most needed:

Breath, unsustained, gives out.

Diminuendo, unsupported, becomes inaudible.

Phrases delivered word by word convey no sense of the whole.

26

National habit of fade-out in speech spills over into song. Our "last word" syndrome could prompt this exchange:

She: Sorry to be late for the audition. My name
is Mary Ann S
m
i
t
h . . . (fade out)

He: Would you spell that? (She does.)
He: Oh, SMITH! (P.S. She did not get the job!)

ACCENTUATE THE NEGATIVE

Along with its mammoth vocabulary, English not unexpectedly has accumulated a large assortment of negative forms. Versatile *no* makes a short and simple answer, an adjective (he is *no* fool), or the first part of a word (*no*body, *no*thing), etc. *Not* appears in copious contractions: *won't, don't, couldn't,* etc. To these add *never, none, nor, neither,* and the prefixes *un-* (*un*aware), *in-* (*in*sensitive), *im-* (*im*placable), including a group of *anti*'s (*anti*social), and many more.

Think of the traps for singers in these negatives, especially the unstressed contractions. If an audience misses a small *-n't* the very opposite idea comes across. "You must(n't) do that!" Or drop *un-* in *unafraid* and the impression of fear, not the lack of it, emerges from the text.

Benet   Moore: The Devil And Daniel Webster

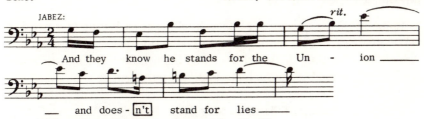

Did we hear "And *does* stand for lies"?

THE DOMINANT SCORE

In daily speech we automatically use the intrinsic cadence of English emanating from the contrast of strong and weak word-types. We stress and unstress, responsive to the pulse of the living language. In song, however, the pulse of the score dominates. The challenging rhythmic and melodic structure of the music, especially when in conflict with the language structure, makes it imperative to establish techniques for preserving the sense stress of the text.

27

ALTERNATIVES AND TECHNIQUES

To create the illusion of strength for words which may have been short-changed by the notation, the singer has other options besides pitch.

Whisper "My country 'tis of thee, sweet land of liberty...." Despite the absence of pitch, whispering the line projects varied stresses to make its meaning clear. Therefore, pitch cannot be the main stress determinant. The singer can choose from an effective variety of adjustments in *quantity* and *quality* of tone:

Volume A word can be sung softer or louder even within prescribed limits.

Intensity A word can be given more energy with inner pressure. Vowels can be heightened and consonants intensified.

Quality The singer has freedom of choice in use of timbre, resonance, and tone color.

Duration Although the composer's note value forbids alteration, some flexibility exists: sometimes it is appropriate to dot a note (tenuto) or to steal from one note to add to another (rubato).

Pauses Music dictates the rests, but an optional quick breath can be taken at the strategic place to signal a strong word. Slight hesitation can call attention to a meaningful expression.

IMPORTANT!

Nothing discussed thus far (or later) should suggest hitting at a word to achieve stress. Well-intentioned over-correction may lead a singer to flail about, chopping the vocal line. The built-in beat of English should always remain *within* the melodic line, *not outside* it.

Recap of "How to Sing Sense in English"

To sing sense. Singers need a ready knowledge of relevant aspects of English structure and the unique stress patterns, or word rhythms, that spring from it.

Significant contrasts. The contrasting stress patterns between strong and weak word-types and between word segments, or syllables, convey the basic *sense stress* (grammatical meaning) of the text.

28

The big four. The main burden of meaning in the language is carried by the four strong word-types: the *noun, active verb, adjective,* and *adverb.* (Knowing their function, not their labels, matters.)

Meaningful delivery. Correctly placed accents on words and syllables (along with clear enunciation) make sense at the listening end.

The basic minimum. Because the *noun* and *active verb* (*thing* plus *action*) are the most important parts of speech, singers must stress these indispensable words above others. Singers should look to the subject, the direct object, and especially to the active verb.

The modifiers. The other two strong word-types of English, *adjectives* and *adverbs,* supply essential meaning and reinforce the *nouns* and *verbs* which they modify.

The vital connection. Diversified modifiers can be either single words or phrases (groups of words). Modifiers appear frequently in inverted positions in poetry. When the modifier is separated from the word modified, singers must find the link between them.

Oversized modifiers. Singers should be careful not to inflate the value of a modifier over the word modified, even when the notation so directs. The more important word is then in danger of losing its identity.

Telegram and headline test. Telegrams feature only indispensable words. In the same manner, performers should deliver messages in song. The stressed strong word-types contained in the messages of texts then stand out in relief from the weak word-types. Headlines, which single out the most telling words of a news story to communicate the main idea, also make good models.

Stress is not interpretation. *Stress*, the grammatical prominence placed upon words, gives the sense of the text — nothing more. *Emphasis* is the special prominence that belongs to interpretation. Sense stress lays the groundwork for interpretation, a personal art.

Final fade-out. In English, key words often appear at the end of the sung line. At this very point, singers tend to weaken breath and tone support. When the significant word fades out, the result is loss of meaning to the whole phrase.

The challenging score. Correct stressing saves the meaning of the text, particularly when the music counterposes conflicting rhythms. When strong word-types are placed on a downbeat or a rise, or have commensurate duration, the music contributes natural stress to these more prominent words. But even when note and word values coincide, the prolonged vowels in song may obscure the word and syllable stress unless singers are sensitive to the stress.

Tools and techniques. In order to create the illusion of strength for words weakened by notation, singers have the advantage of choosing from a variety of adjustments. (For a detailed list see p. 28.)

Section II: The Importance of Unimportant Words

Unstressing, an earmark of English, performs as importantly in making sense in song as does stressing. It is contrast, the essence of our speech rhythms, which makes the sung line and especially the relationships between words clear to the listener. The small connective words,* like those in italics below, contribute their inherent weak beat to the communicative contrasts of weak and strong word-types within the phrase.

CONNECTIVE TISSUE

F. S. Key   Star-Spangled Banner

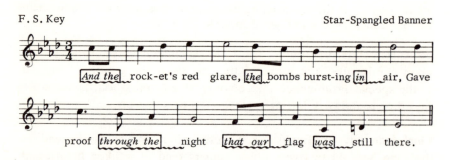

*The weak word-types and syllables of English have very little stress as compared with similar forms in other languages of the vocal repertoire.

The italic words representing the five weak word-types serve to fill out the phrases while remaining subordinate to the strong.

Article *(the)*

Preposition *(in, through)*

Conjunction *(and, that)*

Pronoun *(our)**

Linking verb *(was)*

English continually increases its wealth of dominant words, while subordinant ones, repeated constantly, remain few in number. The ten most frequently used words in the language *(the, of, and, to, a, in, that, it, is,* and *I)* appear, of course, with the same frequency in song. The voice can save itself effort on these unstressed elements in texts. When singers take advantage of this required lessening of energy they enjoy greater ease in sustaining the vocal line.

Moore   Irish: Believe Me, If All Those Endearing Young Charms

WHEN A WORD IS NOT A WORD

From early childhood, we have come to conceive of a word as a letter or group of letters surrounded by white spaces. But weak word-types actually exist in isolation only when printed on a page (or a sheet of music). Despite the spaces before and after, *the, of, and, to,* etc. are not detachable from the next word any more than *pre-* can be detached

---

*Note that *our* in this instance is not technically a pronoun but a weak possessive adjective modifying the noun *flag.*

in *prepare* or *-ish* in *stylish*. The small words, understated in daily talk, are apt to trip singers when they encounter these manifold weak forms, larger than life, in song.

"Believe Me...", having endured and charmed these hundreds of years, presents a classic example of a perfect setting for the words of its text. The pulses of language and of music join in parallel rhythms. Note how the small words in italics are matched by short notes inconspicuously placed in the measures. Nonetheless, somehow singers, transfixed by the music, will frequently accentuate these very words. (The score cannot always be blamed!) The answer to the problem clearly lies in greater awareness of the intrinsic structure of the language and of the role of its weakest members.

Now for a separate look at each weak grouping and its *function* behind the grammatical labels, followed by advice on how best to handle them all.

MOST COMMON, LEAST MEANINGFUL

*Articles** — *the, a, an*: a small set of words attached to a *noun* or *adjective*.

When such non-words become inflated, the succeeding word (always more weighty) wilts. As *the* hits the airwaves, the listener waits expectantly, since nothing as yet has been communicated, and he often keeps right on waiting. Articles should fall on brief, unaccented notes (composers please take notice). If they do not, make it a rule to treat them as if they did.

Are you "ay" singer? *Articles* are meant to carry a neutral vowel, an unassuming one known as schwa, ə,† that quick little sound heard at either end of "**America**." With the article inseparable from the noun, *a man* has the same unstressed initial vowel, ə, as *afraid*. But, in current Americanese, exchanging *ay* for modest *uh*, as in *ay girl*, impairs rhythm and sense.

Schwa, ə, found abundantly in weak words and syllables, is a most useful diminished vowel peculiar to English. Its grayness serves to set off the brightness of other vowels in contrasting patterns of

---

*English articles add limited meaning by qualifying or individualizing nouns (*a* man, *the* man). In other languages, articles are more meaningful: in German, French, and Italian, articles reveal number and gender. Russian manages without these weak words altogether.

†The symbol *schwa*, ə, representing the unstressed vowel in English regardless of spelling, now appears in all standard dictionaries, as well as in IPA (International Phonetic Alphabet).

32

shade and light. A detailed discussion of this interesting sound appears in Chapter IV, pp. 113-16.

THE "BEFORE" GROUP

Prepositions — *pre* (before) -*position:* to place in front of *nouns* or *noun* substitutes.

More common: *to, at, in, of, with*

Most meaningful: *under, up, outside, within, among*

The slight *to*'s, *at*'s and *in*'s fasten to the next word (*to* school, *in* love, *at* home) and are never pried loose except, alas, in song.

Listen to the unmindful singer performing this excerpt:

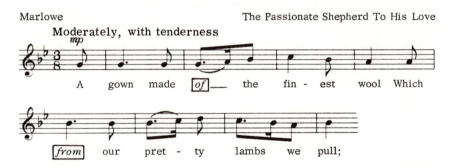

He sings:

> A gown made **of** the finest wool
> Which **from** our pretty lambs we pull;

The problem of the long note on the short preposition has obviously misled our performer. Let us examine the notation:

The preposition *of* on the downbeat is set to two notes occupying two-thirds of the measure; *from* also appears in an equivalent setting of one quarter-note. Faced with this dilemma the singer must find means to reduce the impact of these prepositions (see pp. 37-39). If the over-stress imposed by the music upon these unstressed elements is allowed to go unchallenged, meaning and artistry will inevitably suffer.

THE JOINERS

Conjunctions — *and, but, or,* etc.: literally, the words that join two other words or word groups.

Vocal literature comes fairly riddled with *and*'s into which singers pour wasted energy and emotion. The joiner *and* merely ties together

33

two entities, whether persons, ideas, or things. With little significance in itself, uninflected *and* should be soft-pedaled, despite the temptation of a generous note or favored musical position.

Even in Handel's "*Messiah*," the tradition-honored emphatic repetition of *and* need not be condoned. Can there be any doubt that the less emphasis given to *and,* the more the biblical poetry (especially active verbs) would stand out in dramatic relief?

Short and sweet. Even in fast tempo, singers will breathlessly squeeze every last *a-n-d* into a phrase. To save breath and the sense, use ǝ*nd*, '*nd*, or just plain '*n*.

As in Gilbert and Sullivan:

Banish "ahnd." How often we hear Italianate *ah* issuing from American throats, replacing English ǎ. Blown-up *ahnd* compounds the error of over-emphasis. Why not settle instead for the relaxed English sound, just as euphonious a vowel when well produced. (More on much-abused ǎ in Chapter IV, pp. 99-103).

More expressive joiners. Other *conjunctions* such as *but, or, because* obviously inject more content into texts than bland *and*. Even when more meaningful, however, *conjunctions* as weak word-types should

Teschnemacher   d'Hardelot: Because

Be - cause _ you come to   me __

34

retain their lower status. Feel free to add color with a resounding *but* or a poignant *because*, but not **that** much perhaps...

THE STAND-INS

Pronouns — pro (for) *-nouns*: standing in for *nouns*.

From the variety of *pronouns* here is a sampling: *I, who, yours, which, those, him, mine.*

As a class of words, *pronouns* convey more meaning than the other weak word-types. (Compare *I* and *the, his* and *of*.) Nonetheless, they function typically in subsidiary roles as *noun substitutes* and should remain so in song.

An accentuated *he* or *his* may imply some emotional attitude completely lacking in the text. "*He* loved *his** wife" transforms a casual remark into an innuendo. It is better to curb all impulses to add strength where weakness makes sense.

The most personal.   "Then *I* said...and then *I* saw...*I*...*I*...*I*..." How boring is *I*-oriented chatter in conversation, but no more so than this repetitive personal pronoun when accented in song. After the performer's first *I* or two, the audience has the idea. Besides being irritating, the pronoun satellite overshadows more deserving words.

When, as in song, *I* or *you* substitute commonly for nouns, the active verb takes first place, becoming the catalyst that brings the whole phrase into action.† Countless songs contain this personal pronoun-verb combination.

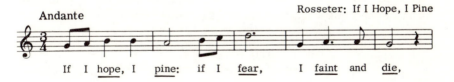

Andante   Rosseter: If I Hope, I Pine

If I hope, I pine: if I fear, I faint and die,

Shade the *I*'s and brighten all six active verbs where the main meaning resides.

The least and most dispensable. *Interrogatory who, what, why* by their very nature call for accentuation. As we take off on a question, we naturally stress the question leader.

*Note that *his* in this instance is technically not a pronoun but a weak possessive adjective modifying the noun *wife*.

†The primacy of *noun* and *verb* is discussed on pp. 23-24.

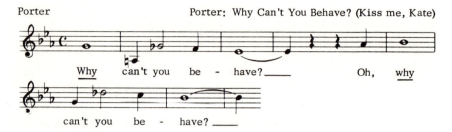

Porter

Porter: Why Can't You Behave? (Kiss me, Kate)

Why can't you be - have?____ Oh, why

can't you be - have? ____

Demonstrative, an apt term, describes the stronger pronouns *that, this, these,* etc. (When modifying a noun these are technically demonstrative adjectives).

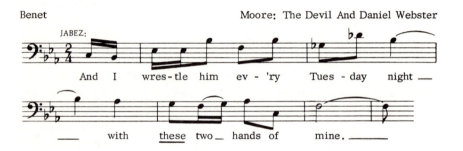

Benet

Moore: The Devil And Daniel Webster

JABEZ:

And I wres-tle him ev-'ry Tues - day night ___

___ with these two ___ hands of mine. _____

Relative pronouns that, which, whom are among the weakest. In "the man *that* I love" ("the man I love"), dispensable *that* exemplifies all those we omit in conversation. Why build them up in song?

> "Who is Silvia? What is she,
> That all our swains commend her?"

THE ASSISTANTS

Auxiliary, or *helping, verbs* provide assistance to the all-powerful active verbs (*has* gone, *will* sing, *is* laughing). Another weak variety, the *linking verb,* serves to fill out innumerable phrases (*he is handsome,* or more likely with the contraction: *he's handsome*).

The contractions they undergo prove the weak nature of these verbs. In English we literally compress the size of these feeble forms to strengthen the dynamic ones. But when music fills the air, with the big note on the small verb, the reverse may take place. ("She *is* a pretty girl." The listener reacts: "Who said she wasn't?")

INEVITABLE EXCEPTIONS

Within life and literature, the uncolored word-types operate mainly in their usual non-emphatic contexts. Obvious exceptions calling for emphasis invariably occur.

> "You mean **the** (thee) Fifth Symphony?"
> "Where are you **from**?"
> "**And** one, **and** two, **and** three, **and** four."
> "I **can** sing high C!"
> "**Was** I?" "Who, **me**?" "Not **him**!"

Here the repeated preposition *about* has interpretive stress which the notation reinforces.

Floyd   Floyd: Susannah

What's it all a-bout, Sam?   What's it all a-bout?_

NOTATION AND THE WEAK WORD

When speechlike tempo and unstressed notation accommodate unstressed words in texts, the natural rhythm of the language is preserved. But since the nature of music tends to elongate speech sounds, subordinate words and syllables in song produce problems in adjustment of word and note. Singers constantly have to counterbalance the impact on the small word of the long note, of the sudden high note or descent, or of a commanding position in the measure. Suggestions for intensifying a key word threatened by inadequate note values appear on pp. 28-29. Now in reverse, what can be done to demote a lesser word promoted to prominence by the music?

Reduce volume and intensity. While note values remain constant, pressure values can fluctuate. Practiced control of inner pressure can subdue the too long and too prominent note.

The thirst — that from the soul — doth rise

Even with *Mezzo forte* indicated, the experienced singer would soften and play down the preposition *from* on the elevated, long *e* flat. The object-noun *soul,* that descends two notes on the downbeat to carry the musical stress, should be further intensified to shade by contrast the too prominent *from.*

Reduce vowel. Toning down the vowel toward a more neutral sound can be counted on to shrink a protrusive note on a weak word:

Drink To Me Only With Thine Eyes

But might I of Jove's nec - tar sup, —

The preposition *of,* here on the longest note in the measure, benefits from the neutralizing treatment of mixing schwa, ə *(uh),* with a muted *ah* to form the diminished vowel in *of.* (For discussion of the diminished vowels of English, see pp. 118-120.) The indicated crescendo (*poco cresc.*) which appears over *of* should obviously be postponed until the following words: *Jove's nectar sup.*

Reduce duration. To meet this problem of too generous notes, also look to other words in the vicinity. Heighten these to offset the problem ones. Create the illusion of a shorter word by abbreviating vowels and lengthening consonants.

Hindemith: The Wild Flowers Song

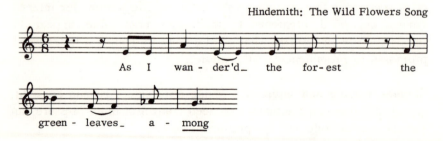

As I wan - der'd — the for - est the

green - leaves — a - mong

38

Begin by standing the inverted phrase on its feet: "As I wandered among the green leaves (in) the forest...." This useful practice of righting the phrase reveals its true structure. We find here that the preposition *among*, a weak word, has been placed conspicuously on the downbeat and dotted quarter-note.

The hum of both consonants *m* and *ng*, when prolonged (but not too long), will give the impression of a shorter vowel. Also in adjacent *leaves*, the *ē* vowel on two notes, when brightened, will overshadow the vowel in the syllable *-mong*. Thus *among* is held down to size with the help of descending notation.

Change quality. Modulation of tone color does much to weaken overly strenuous notation. These changes in quality, however, must not be abrupt or out of harmony with the rest of the line.

Stay within the framework. All remedies call for comparative, and not absolute, measures. To project the illusion of weakness, subordinate words can be adjusted in volume, intensity, duration, and quality. Any adjustment, however, should operate in relation to the stronger words in the phrase.

Again, not interpretation. It is essential, in order to make sense in singing, to preserve the weak beat of English in contrast to the strong, with techniques of illusion if necessary. Individual response to the text, however, may inspire the interpreter to highlight selectively a weak pronoun, an auxiliary verb, or even an *and* as in this excerpt:

Dowland: Come Again

The sense stress prepares interpretive ground for the artist. He has the creative choice of exceptional accent on structurally subordinate words.

Recap of "The Importance of Unimportant Words"

Role of weak stress. In order to sing sense, correct unstressing of subordinate words is as important as stressing the more prominent. Contrast of weak word-types with strong gives communicative rhythms of English to texts. Unstressed words and syllables in English have very little accent compared with other languages in the vocal repertoire.

Connective function. The five weak word-types, satellites of the strong, serve to fill out the meaning in phrases and make the statement complete.

Energy saved. Performers should take advantage of the required lessening of effort in singing subordinate words.

Non-detachable words. These minor items exist in isolation only when printed. When spoken or sung, they cannot be severed from the next word any more than a prefix can be separated in a word (*pre*pare).

Five weak word-types.

1. *Articles* — *a, the, an* — Weakest of the five, they have little meaning in themselves. The accented "ay" should never be used as an article.

2. *Prepositions* — *to, at, with,* etc. — Preposition means "to come before" some strong word-type. More meaningful forms include, *under, above, over,* etc.

3. *Conjunctions* — *but, or, and,* etc. — The most common of all, *and,* is a notorious energy stealer. *"Ahnd"* must be shunned altogether.

4. *Pronouns* — *I, he, them,* etc. — These noun substitutes are generally more significant than the other weak word-types while remaining subordinate to the noun.
The repetitive *personal pronoun, I,* when stressed, becomes tedious. *Interrogatory* (who, what, why) and *demonstrative* (these, that) *pronouns* by their very nature call for accentuation.

5. *Auxiliary verbs* — *am, is, will,* etc. — are also called *helping verbs,* the main meaning residing in the active verb (am going, is laughing).

This musical excerpt demonstrates repeated use of all five of the weak word-types.

Blitzstein   Blitzstein: Regina

In this excerpt, the subordinate words are crossed out so that the prominent ones stand out. The notes, repetitive and mainly of equal duration, make it necessary to use techniques to help give the illusion of less stress on the weak words.

Bishop   Rorem: Visits To St. Elizabeths

Always exceptions. When special emphasis is desired for interpretive purposes, all five weak word-types can receive exceptional stress.

Tools and techniques. In song there is always greater danger of over-stating the weak word-types than of understating the strong. Where weakness makes more sense, accentuation will invariably confuse the listener. In order to create the illusion of weakness for words strength-ened by notation, singers have the advantage of choosing from a variety of adjustments. (For a detailed list, see pp. 37-39.)

Section III: Rhythms Within Words

The vivid contrasts of strong and weak syllables is an ancient beat built into English speech, poetry, and song these many centuries. What a boon to the art of singing and what a pity to waste this natural resource!

Of course we all know where accents occur: we certainly would not say *mu*sic instead of **mu**sic. But propelled on the wings of song, do we perhaps forget and sing *mu*sic after all? From concert hall and opera stage, audiences are assailed by such non-English as *beauteeful* or *angel*. We may smile at the foreigner who scrambles syllables, but for singers this is no laughing matter. Just as a wrong note jars, in the same way *bless***ed**, *glo***ree**, and *moun***tain** cause us to squirm.

Surely the performer's plaint, "But it's the *score* — what can *I* do!" needs answering. However, before dealing with the dilemma of score *versus* word, a once-over-lightly review of the variety of our word rhythms is in order.

THE PULSE OF SYLLABLES

The metrical arrangement of strong and weak segments within words, called *syllable stress,* performs as an integral part of English pronunciation. When syllables are incorrectly accented, every vowel or consonant might be enunciated precisely and yet the words would not be understood (marri**age**, eter**nal**, lova**ble**).

A syllable is one or more speech sounds forming an uninterrupted unit of the spoken language which phonetically is the next higher order above a speech sound. A syllable can be a whole word *(song)* or the recognizable subdivision of a word with a single vowel sound (*mu-sic*). Linguistic theory describes the syllable as a single pulse of sound energy; thus a polysyllabic word would consist of two or more pulses with the main accented one described as the peak of sonority (*a-***waken***).

The listener finds it difficult to recognize individual speech sounds, but recognition of the syllable on which word rhythm depends is universal. People hear three syllables in re/mem/ber, but how many know there are three *e*'s, two *m*'s, etc.? Both physiological (its bodily impulse) and acoustical (its impression on the ear), the syllable can be regarded as that irreducible unit of expression which the singer must project clearly for the audience to perceive.

Be - lieve me

Here the music adds an extra pulse to the first syllable of *believe*. If it is correctly sung, the audience should still perceive only a single syllable.*

UNIQUELY ENGLISH

Probably the most distinctive feature of the language is the richly varied stress arrangements within words of more than one syllable. Moreover, the stressed syllable (the peak of sonority) can occur in any position in an English word. We steal strength from one syllable to empower another; the robbed portion of the word becomes shorter, its vowel weakening to a more neutral sound, usually *schwa* (**ə**meric**ə**n). Thus contrasting accented and unaccented syllables give and take color from the vowels and energy from the consonants. A shift in syllable stress can alter the meaning of an English word (**des**ert, de**sert**; **ob**ject, ob**ject**).

The stress/time feature of English syllables (shorter or longer depending on accentuation) is unique among the usual tongues of the vocal repertoire.†

Compare English *umbrella* with Italian *ombrello,* both derived from the Latin, and both stressed on the second syllable. The difference is that in *ombrello* the unstressed vowels of the first and last syllables do not alter, retaining their original sound [o]. In *umbrella*, these vowels have both diminished to *schwa* [ə]. Even the spelling altered in the process.

THE VARIETY OF RHYTHMS

Read these words aloud. The strong syllables are marked / , the weak ones ∪ , while the notes approximate the word rhythms. Terms of poetic meter are also used to show the beat in words. Can the beat in the language be felt with the same immediacy as that in music?

---

*First two words of the opening phrase of "Believe me if all those endearing young charms," Old Irish Melody, *Arnold Book of Old Songs*, p. 31.

†The Romance languages, including Italian, do not (as in English) alter the vowel in the weak syllable. In German, while the neutral *schwa* does appear in the final weak syllable of words, its use is much more limited than in English (*liebe*).

1. laughter, happy, singing — ♩ ♪ *(trochaic)*
2. deceive, alone, concern — ♪ ♩ *(iambic)*
3. beautiful, suddenly, happiness — ♩ ♪ ♪ *(dactylic)*
4. understand, disappear, masquerade — ♪ ♪ ♩ *(anapestic)*
5. imagine, romantic, confusion — ♪ ♩ ♪ *(amphibrachic)*
6. sunset, daybreak, mishmash — ♩ ♩ *(spondaic)*

These six varieties,† of which the first three are most numerous, account for the main syllable patterns, spoken and sung. Number one, the ubiquitous trochee (laughter), is by far the most common. Note this persistent pattern (/ ∪) of the marked words below:

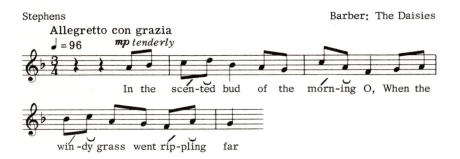

Stephens   Barber: The Daisies

Allegretto con grazia
♩ = 96   *mp tenderly*

In the   scen-ted bud   of   the   morn-ing O, When the

win-dy grass went rip-pling   far

Because of their relatively infrequent appearance in song, four- and five-syllable words have been omitted from the listing. When American singers correctly accent the key segment in these many-syllabled words, the others readily fall into place. Words pronounced **hon**or*ably*, **un**hap*piness*, *inter*pre**ta**tion emerge as entirely comprehensible to listeners.

Should singers commit to memory the Greek terms for these six varieties of poetic syllable stress? Here again labels do not matter, especially with such uncommon ones. What does matter is to build into

44

the voice mechanism the communicative word rhythms of English. Even formidable musical treatment need not intimidate singers who respond positively to the pulsation of words within English song.

WHEN WORD MEETS SCORE

When the score rides over the word, trochaic **mo**_ther_ may turn into iambic mo**ther**, or dactylic **love**_liness_ to convert to anapestic _love_**liness**. Unequal syllables, as in _ná-tiŏn, ăt-témpt, lít-tlĕ_, are often set to two equal notes in music. The performer has the responsibility, with illusory techniques, to restore the original rhythms.

 hópe-lĕss

At first glance the set-up really looks hopeless, if delivered exactly as notated. The weak element -_less_ would then sail strongly forth to make the listener wonder what indeed was _less_ than what!

First lean on _hope-,_ the primary syllable, and hold on to the eighth-note. Feature a good round _oh_ for almost every particle of the count; voiceless _h_ and _p_ consume a mere fragment of the time value.

Go to work on the weak syllable -_less,_ which rests uneasily on the elevated dotted-quarter-note:

Deliver with modulated intensity.

Sing on _l,_ a sonorous consonant, to use up some of the dotted quarter-note.

Diminish the vowel _eh_ in -_less_ toward the weaker blend of _eh_ and _ih._

Hold the _ss_ (actually only one _s_ sound), a short voiceless sibilant, to fill out the count (perhaps like a sigh?).

With similar techniques, the singer can make a happier marriage of convenience between other mismatched words and notes.

Now achieve the same reduced effect on the indicated weak syllables on the longer notes in these song excerpts:

Rossetti   Hageman: When I Am Dead, My Dearest

When I am dead, my dear-est, Nor sha-dy cy-press trees—

45

THE WEAK VOWELS

Since music will slow and elongate syllables, performers find they must deliberately enlarge in song what they reduce automatically in speech. But whether spoken or sung, brief schwa [ə], familiar as *uh*, is the chief answer for unstressed portions of words.

ə-fraid   dra-mə̆   sing-ə̆r*

INTERCHANGEABLE WEAK VOWELS

The vowel *ih* (i) is also used as a neutralized vowel in English, though less frequently than *uh* [ə]. In many words in the unstressed syllables we can use either sound or a blend of the two. (See discussion of all neutralized vowels, pp. 118-120.)

children   parable   wanton   religion

For song, *ih* often makes the better choice, contributing a brighter sound. Also use *ih* whenever possible in unstressed syllables of words like *deceive, beneath, reward, prepare.*

When the prefixed *de-, be-, re-, pre-* are held on long notes, the vowel *ih* begins to sound awkward. Then use ē, unstressed, making sure to shade its brightness to accommodate the weak syllable.

But avoid pronouncing words naturally stressed ◡ / as / / (*pree- pare, dee-ceive, bee-neath*). Such flattening of intrinsic rhythms also spreads confusion. "*Bee*-hold!" Who could blame the listener for mistaking the weak syllable for an insect?

*A blend of *schwa* plus *r* [ər], the *er* is the common unstressed counterpart of the stressed vowel in *fern, bird,* etc. The *r* in this weak position (sing*er*) is more color than consonant.

SHUN "SHUN"

Eisenstein   Strauss: Die Fledermaus

My se-lec-[tion] is per-fec-[tion] The di-rec-[tion] of her glance

This excerpt is typical of the rhymed translations, so partial to exaggerated "shuns" which have the same note value as the important accented syllable. Handle this final weakest segment by getting to the *n* fast and holding its hum longer. The depleted vowel between *sh* and *n* (sh — n) then becomes the shortest distance between two consonants. We also have *ex-* words and *en-* words, *-less* words, *-ful* wŏrds, and *-ure* words (*ex*alt, *en*joy, end*less*, hope*ful*, plea*sure*, all calling for schwa [ə] or a kindred diminished vowel. Relaxed and reduced, these neutral sounds supply the essential weak beat to the copious unstressed syllables of English.

NOTATION AND THE SYLLABLE

To co-ordinate syllables and notation, invoke the rules applying to similar problems of strong and weak word-types within phrases (pp. 37 and 39).

Always adhere to correct syllable stress, checking an American dictionary when in doubt. Though frustrated by notation, do the best to create the illusion of accurate accents within words.

Although *every* looks like a word with three syllables, we speak and sing only two. Sing the vowel *eh* in *every* on the first two notes.

Broadly   Byrd: O Mistress Mine

Ev - ĕr - y wise man's son _____ doth know

Balance the dynamics. With all the concern for the weak syllable, the need to keep the strong one dominant should not be overlooked. Its strong pulse demands vibrant vowels and consonants to balance the weaker pulse of the lesser syllable. Contrast communicates the word, with the strong segment requiring reinforcement in intensity and/or volume, duration, and color.

47

The excerpt below demonstrates the strong stresses in the phrase. Note in particular the accents on underlined key syllables and strong monosyllabic words within the musical design.

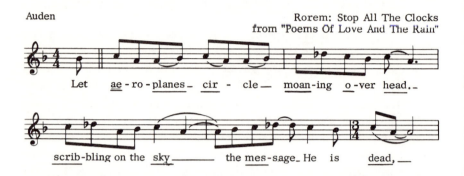

Keep oneness in mind. In a setting of more than one note, a syllable runs the risk of losing its individual identity. Despite the dictates of the notation, the impression of a cohesive segment should be maintained as it appears in the word.

As the vowels above move from one note to another within a syllable, hold on strongly to their recognizable sounds. Prevent added vowels from creeping in to distort them. The consonants *m* and *n* move on humming pitches, the percussive *d, p,* and *k* have time for exceptional clarity.

Make certain not to lose the important last word *care* on the low note.

Leave well enough alone. When music and text are compatible, resist plying the strong beats with extra pressure or the effect will be labored and plodding. When music contradicts text, never hit at a syllable to impose stress upon it, but use subtler techniques to achieve the desired result.

Not "rapchōōr." Strong and weak stresses in syllables pertain to correct pronunciation of words and *not* their interpretation. Sing *rapture* with all the fire and force imaginable, but please, vent most of it on the *first* syllable!

But when faced with this...

heav-en - leee

Give up!

A musical setting such as this may resist all valiant efforts to adjust words and notation. Try as singers will to decrescendo, mute the tone, or diminish the vowel, the escalated *b* flat on the half-note will remain too big for the little *-ly* syllable.

Recap of "Rhythms Within Words"

A distinctive feature. Within words, the varied arrangements of syllables and their contrasts of strong and weak stress are more marked in English than in other languages. In addition, the accented syllable can occur in any position in English words.

The built-in beat communicates. Correct stress of word segments is an integral part of English pronunciation. Incorrect accents render words unintelligible to the listener.

Syllable defined. The syllable, consisting of one or more speech sounds, is an uninterrupted, irreducible, recognizable unit of the spoken language, and a single pulse of sound energy.

The varied rhythms. Singers need to become familiar particularly with the rhythms of six main syllable patterns of English words described on p. 44. The strong subdivisions of words are marked with a slash line (/), the weak with a breve (ᴜ).

The practice of marking will develop sensitivity to these essential accents and non-accents. When score and text are in conflict, singers find this device especially useful.

The diminished vowel. The weakening of non-accented vowels is unique to English. In song or speech, the neutral *schwa* is the main vowel for the unstressed subdivision of a word. Other vowels perform a like role, especially *ih*, which is frequently interchangeable with *schwa*. In slow tempo, a bland blend of *uh*, *ih*, and *eh* makes the best answer. In the elongated weak syllables in these excerpts, try to produce a muted blend of the three weak vowel sounds.

Wylie   Rorem: On A Singing Girl

Calm and moderate

best   Is voice-less   in a   sud-den Night _   O love-li-est

Symonds   Dello Joio: Farewell

Adagio

As   thou go - est __   morn will be

Beware of flattening the contrasts. The tendency of the score to ride over the natural stress can destroy the innate weak-strong syllable patterns essential to meaning. Also the over-accentuation of weak syllables in speech (*ree-ceive*, *dee-clare*) spills over into song.

Make the most of consonants. These lip, teeth, and tongue shapes play an important role in stressing and unstressing. The initial consonant that begins a strong syllable remains strong and should be stressed (de-*light*, *mo*-ther).

Tools and techniques. To handle the problems of syllable accent in song:

Analyze the word and its setting.

Recognize the beat of the word and try to match it to notation.

When conflict arises, create the illusion of accurate stress to preserve the rhythm within the word.

If a syllable is set to two or more notes, try to hold on to the impression of "oneness." Also, keep the vowel shape from becoming distorted.

All recommended techniques are designed to maintain the natural built-in accents within words. Added emphasis on strong segments, or further softening of weak ones reflect the emotional response of individual interpreters.

Know when to give up.   Some notation, especially in the highest or lowest reaches of the voice, resists all efforts to maneuver a compromise with the text. When the notation is so obviously stacked against the words, singers should not strive to preserve words beyond the point of no return.

What We Covered and Discovered

Joyce

Barber: Rain Has Fallen

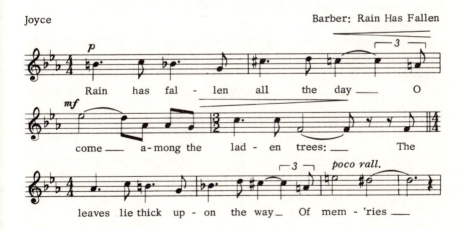

WORKING METHOD

To summarize the three sections of this refresher course, *Structure, Sense, and Stress*, the above musical excerpt demonstrates the assembling of intrinsic English stresses into one over-all pattern. The markings reveal the pattern of contrasting weak and strong word-types within phrases and syllables within words.

In scanning any phrase, identify and mark:

four strong word-types (encircle).

five weak ones (keep outside of circles).

six typical rhythm patterns within words (mark all syllables).

Now encircle the strong words and mark all stresses in this phrase from the musical excerpt above:

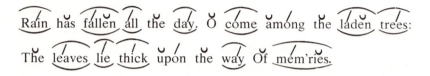

The individual weak and strong beats assembled into this over-all rhythmic design when sung in sequence will bring clarity to the phrase as a whole.

Weigh word and note values. While in "Rain Has Fallen" the musical notation matches the word stress with unusual fidelity, presenting few adjustment problems, the text still requires careful perusal of stress patterns.

In the second phrase for example, watch the active verb *lie*, making sure to sing the short eighth-note with intensity, consistent with the *p (piano)*.

Reduce dynamically the impact on the second syllable in *upon,* a weak word-type.

The inner beat of the language continues within the forward movement of the vocal line. The pulsation beneath these words and their segments will add an eloquent lilt to this as well as to all new and old songs performed in English.

FINALLY

Responsive to the underlying structure of the language, singers successfully meet the challenges of musical structure and deliver a fusion of words and music.

But even the skilled artist, sensitive to the inner life of words, may experience difficulty when confronted by a musical impasse. A sudden leap, an elaborate run, or the onset of an extremely high or low tessitura may force him to sacrifice briefly the clarity of the text. If he has sung the song with supple adjustment of word and note, his audience, grateful for his lucid delivery until that precarious musical moment, will overlook the few words they might miss.

But before such expertise is possible, conditioned reflexes of old habits have to be dislodged. These will give way as conscientious singers-in-English learn new techniques and condition new reflexes.

CHAPTER THREE

ENGLISH,

A LEGATO LANGUAGE

FOURSCORENSEVNYEARSAGO

The eye sees this famous phrase as strange; the ear hears it as familiar. To deliver the Gettysburg Address effectively, the speaker must pull words together into meaningful clusters and link syllables in chains of articulation. Just as blank spaces between notes exist only visually for purposes of identification, so spaces between words lack reality for the ear.

However well singers may grasp the sense stress patterns of English and master its isolated sounds, they will still fail to communicate the language if they do not set these sounds in motion in distinct linked clusters. English demands *linkage** for clear speech and especially for clear song. To the definition of the term *legato* in music which means without abrupt or perceptible break in movement and in a manner smooth and connected between successive tones, we should add *and also between words*.

Singers may choose to stop within a phrase for a quick breath, for

---

*A foreigner hears only a series of strange, *linked* combinations and not separate words in English. So with us. How many words do we hear in *dusvidanya,* the Russian expression for "goodbye"?

vocal effect, or interpretive color; but until an indicated rest signals a pause, no sound in the language, of itself, need sever the sung line. For English to be beautiful and intelligible, vowels join consonants in a non-stop flow of sound and sense.

SCIENTIFIC LEGATO

Legato forms the basis of both the technique of the artist and the response of the audience to beautiful singing. Not only an esthetic but also an acoustical principle provides a strong supportive basis for *linkage* in speech and song.

How does the receiver (listener) discern messages from the sender (singer)? Not in disjointed sounds or words, but in a continuity out of which coherent language patterns emerge. Those out front perceive language acoustically in blends of vowels and consonants, technically termed *smear*.* It follows, therefore, that performers must produce such blends in order to get through to the receiving end.

With hearing attuned to linkage, the listener's nervous system reacts adversely to gaps in the sung line. His frustration mounts when he discerns only a succession of vowels but few, if any, consonants. Thus listening perception, preconditioned to distinct and blended forms (*smear*), seeks automatically (and vainly) to fill in the voids. The listener would indeed become frustrated and probably tune out the words altogether if instead of this:

Joyce

Barber: I Hear An Army

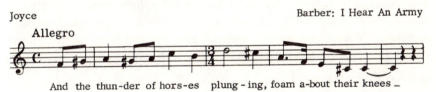

And the thun-der of hors-es plung - ing, foam a-bout their knees _

he heard something like "an the undah horse plungi, foa abou thei knee."

THE TWO-WAY PROCESS

Smear, essential to listening, calls for *slur,*† a matching concept essential to singing. Also an acoustical term, *slur* means obligatory linking of

---

*Smear, the technical acoustical term, is not to be confused with staining and smudging.

†The term *slur* should not be confused with the unfavorable connotation often given the word as in *slurred speech:* the substitution or omission of a sound or series of sounds.

phonetic elements by the performer in order to satisfy the ear. To reinforce this *smear-slur* process for the comprehension of song texts, the performer must produce clear, interconnected sounds.

Slow motion reveals how the slur process works. Try this example: Begin intoning the word *man*. Feel the vibration of *m* which spills over into the vowel *a* ... prolong *a* ... now feel the vibration of *n* begin before the sound of *a* ceases ... then as the vowel melts away, *n* continues its hum alone.

Note that the vowel *a* reflects both the *m* it follows and the *n* it precedes. Actually, were it not for the enunciation of slower vowels in juxtaposition to faster consonants, we would scarcely be able to distinguish the varied tongue-teeth-lip shapes of the consonants. Thus we need slur to identify what has gone before as well as to signal what comes next.

Vowels and consonants mutually modify and color each other in the slur process, but still retain their individual characters.

Nothing in this exposition of slur as an acoustical principle should suggest any crooning, sliding, bending of tones, or scooping between them nor that the consonant should be anticipated ahead of time. Indeed, in order for the vowel to fulfill its part as main carrier of the phrase, it must be held to full length for the purpose of identifying the preceding and the following consonants. Of course, if consonants are under-articulated the balance will be destroyed (the main problem in singing). The term *slur*, because of its possible unfortunate connotation, had best be relegated to its *smear-slur* acoustical context. *Linking, joining, blending*, or *merging* (but not *elision**) will have to substitute in the absence of a more exact and "unloaded" expression.

BOUND TOGETHER

In the process of linkage, the formation of a given sound begins *prior* to the release of the preceding one; and then in turn it merges into the oncoming vowel or consonant. In other words, the singer before completing one sound makes ready for the next in an unceasing progression and interaction.

The definition of *legato*, from the Italian word means *bound* as in "bound together."

---

*The word *elision*, often used erroneously in this connection, does not mean merely the carrying over of one sound to the next, but involves also the omission of some element in a word (Chris/mas, han/kerchief). A kindred elision occurs in instrumental notation.

56

Now test the definition in this one-long-word approach:

Say: "Metro**po**litan" then: "What a **love**ly day."

Do you feel the same five pulses within the four-word sentence as within the single word?

Now the same approach with notation:

Sing:

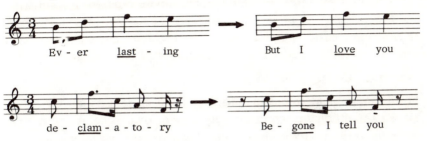

Ev - er   last - ing   But   I   love   you

de - clam - a - to - ry   Be - gone   I   tell   you

Q.E.D.: Words, spoken and sung, are bound to each other in the same manner as syllables are within a word.

A LESSON IN LIAISON

That traditional feature of the French language, *liaison,* helps to elucidate English linkage. The Gallic tongue forges a strong link between a word ending in a consonant and a word beginning with a vowel. In French, the phrase *je vous aime* becomes *je vou zaime.* In English *those eyes* never becomes *tho zeyes.* French usage furnishes an excellent linguistic model to follow, but with this signal difference: In English, the final *z* sound in *those*, carried over to the next word *eyes*, retains the unstressed character of a *final* sound. French *liaison,* on the other hand, imparts to the *z* sound of *vous* the impact of an *initial* sound in a word (*zaime*).

The rule: In English, as we link the final weak consonant to the next word, the consonant holds to its original intensity, neither more nor less. Thus, *and all* should never give the impression of *an dall.*

SOME CLASSIC BLOOPERS

glorious wine	*(glorious swine)*
before I'm old	*(before I mold)*
this, our food	*(this sour food)*

The error of incorrect linkage and misguided stress common to these amusing examples lies in treating final consonants as initial sounds of the next word. It has already been observed that while this makes good French, it makes bad English.

With correct stress and without breaking the continuity of tone, compare the difference between *glorious wine* and *glorious swine*. In the first the whole word *wine* is stressed, including the *w*. The final *s* in *glorious* must remain weak to avoid *wine* becoming *swine*.

Some choral directors and coaches advise separating word from word in an effort to prevent the possibility of such confusion. But why endanger the legato of a phrase when the problem can be circumvented with skillful techniques of correct English stress and linkage?

THE MAIN VEHICLE OF LEGATO

From the moment voice students first stand up to a piano, the vowel takes its traditional place at the very core of their vocal training. Very early in continuous vocalizing, they learn vowel-to-vowel legato. At a more advanced stage, singers develop consistency of vowel tone and of color, so necessary to the legato line.

For its basic role in legato the vowel must be fully sustained until it meets and blends, with a slight crescendo, into the shape of the consonant. Singers should guard against losing the recognizable shape of prolonged vowels. If the mouth contour is permitted to slacken and the breath support to waver, the intended vowel gives way to a distortion unrecognizable out front.

Most important: However mellifluous it may sound, vowel-to-vowel legato with consonants neglected becomes gibberish.

CONSONANT MEANS "TO SOUND WITH"

The discredited notion that English consonants impair the lyricism of the voice still persists. As a result, many singers, fearful of endangering their hard-won vowel tone, approach consonants with apprehension. Far from being impediments, these vital sounds actually enhance the vocal flow.

In a reciprocal process, vowels lend consonants clarity and carrying power as consonants in turn set vowels going, energizing them onward to the end of the phrase. In lyric linkage, consonants lead the forward drive of the language in a continuing series of connecting syllables. Thus consonants play twin roles as the chief instruments of intelligibility and as vibrant contributors of color to the fabric of song.

Obviously, a precondition for the active partnership of vowels and consonants is their accurate production* and skillful connection.

*Chapters IV and V deal in detail with the sixteen vowels and twenty-five consonants of American English.

CONSONANTS ON THE MOVE

Voiced assets. The fifteen English consonants that involve vocal cord vibration add greatly to the nonstop effect of continuous tone. But to the detriment of pronunciation and legato, unvoicing these vibrating shapes is common practice, especially at the ends of words. Note the prime example of the final *s* in countless words which is actually a *z* sound. This fine, brief buzz of a consonant — as in *begins*(z), *songs*(z), *verses*(z) — when articulated as an unvoiced sibilant becomes a down-graded noise element. This omnipresent letter, *s*, when properly pronounced *z*, bridges sonorously to the next word.*

Voiceless, not soundless. Ten so-called voiceless consonants produce a variety of *sound effects* that ride on the breath along with the vowel. They resemble sound effects often heard from the tympani section of an orchestra. Their deft interjection of voicelessness, particularly of the continuants† (*s, sh, f, th*), aids the indissoluble linking that legato requires. Immune to scooping or hard attack, these pitchless shapes make the smoothest transitions to the next higher or lower note.

Here the final *s* in the word *miss* (two letters but one sound)‡ bridges effortlessly to the next word. Caution: The *s*, as a final weak consonant, when carried over must not be stressed.

Misnamed stop-plosives. The percussive consonants (*p, t, k, b, d, g*) neither stop nor explode nor break the line. Only at the ends of phrases do these clear-cut sounds come to an abrupt halt, and then with a percussive effect, not a gust of air.§

*Some final *s*'s are pronounced *s* (*lights, takes*). See rules for *s* and *z* on p. 194.

†*Continuants:* Voiceless or voiced consonants that can be held (unlike the *plosives* that cannot).

‡There are only double letters, not double sounds, within words in English.

§The consonants *ch* and *j* are kindred sounds to the plosives and share some of the same characteristics, particularly their percussive effect at the ends of phrases.

59

To preserve unbroken legato: Prepare the vowel in advance, and then in one movement, deliver it together with the consonant in a single pattern holding the jaw steady. The rule: Plosives are produced in the shape of the following sound (pp. 206-18 and 233-52).

WORDS DIVIDED AS SUNG

My cou - ntry 'ti - zo-vthee

This division of a phrase in which each segment begins with a consonant, while perhaps difficult to read, becomes good legato when sung. Syllabication in dictionaries (and song texts) is often unsuitable for singing.

Here are examples of such rearrangement for singing:

As Printed		*As Sung*	
lov-ing	end-ed	**lo**-ving	**en**-ded
heav-en	rit-u-al	**hea**-ven	**ri**-tu-al
pal-ace	leg-end-a-ry	**pa**-lace	**le**-gen-da-ry

Note: If the *As Printed* arrangement were followed literally, the division of syllables would break the legato. In the *As Sung* column, the stronger first syllables are in bold type to emphasize the correct stress for these words.

HOW LONG IS A CONSONANT?

The answer to this question generally calls forth a variety of opinions, some fanciful. For example, singers are sometimes advised to slip consonants *in-between*, (Between what? one wonders.) Such advice implies that these vital shapes have neither substance nor existence of their own in time and space.

Conscientious attempts have been made to chart tangible duration by placing consonants on imaginary grace notes, or by exact sub-divided notation, or by other means. We must, of course, accord consonants the reality of existence despite the difficulty of determining exactly how much time value is to be allotted.

The length of a consonant depends on various factors: the given notation, the tempo, its position in a word, its position in a measure, and also the character of the sound itself. The more sonorous consonants (*m, n, l*) deserve longer duration than the fragmentary percussive shapes or the buzzing and sibilant sounds.

Where then does the time come from? Mainly from the vowel. The following break-down, not to be considered exact, demonstrates approximate and comparative durations of consonants as related to the vowel.

These examples are based on a whole note representing four beats. Note that vowel duration changes, depending on the character and length of the consonant. All suggested allotted time values are, of course, approximate.

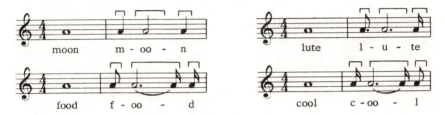

CONSONANTS BETWEEN PITCH CHANGES

Transitions in song call for flexibility, arbitrary opinions notwithstanding. Notation, tempo, vocal materials, and interpretation — all these factors must inevitably influence the choice of where to place a consonant in transition from one pitch to another. As the prime mover of syllable and phrase, its impetus is forward toward the next note. Regardless of which note receives the consonant (and with vigilant avoidance of scooping and sliding), the legato line remains firm and undisturbed.

Consonants in general move ahead whether traveling to a higher or lower note, as below.*

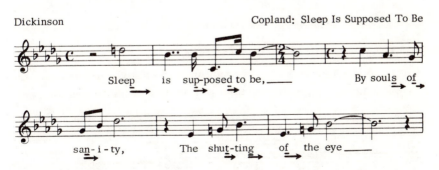

*The following four musical excerpts are from Aaron Copland's song cycle *Twelve Poems of Emily Dickinson.*

61

Sustained consonants (such as *m*, *n*, and sometimes *l*) are begun ahead of time and sung through the bar line. The *m* in both *May*'s below begins at the end of the previous measure and is sung on the pitch of the downbeat.

Dickinson   Copland: When They Come Back

An inflexible rule that *v* always be sung on the lower note would deprive the singer of the choice of perhaps a more dramatic effect with *v* on the higher note.

Dickinson   Copland: Going To Heaven!

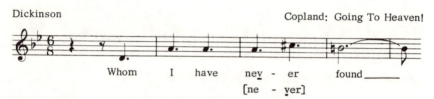

Although *k* would generally link to the next syllable, the singer may seek a more lyric effect with the *k* on the lower note.

Dickinson   Copland: Sleep Is Supposed To Be

The rule: Above all, maintain the legato.

RECITATIVES FOR LEGATO PRACTICE

Closer to the spoken language than arias, recitatives in particular call for binding word to word and note to note in a seamless legato.

Duncan   Britten: The Rape Of Lucretia

62

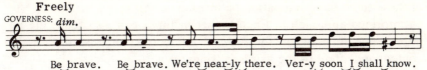

Freely
GOVERNESS: *dim.*

Be brave.   Be brave. We're near-ly there. Ver-y soon I shall know.

These examples demonstrate characteristics common to recitatives:

Tempo and pitch changes are speechlike.

Notation parallels stress patterns of the words.

The tessitura lies in the middle of the voice.

There is greater freedom and flexibility in execution.

The singer can transfer to more complex areas of song the legato skill acquired in the simpler musical form of recitatives.

UNDERSTANDING ENGLISH INFLECTION

Though the effects of inflection patterns on song would seem to be the exclusive concern of the composer, the singer can benefit from a technical understanding of simple English speech tunes.

These are composed of three basic legato curves:

up ➚ for questions ("Are you ready?")

down ➘ for statements ("Not quite yet.")

down-up or *up-down* for variations. ("Hello?")

("Please!")

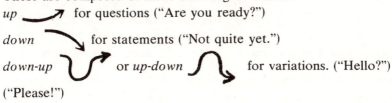

Mozart: Marriage Of Figaro

Su- san-na?   No, it's   not

The usual inflections — non-emphatic — are short tonal ascent ➚ or descent ➘ When the curve is greater a new element is added, the emotional:

"Stop." ➘   "Stop!" ➘   "Stop!!" ➘   The last is highly charged. In music this pattern of emotional curve is often intensified.

63

Except for recitatives, the performer can only make limited use of these three basic intonation patterns and their many variations. But an informed approach to English speech tunes can also serve the interpreter at times when the musical inflections correspond with the content and intent of the words he sings.

No! I'll nev - er yield_ to your will!

Note: The emotional sweep verbally and musically is carried through two octaves.

ECONOMY OF OPERATION

Consonants between words. When the same consonants meet between words, prepare the first consonant, hold it slightly, then articulate and stress the second. This action gives the listener the impression of two consonants.*

hold execute hold execute
(f) (f) (k) (k)
enough freedom black cat

When vowel meets vowel. To link identical vowels between words (*the evening, though old*), prolong the shared vowel but lean on the second vowel with a slight crescendo (*the evening*). This blending technique will forestall a glottal attack. If the interval between vowels is long, a separation may be necessary.

Partners in production. When two adjacent consonants are cognates† (*half voice, what dream*), prepare the first consonant and execute the second (with light stress).

Related consonants. Some adjacent consonants, while neither iden-

---

*The same action of holding the first consonant and executing the second occurs in Italian (*frammenta*).

†*Cognates* is the speech term for two consonants similarly produced, one of which is voiced and the other voiceless. There are nine such pairs in English (*f-v, t-d, b-p, s-z,* etc.).

tical nor cognates, are closely connected in articulatory movement. Link *t* and *l* in *lately* (both tongue-tip shapes) in co-ordinated action to obviate the awkward *latuhly*.

Adjacent percussives. The lip, teeth, and tongue shapes (*p, b, t, d, k, g*) are related in the hold-release action of their sound effects.

*(ba**d** g**irl**, grea**t** **c**oncert).* To preserve legato flow, deliver these percussive consonants clearly and rapidly, holding the jaw steady and *without spillage of breath*.

Think link. Whether *identical, partners, related,* or *unrelated,* all consonants merge with each other and with vowels in an ever-moving, lucid legato. Particularly consonants in clusters between words require careful articulation and co-ordination (*memori**z**e**d** **sc**ore*).
z d s k

In slow tempi. These linking techniques pertain mainly to moderate and fast tempi. It is usually necessary in a slow tempo to pronounce both sounds between words (*than**k** **G**od*). Do not, however, allow cutoff of breath or actual separation at the apparent juncture between *thank* and *God*. The legato remains undisturbed.

FAMILIARITY BREEDS CONTENT

True lyric linkage encompasses all the sounds of language and music with none sloughed off. Obviously a requisite for such artistry in English is thorough familiarity with its sixteen vowels and twenty-five consonants.

If American singers would develop a legato approach in speaking — with well-supported longer phrases, fewer stops without purpose, and linked sounds — the carry-over would bring security to their legato delivery in song.

PUNCTUATION PITFALL

A mechanical halt at a comma,* as if it were a red light, contributes

---

*The marks of punctuation designed primarily for silent reading do not necessarily make sense when spoken or sung. To punctuate the phrases he performs, the artist assumes the right to create his own effects in re-creating the intent of the text and not to be bound by typographical convention. To follow stop signs automatically results in trite delivery.

nothing but a break in the line. In "My love is like a red, red rose," the comma, if heard as a pause between the two *red*'s, would sound all wrong to the ear.

ACROSS THE BOUNDARIES

The danger of breaking the legato flow is greatest at change points between words. While singers grasp the need for linking sounds within words, it is between words that they often falter.

Just as the voice moves through the bar lines, so the vowels and consonants should connect across boundaries of words in an interlocking chain of notes and syllables. The listener hears the sung phrase like a long polysyllabic word out of which his mind sorts a coherent flow of syllables into language.

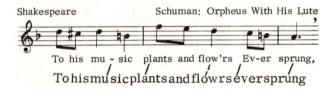

STACCATO/LEGATO

Staccato is not, as often supposed, the opposite of *legato*. The stylistic effect merely gives the illusion of separate impulses without breaking the line. Important: Support the detached notes firmly on the breath *within* the over-all legato of the phrase. In order not to lose intelligibility pronounce crisply and hold on, as well, to the stress patterns of the words.

This excerpt calls for staccato in two selected phrases. The effects should be delivered without breaking the legato implicit in the over-all phrase.

66

PRESTO TEMPO

When the score begins to race, singers, unless fortified by supportive techniques, end up breathless and unintelligible. The remedy is *to lean on the vowels,* particularly those of key words, and to let the consonants follow along. To punch away determinedly at the consonants in the mistaken idea that this will bring clarity results only in unvocal production and loss of meaning.

In the following excerpts, to hold the line stable sing from vowel to vowel carrying the consonants along to bridge syllables and words. Keep to the strong stresses on words as indicated.

For this excerpt, visualize the same markings for vowels and stress as in the one above.

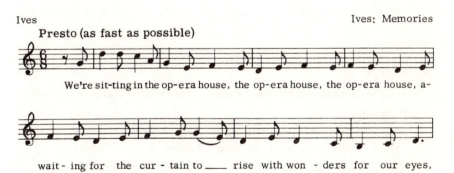

THE BEAT UNDERNEATH

All our spoken and sung phrases consist of a succession of stressed and unstressed elements moving forward. The continuous contrasts transmit acoustic signals of meaning to listening ears, somewhat like the intermittent beep-beeps of an electronic sending device.

Legato does not mean a softened or lax line devoid of these rhythms. The correct, communicative stress and unstress of English words and syllables must continue like an inner pulse within the smoothly sung phrase.

UNDERLYING CONCEPT

The principle of the whole as greater than the sum of its parts is fundamental to the art of legato singing. Thus even though a rest may briefly break the continuity of music and text, the thought is always carried forward. This process is repeated through the whole song to the last sung sound, and beyond, ending only when the accompaniment ceases.

SOME FINAL DON'T'S AND DO'S FOR LEGATO

Reject:

Hampering patterns from speech

False notions about English consonants

Word-by-word delivery that loses listeners and energy

Breaking the legato by careless articulation

Unmotivated stops and badly placed quick breaths

Automatic response to punctuation

Weakening the line by cutting off vowels too soon in advance of consonants

Bending, crooning, scooping, sliding transitions between pitches.

Remember:

The main vehicle of linkage-legato is the sustained and recognizable vowel.

A consonant, whether printed as part of the previous or the next word, leads syllables in the forward drive of word rhythms.

No English vowel or consonant need interrupt the momentum of the phrase. English does not cut the vocal flow; singers do.

The practice of seeing and feeling connected sounds *in advance* reinforces legato singing.

To reach the listener preconditioned to hearing the language in blended forms (*smear*), singers are required to produce clear, linked sounds (*slur*). (See acoustical concept of *smear-slur*, pp. 55-56.)

Consonants have existence in time and space.

The economical co-ordinations of consonants save breath and strengthen the illusion of continuous tone.

The handling of consonants in transitions between pitches calls for skill and flexibility.

The final consonant in English, when linked to the next word, remains weak and is never stressed.

French liaison makes a good model for English linkage despite differences in stress.

IN CONCLUSION

Oriented always toward the audience, the artist delivers the text-message in the form that most insures accurate reception at the listening end. He makes expert use of linkage-legato, an amalgam of parallel techniques welding language and music together in beauty and intelligibility. He counteracts all interference with the sustained flow of firmly linked elements of limpid language, which he makes certain to underscore with intrinsic English word rhythms.

Thus, as a creator of American *bel canto*, the artist reflects and validates the superb singability of English.

CHAPTER FOUR

THE VOWEL CONTENT
OF AMERICAN ENGLISH

Vowel Essentials for Eye and Ear

THE MAIN BODY OF TONE

To dramatize the major role of vowel and consonant, experiment by extracting from this phrase first all vowels, then all consonants.

Foster: I Dream Of Jeanie

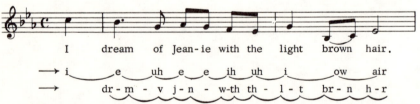

When all the vowels are sounded in a chain, the result is pleasing, perhaps, but gibberish. When the consonants are linked through the dashes, the result almost makes sense. Consonants divorced from vowels may sound like some strange dialect or a slowed-down record, but meaning comes through. With vowels contributing the main body of tone and consonants the main meaning, the singer must unite them firmly in a partnership of sound and sense.

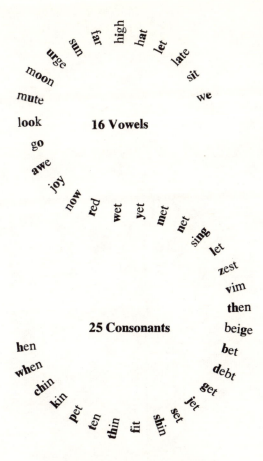

hat
far
let
sun
late
urge
sit
moon
mute
we
look   **16 Vowels**
go
awe
joy
now
red
wet
yet
met
net
sing
let
zest
vim
then
25 Consonants   beige
hen   bet
when   debt
chin   get
kin   jet
pet   set
ten   thin   fit   shin

"S for Speech and Song"

THE LANGUAGE AT A GLANCE

Winding about the letter S, appears the American English alphabet of pronunciation, sixteen vowels and twenty-five consonants. Forty-one in all, they represent a galaxy of tonal shades, shapes, and sound effects which, when faithfully executed, determine the clarity of English texts.

VOWEL PRODUCTION ASSEMBLY LINE

The following impressionistic design broadly conveys what happens in the body during the creation of the resonance phenomenon called

Vowel Production Assembly Line

a vowel. The process in slow motion is as follows: the brain flashes a message to enunciate the chosen vowel; the breath instantly causes the vocal cords to vibrate as the vowel shaping begins; the breath supports the emerging vowel shape from one resonating cavity to another, setting off sympathetic vibration toward head and chest; the articulators contribute the final shaping; and the breath, conveying the vowel in finished form out through the lips, is converted into sound waves that travel to the ears of the listener.

THE MECHANICS

Involved in the production are three main cavities: the throat (just above the cords), the nose (behind, not in it, actually the nasal pharynx) and, most important of all resonators, the mouth (the oral cavity). The shape and quality of vocal tones are molded through changes in these resonating areas and amplified by sympathetic vibration.

Except for the hard palate (roof of the mouth), all the articulatory organs within the oral cavity are endowed with considerable flexibility. The soft palate (that spongy mass behind the hard palate) and the uvula (the pendulous lob at its center) can be elevated to increase the size of the back of the mouth. Even with its tip at rest against or below the lower teeth for all vowels, the tongue, that essential shaping device, can execute a variety of pliant and subtle movements. The lips, whether rounding or unrounding, follow through to give the vowel its final shaping. The jaw remains a relaxed adjunct to production as it shifts, rises, and lowers.

Thus each vowel has its own distinctive pattern of shaped resonance by means of which the listener can distinguish it from all other vowels. The singer's task is to mold sixteen individual English vowels with maximum resonance of tone and without sacrifice of the recognizable sound of each.

VOWEL SYMBOLS EXPLAINED

Dictionary. The most widely known dictionary symbols have been selected as principal guide to the pronunciation of the vowels and consonants.

IPA. The International Phonetic Alphabet, more or less familiar to singers, represents a more precise system of speech sounds. IPA symbols are here utilized as additional identification.

73

Ah, ih, eh, and uh. These forms, especially *ah*, so popular among singers, are also included in the material whenever pertinent. *Note:* The sixteen vowels are listed in the order in which they are studied.

Vowels and Symbols

Dictionary	IPA	Key Word	Other Forms
ē	[i]	beat	
ĭ	[ɪ]	bit	ih
ā	[eɪ]	bait	
ĕ	[ɛ]	bet	eh
ă	[æ]	bat	
ī	[aɪ]	bite	
ä	[ɑ]	bard	ah
ŭ	[ʌ]	butt	uh
ə	[ə]	about	
ûr	[ɝ]	bird	
ər	[ɚ]	bother	
o͞o	[u]	fool	
ū	[ju]	fuel	
o͝o	[ʊ]	full	
ō	[ou]	foal	
ô	[ɔ]	fall	
oi	[ɔɪ]	foil	
ou	[aʊ]	foul	

Note: the symbol /â/ [ɛ ə], always followed by /r/ and found only in words like *fair*, *bear*, and *there*, is not listed among the sixteen vowels. (See p. 154)

VOWEL LADDER I: THE SIXTEEN

The vowels from one to sixteen are arranged in descending order based on gradual progressions for seven unrounded vowels from most closed to most open mouth formation and from highest to lowest front arch of the tongue; for seven rounded vowels, the progression is from highest to lowest back arch and from smallest circle to largest oval shape of the lips. The two *central vowels*, unrounded *ŭ* and rounded *ûr* and

their weak counterparts, ə and ər, appear between the ladders.* Note·
that there are eight unrounded and eight rounded vowels in American
English.

Vowel Ladder I: The Sixteen Vowels of American English

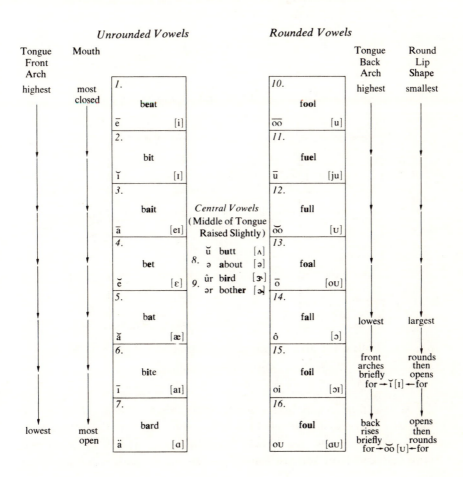

Unrounded Vowels   *Rounded Vowels*

Tongue Front Arch	Mouth				Tongue Back Arch	Round Lip Shape
highest	most closed	*1.* beat ē [i]		*10.* fool ōō [u]	highest	smallest
		2. bit ĭ [ɪ]		*11.* fuel ū [ju]		
		3. bait ā [eɪ]	*Central Vowels* (Middle of Tongue Raised Slightly)	*12.* full o͝o [ʊ]		
		4. bet ĕ [ɛ]	*8.* ŭ butt [ʌ] ə about [ə] *9.* ûr bird [ɝ] ər bother [ɚ]	*13.* foal ō [ou]		
		5. bat ă [æ]		*14.* fall ô [ɔ]	lowest	largest
		6. bite ī [aɪ]		*15.* foil oi [ɔɪ]	front arches briefly for → ĭ [ɪ] ← for	rounds then opens
lowest	most open	*7.* bard ä [ɑ]		*16.* foul ou [aʊ]	back rises briefly for → ōō [ʊ] ← for	opens then rounds

*The first syllable in *about* is listed as the weak counterpart of the stressed vowel in *butt*: the second syllable in *bother*, as the weak counterpart of the stressed vowel in *bird*. These unstressed versions of /ŭ/, No. 8, and /ûr/, No. 9 on the ladder, are generally classified as additional vowels. While stressing does affect the vowel, the qualitative difference does not appear great enough to warrant such classification.

75

VOWEL LADDER II: THE COMPOUND VOWELS

IPA symbols represent the approximate two-vowel blend of diphthongs in these words: **raise** [eɪ]; **thy** [aɪ]; **lone** [ou]; **voice** [ɔɪ]; **now** [aʊ]. Sing all five with words and music:

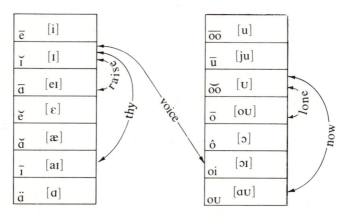

Vowel Ladder II: The Five Compound Vowels

Follow the arrows that show the merging of two vowels
into a third sound.

These long compound vowels, or diphthongs,* should be reproduced in song as single syllables and without loss to the integrity of
their speech sounds (see Vowel Guidelines, pp. 81-82). Observe that
both [eɪ] and [ou] require only one step up the ladder toward their

---

*The English diphthong is defined (in *Webster's Third International Dictionary
Unabridged*) as "a gliding *monosyllabic* speech item that starts at or *near* the
articulatory position for one vowel and moves to or *toward* the position for another,
and that is usually indicated in phonetic transcription by two symbols, representing
often only *approximately* the beginning and ending limits of the glide." (Italics
by the author.)

second elements, [ɪ] and [ʊ]. As a consequence, their "diphthong" character is hardly apparent, whereas [ɔɪ] and [ɑʊ], with longer routes to traverse, sound closer to the concept of two blended vowels. Note: The second vowel element is always a shorter vowel.

VOWEL LADDER III: MODIFICATION

The use of words and music notation clarifies the modification process. For singing in extreme registers, the sound and shape of most vowels change, but the listener continues to hear the original word. Dotted lines with arrows indicate the approximate routes the vowels travel.

Vowel Ladder III: Modification for Extreme Registers

Note: The vowels /ĭ/ (*fit*), /o͝o/ (*full*), /ŭ/ (*love*), and /ô/ (*caught*) are relatively stable at all pitch levels and thus the words remain unchanged.

77

The action. The ladder structure illustrates the modification from a relatively closed vowel to a more open one as the soprano voice approaches its highest reaches. The descent is from one rung of the ladder to the next below, beginning with the closed vowel $\bar{e}$ (**heat**) to the more open $\breve{i}$ (**hit**) until $\ddot{a}$ (**calm**) moves toward the middle vowel $\breve{u}$ (**love**). On the second ladder, beginning with $\overline{oo}$ (**fool**), the same process takes place down to oi (**joy**) and ou (**sound**). These compound vowels follow the same adjustment as $\hat{o}$ (**caught**) and $\ddot{a}$ (**calm**) except for their special diphthong blend. Follow all the dotted lines to the arrows which point toward the modified vowel sounds.

An approximate directive. As pitches rise, the original vowel shape alters in the given direction but not necessarily all the way. Thus the movements toward substitute vowels are not as well defined as indicated. Although the ladder can offer only an approximate guide to modification, the search for a modified, yet recognizable, sound should be made close to the indicated area.

The different ranges. Although sopranos generally have higher tessitura than tenors and thus a greater need for modification, tenors can also benefit from use of the same approximate routes to less strained vocal production. Mezzo-sopranos require more or less the same adjustment in the highest ranges as do sopranos. As for baritones and basses, the modification (also approximate) proceeds from more open to more closed vowel in reverse of the soprano. The deep, darker tones of these male voices tend to move toward a brighter sound as their pitch descends (*hit* to *heat*, *let* to *late*, etc.).

Vowel Guidelines

AN AMERICAN STANDARD

Pronunciation of the sixteen representative vowels or phonemes scrutinized in this chapter is based on the speech patterns of live models in all media — actors, singers, commentators — who exert the greatest influence on American English usage. With the aim of featuring the vowel sounds most readily identifiable in the country as a whole, obtrusive localisms have been screened out. When put to use in the field of song, high standards of voice production elevate these vowels to meet the communicative and esthetic demands of vocal literature.

Singers should perfect and perform those vowel sounds to which audiences, nationally, are attuned.

NOT A BOOK ON VOICE PRODUCTION

The task ahead concerns itself primarily with the vowel as a conveyor of meaning, for without accurate vowels, however toneful, nebulous words of texts will lose the listener. With sound and sense held inseparable, singers need sacrifice neither tonal quality nor the character of meaningful vowels.

If singing can be learned, so can diction. No one is "born" with beautiful diction.

WHY BEGIN WITH VOWELS?

Because the singer does. From the first lesson, the voice trains on a diet of vowel routines that continue in daily workouts for vocal fitness.

Singers tend to shy away from anything that might seem to endanger their hard-won vocal quality. At the start they approach the study of vowel enunciation with apprehension, though it vanishes once they master accurate and resonant sounds.

We do not have, as often assumed, five vowels (*a, e, i, o, u*): we have five *letters* and sixteen vowel *sounds* commanding the same inherent beauty as the Italian. We have nine more vowels than in the land of *bel canto*; and if the singability of a language were measured by its vowel content, ours would come out ahead!

The vowel, enthroned as the tonal center of all words, bestows clarity on consonants as it carries them along.

THE BASIC FALLACY

Vocalizing exclusively on Italian vowels will not produce good English diction. Thinking in one language and singing in another accounts for the hybrid Italian-English diction so often heard. While some American performers can manage fine diction despite this Italian to English gymnastic, the technique spells danger for the majority. Vowels should be implanted into the tone in their natural form and not artificially transplanted.

The exclusively English vowel in the word *love*, easily the most common word in song, is rarely, if ever, made part of a vocalise. Small wonder, then, that we hear so many "lahve's" or "lawve's"!

All sixteen English vowels should form the basis of vocalises to insure the delivery of unadulterated English.

THE CHICKEN OR THE EGG

Is the tone built into the vowel or the vowel into the tone? The performer who produces a tone and then attempts to stamp the character of individual vowels upon it runs the risk of deforming the vowel. But when learned sensations associated with an accurate vowel anticipate the onset of tone, such integration of vowel sound and tone creates a higher level of both.

Mold the sixteen tonal shapes (vowels and tone built together) into the voice system for intelligible performance.

THE SPOKEN AND SUNG VOWEL

For each vowel there are certain boundaries or space limits within the mouth or oral cavity.* So long as the vowel is produced within these boundaries it will communicate as intended by the performer. But if the singer over-reaches these limits, the listener will receive the impression of quite another sound.

Over and above the spoken form, the sung vowel involves *more vitalized articulators; more varied degrees of intensity; firmer support of breath pressure; more open, released jaw; augmented vowel size; prescribed pitches; and an enlarged resonating system.* (See Vowel Production Assembly Line, p. 72). The stable position for an accurate vowel in song relates to its position in speech, but with an adjustment taking place at the singing level.

There is no absolutely fixed vowel position, only an approximate and useful guide established by the spoken phoneme.†

THE AH-STRICKEN SINGER

Super-sound *ah* rides high in the world of song. In English, however,

---

*The What to Do sections in the vowel study that follows offer a guide to the approximate boundaries of correct enunciation for each vowel sound.

†Phoneme: A sound readily recognizable and distinctive in a language which changes the meaning of a word by its presence (c*a*p, c*o*p). In French, for example, in "Je vous hais" ("I hate you"), the *h* is silent, but when uttered emotionally can be aspirated. However this does not make *h* a French phoneme. To us the difference between *it* and *hit*, *at* and *hat*, etc., establishes *h* as an English phoneme.

other glamorous vowels such as /ā/ or /ō/ outnumber *ah* by far. Singers have allowed themselves to be misled into relating all vowels to the "perfect" open sound of international *ah*. This approach has become a permissive device to project a free tone without taking the trouble to shape an authentic vowel. Fifteen other English vowels are often the victims.

English offers a galaxy of vowels, all essential and all resonant, for the embellishment of vocal literature.

TO ROUND OR NOT TO ROUND

Some singers are taught lip-rounding for almost all English vowels especially to achieve "darker" sounds. Others are encouraged to play down such lip movement regardless of the intrinsic shape of a given vowel. Diction teachers, however, line up unequivocally in favor of rounding or not rounding English vowels as each requires.

Considerable changes of pitch, and often volume, affect the prescribed lip shape. However, despite the more open, released jaw, etc., lip-rounding, while necessarily modified, remains essential to the production of individual vowels in singing.

Of the sixteen English vowels, eight require lip-rounding in whole or in part for the delivery of recognizable sounds.

DIPHTHONG EQUATION: 1+1=1

When not confused by the theory that diphthongs are composed of two distinct, separable vowels, singers enunciate these ordinary English sounds quite naturally as single entities.

To allay the fears caused by the misunderstood glide between the two merging sounds of a diphthong, note the definition of a glide: "to pass or taper off into something different gradually and imperceptibly by slight progressive changes" (*Webster, Unabridged*). In other words, both vowels modify in a blending action to form a third sound, a distinctive English vowel.*

The first element is the predominant one blending gradually toward the lesser element, the second. (Actually, both vowels merely approximate their original shapes.) Since it is impossible to pinpoint an exact moment of transition, pronouncing two separate vowels can only pro-

---

*Diphthongs are conventionally classified apart from vowels. Since vowels are variants of diphthongs, and vice versa, diphthongs in this chapter are listed and discussed along with other vowels in logical sequence.

duce an inaccurate and artificial sound. (See Vowel Ladder II, p. 76).

The five English diphthongs are actually compound vowels, each the close and unique union of two vowel qualities in one syllable.

DIVIDE ONLY TO CONQUER

While singers need to absorb the separate identities of sixteen vocalic shapes, they should resist the temptation in vocalizing to linger too long on these disembodied elements.

Vowels combined with consonants into word clusters and supported by music make the most favorable material for study and practice. The voice mechanism remembers best through muscle and stored sensation what it experiences in the flow of song. And the listeners' cues for recognition of a distinct vowel come not from its sustained isolation, but from the correct movement of the articulators from consonants to vowels and back to consonants.

The important step of vocalizing on fragments should give way as soon as possible to singing words and phrases.

Study Plan for Vowels

FROM SPEECH TO SONG

The order in which the vowels in standard American usage are studied is the order of *Vowel Ladder I* (p. 75). Moving from the first vowel *e*, (**see**) to the sixteenth *ou* (**out**) involves a progressive change, from one vowel to the next in tongue arching, lip shape, and mouth opening.

The plan of study followed for each vowel is designed to facilitate treating them individually, whether in or out of sequence.

Vowel introduced: The dictionary and IPA symbols for the vowel, a list of word examples and various spellings, the general description and usage of the target sound and its occurrence in foreign languages.

What to do: An analysis of the basic speech approach to production of each vowel sound (tongue position, lip and mouth formation) as a secure, general guide to the sung vowel.*

*To avoid possible confusion with established methods of voice training, several traditional speech terms have been omitted: the classification of vowels as *front*, *middle*, and *back*, and of tongue movements as *tense* or *lax*. Also omitted is discussion of jaw action. Due to the varied and individual nature of jaw positions, the question is best left to the discretion of singers and voice teachers.

What Not to Do: Pitfalls to avoid in producing the vowel, including a listing of common local mispronunciations in the United States, especially the national problem of nasal speech.

PROGRESSIVE PRACTICE
A short poetry selection to be spoken.

First Say: Instructions on how to speak the target vowel in context.

Next Chant: Included in special cases for additional practice.

Then Sing: The same selection adjusted to an improvised musical fragment.

SINGING THE VOWEL
Note: For general discussion of adjustment of the vowel from speech to song, see *Vowel Guidelines*, p. 80.

Distortions to Avoid.   A discussion of the main problems encountered in singing the target vowel.

Vocalize.   Instructions for effective drills of vowel sound. (For transitions of extreme registers, see *Vowel Ladder III*, pp. 77-78.) *Vowel Wheels*, a series of comparative exercises, included for extensive drill.

Kinesthetics.   Analysis of sensory responses to accurate production of the sung vowel; the building of reflexes into the voice mechanism.

MATCHING TO MUSIC
Finally, a musical excerpt, selected from repertoire materials, with several examples of the target vowel; analysis of setting, pitch, duration, and position of vowel in word and measure; as well as the effect of English stress and unstress.

The Sixteen Vowels of American English

ē [i]

he, **feel**, **peace**, scene, **grieve**, deceive, regime, **people**
Common vowel; long, bright sound (the sound is name of letter).
Usage: /ē/ appears mainly in strong word-types and stressed syllables. Article *the* pronounced *thee* before vowels, but always unstressed, as in *the ideal*. Standard American: unstressed short /ē/ (instead of /ĭ/) in weak, final syllables (tenderly, happy); in verb endings (marries); and in plurals (charities).
/ē/ appears in Italian, French, and German.

WHAT TO DO /ē/

Tongue Position: Tip firmly held behind lower front teeth. Front arched forward nearly to hard palate (most forward and highest· in mouth of all sixteen vowels). Sides aligned with upper molars.

Lip Shape: Unrounded, horizontal.

Mouth Opening: Narrowest opening of all unrounded English vowels.

WHAT NOT TO DO /ē/

Do *not* grin, spreading lips or pulling back at corners.
Do *not* tense throat muscles or jaw.
Do *not* flatten tongue; keep arched.

Speech Localisms to Avoid: Tendency to nasalize words like *seem*, *neat*.

Drawling /ē/ into limp shape with an added vowel (feel ——➤ feeuhl).

PROGRESSIVE PRACTICE FOR /ē/

> Over the ripening peach
>> Buzzes the bee.
> Splash on the billowy beach
>> Tumbles the sea.
> But the peach
> And the beach
> They are each
> Nothing to me!
>> W. S. Gilbert

First Say: Practice verse with good speech tone, connecting sounds and words in linked flow.

Adhere to correct stress patterns of words and syllables.

Execute long, level /ē/'s with forward "ring" (think double *ee*).

Note that the *-y* in *billowy* is pronounced as an unstressed /ē/.

Match all /ē/'s whether followed by consonants (p*ea*ch) or open-ended (*sea*).

Then Sing: Song has been described as intensified, elongated speech. As you improvise a melody in free-form style, hold on to the speech shape for /ē/ practiced in reading verse aloud.

SINGING /ē/

Distortions to Avoid: Constricted production with retracted lips and overly arched tongue.

Lax production with limp tongue.

Replacement of typical, more open English /ē/ with more closed and abbreviated European version.

Vocalize: This international sound is the foundation for countless classical vocalises. Use any of these, making sure, however, to drill the English vowel /ē/ and not some foreign variety. For Vowel Wheel, see p. 98.

Kinesthetics: Cultivate the sensation of action and co-ordination in lips, tongue, mouth, and resonating cavities (all the active and reactive parts in the "production line") in forming the target vowel, /ē/, with firm breath support. Establish shape and feedback of relatively longer and untensed English sound.

Feel tongue-tip secure against back of lower front teeth and front of tongue arching as sides make contact with upper back teeth.

Hold intact the relaxed horizontal lip shape during phonation. (Stability of this mouth mold reinforces accuracy of sung /ē/.)

MATCHING TO MUSIC /ē/ [i]

In singing this excerpt work for accurate target vowel.

Heed the sense stress:

She bid me take love easy. As the leaves grow on the tree.

Folk Song: Down By The Sally Gardens

Moderato

She bid me take love eas - y, As the leaves grow on the tree.

Word and Setting	*Delivery*
(1) She	Pronoun is on upbeat, do not stress /ē/
(2) me —	Keep /ē/ stable on moving eighth notes
(3) ea - sy	Distinguish between first, bright, stressed /ē/ and second, unstressed, shorter /ē/

86

(4) Strong word is on downbeat; sing bright
/ē/ and voice all consonants

leaves

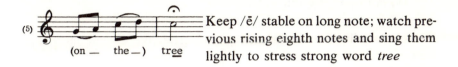

(5) Keep /ē/ stable on long note; watch previous rising eighth notes and sing them
lightly to stress strong word *tree*

(on — the —) tree

Final Note: The /ē/, highest and most forward of vowel sounds, should be free and unconstricted.

The English vowel is longer and less tense than its Italian or French counterpart.

The standard pronunciation for weak syllables (easy) is an unaccented /ē/ and not an /ĭ/.

ĭ [ɪ]

it, lips, build, lyric, been, pretty, busy, women, individual, beautiful, singing (and all other "ing" words).

Characteristic and common short* English vowel.

Usage: Very serviceable sound in weak and strong positions and frequently interchangeable with *schwa*, [ə], as weakened vowel: delicate, notion, emphasis.

Appears in German, but not in Italian or French.

WHAT TO DO /ĭ/

Tongue Position: More released than /ē/. Tip rests behind lower front teeth. Front arched slightly less than for /ē/ but still high in the mouth. Sides aligned with upper teeth.

Lip Shape: Untensed, unrounded, horizontal.

Mouth Opening: Drops slightly from /ē/, more open.

*The designation *short* applies more specifically to speech, since in song the notation governs vowel length. However, when sung, the recognizable character of the "short" vowel must be retained.

WHAT NOT TO DO /ĭ/

Do *not* let sound fall back into throat.

Do *not* keep tongue too slack or too low in mouth.

Do *not* open jaw too wide.

Speech Localisms to Avoid: Throaty, grunt-like sound, more like *uh* (sister ⟶ si-uhster).

Substitution (mostly Southern) of /ĕ/ for /ĭ/ (*hem* for *him*) and vice versa.

Affectation of /ĭ/ vowel in "-ly" endings (love**lih**). Standard-American usage is unstressed /ē/ for this final syllable.

PROGRESSIVE PRACTICE FOR /ĭ/

> The moving finger writes; and, having writ,
> Moves on: nor all your piety nor wit,
> Shall lure it back to cancel half a line...
>
> Omar Khayyám (Fitzgerald)

> And since to look at things in bloom
> Fifty springs are little room...
>
> A. E. Housman

First Say: Practice the typically released quality of /ĭ/ in the excerpts making sure to focus *forward* on the hard palate. (Released does not mean sluggish.)

Note that both *e*'s in *piety* and *cancel* are pronounced /ĭ/ or closer to schwa, /ə/.

Next Chant: As you intone the words of the same lines, all the sounds will lengthen. The objective is to hold on to the character of the short target sound /ĭ/ despite its added length. Even in speaking we often prolong vowels in some emphatic context. "I'm fifty...fiiiifty!" she exclaimed. And the vowel remains clear.

Then Sing: Again, fashion some melodic lines. Carry over the spoken and chanted enunciation of all examples of the target vowel. Try to reproduce this intrinsically clear, simple sound. Do this wherever the pitch changes may lead.

SINGING /ĭ/

Distortions to Avoid: Heard all too frequently is /ē/ for /ĭ/ ("I love heem"), a carry-over from Italian, which has no /ĭ/ vowel.

Spoken often in a slip-shod manner, a guttural variety spilling over into song ("Don't do **uht**").

Vocalize: American singers reveal insecurity with /ĭ/, this rarely vocalized vowel which, typically English, has an innate lovely quality. Now set about building the accurate vowel into the voice mechanism beginning with familiar vocalises. For Vowel Wheel, see p. 98.

Kinesthetics: Develop feeling of two different yet somewhat similar contours for /ĭ/ and /ē/. With both vowels feel sensation of tongue, *high,* arching in mouth. With /ĭ/, however, the tongue drops slightly, releasing some of the tension. Establish the movement as distinctly performed in the same area for both vowels, with auditory feedback of /ē/ more sustained and brilliant, and auditory feedback of /ĭ/ more abbreviated, open, but *still bright.* Build these comparative sensory responses into mechanism firmly so as to avoid the common intrusion of foreign-sounding /ē/ for /ĭ/ in English song.

MATCHING TO MUSIC /ĭ/ [ɪ]

In singing this excerpt work for accurate target vowel.

Heed the sense stress:
All Heaven would I give and eternal bliss If I still could sometimes kiss you so

Büchner   Berg: Wozzeck

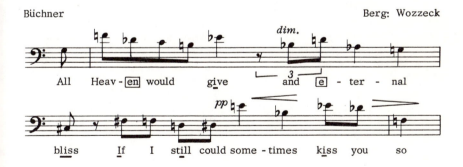

89

give

Sing released /ĭ/ (stable at all pitch levels) in strong active verbs

bliss

Use downbeat to stress noun; sing recognizable /ĭ/; do not tense toward /ē/

(bliss),   If   I

Do not over-emphasize conjunction *if* on higher note

still   (could)

Keep adverb *still* stressed in relation to other eighth notes; voice a resonant /l/

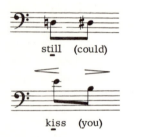

kiss   (you)

Use indicated crescendo to stress key word on fairly high note (only an eighth)

Final Note: The vowel /ĭ/ is a characteristic English sound often distorted.

The substitution of /ē/, a common fault, should be avoided.

A recognizable /ĭ/, although more relaxed than /ē/, is also bright and forward. The vowel in the weak syllables in *heaven* and in **e**ternal should be pronounced /ĭ/, especially with moderate to fast tempo.

ā[eɪ]

ate, day, fate, break, grey, reign, afraid, ancient, nature

Characteristic, long English vowel; technically a diphthong;* traditionally listed separately. (The sound is name of letter *a*, first in alphabet.)

Note: IPA symbol [eɪ] clarifies the diphthong pattern.

Appears in shorter, tenser versions in Italian, French, and German.

WHAT TO DO /ā/

Tongue Position: Tip down behind lower teeth. Front arched gently. Sides aligned with upper teeth, touching lightly. Then sides rise and front arches with minimal movement as sound extends toward /ĭ/.

Lip Shape: Remains unrounded throughout production, horizontal.

Mouth Opening: More open than /ē/ and /ĭ/ (halfway down Vowel Ladder I to /ä/).

Compound Vowel /ā/ [eɪ] in Slow Motion

Crest of sound

e e e **e eɪ** ɪ ɪ

Two vowel elements gradually blend into a single unit — the first element longer and stressed, the second shorter and unstressed. Both sounds merge at the approximate crest of the diphthong pattern.

WHAT NOT TO DO /ā/

Do *not* drop jaw too much; (/ā/ is relatively released, not lax vowel).

Do *not* tense lips and tongue.

Do *not* change mouth opening or move jaw while enunciating vowel.

---

*Diphthong: a composite two-vowel unit belonging to a single syllable. More precisely, it is the recognizable form of the extension of one given vowel rather than the joining together of two different vowels. All diphthongs, therefore, are treated here as single, long, distinctive vowels.

Speech Localisms to Avoid: Tense, nasalized /ā/, especially when adjacent to /m/ or /n/ (**saint, name, feign**).

Drawled, misshapen /ā/ with added vowel (**fate ⟶ fā-uht** or **fail ⟶ fā-uhl**).

PROGRESSIVE PRACTICE FOR /ā/

> But when I came to man's estate,
> With **hey**, ho, the wind and the **rain**,
> 'Gainst* knaves and thieves men shut their **gates**,
> For the **rain** it **raineth** every **day**.
>
> Shakespeare

First Say: Always practice with good speech tone. Observe how "natural" and uncomplicated /ā/ sounds when spoken and how readily identifiable to listeners. Avoid any taint of nasality.

Match all /ā/'s carefully, keeping them long and level.

In open-ended words like *day* and *hey*, the vowel tends to be longer, ending in a brief /ĭ/ off-glide. When, as in most words, a consonant follows (**estate, rain, knaves**), do not permit an off-glide.

Next Chant: As a stepping stone to sung sound chant the same verses. Make sure when intoning protracted /ā/'s that you faithfully transfer the spoken vowel. Be careful not to lose pitch on these sustained /ā/'s. Hold their shape stable.

Then Sing: Once again with a tune of your own setting the above text to music, try to adjust spoken and chanted /ā/'s to sung /ā/'s, keeping the correct vowel sound.

SINGING /ā/

Distortions to Avoid: Short, Italian hybrid, superimposed on English song.

---

*Note: In British English *'gainst* is pronounced with /ā/, in American English with /ĕ/.

92

An /ā/ sung as two separate, divisible vowels, by holding /ā/ to abnormal length and tacking on an abrupt /ĭ/ (often /ē/), *say* ⟶ sāee.

The very closed, pinched /ā/ which comes across as /ē/ (*fate* ⟶ feet).

Vocalize: Drill /ā/ on familiar vocalises and on intervals of seconds. Hold the vowel shape steady. For Vowel Wheel, see p. 98.

Kinesthetics: Establish the sensation and co-ordination of /ā/ as single entity. Feel gradual shift as tongue moves from high arched position to slightly higher position, simply extending the vowel shape toward /ĭ/ without actually reaching it. Feel that, as tongue moves, the mouth shape remains stable. The brief blending action molds this distinctive English sound.

Build sensory responses into resonating system to achieve a sonorous tone with consistent auditory feedback.

MATCHING TO MUSIC /ā/ [eɪ]

In singing this excerpt work for accurate target vowel.
Heed the sense stress:

When I am laid, am laid in earth may my wrongs create no trouble, no trouble in thy breast.

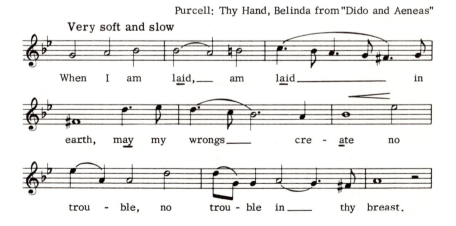

Purcell: Thy Hand, Belinda from "Dido and Aeneas"

Very soft and slow

When I am laid,__ am laid_____ in earth, may my wrongs____ cre - ate no trou - ble, no trou - ble in ___ thy breast.

Words and Settings	Delivery

laid ___

laid _____

Keep /ā/'s stable and firm; do not sep-arate into two sounds; the first setting on two half-notes must be held firm and not be allowed to sag; the second on the five-note descent also requires con-trol to keep the vowel from distorting

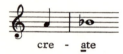

(earth)   may

Enunciate clearly but do not over-emphasize this helping verb despite upward leap

cre - ate

Use favorable notation to full advantage keeping /ā/ relaxed and consistent on long note

Final Note: This vowel is a blend of two related elements to form a distinctive third sound.

The use of the Italian or French sound, shorter and more tense, imparts a foreign flavor to English song.

ĕ [ɛ]

let, men, said, friend, many, bury, pleasure, heaven, welcome
Characteristic English vowel, short released sound.

Usage: /ĕ/ is preferred pronunciation in Standard American; /ā/ also heard (leg ⟶ lāg) but not recommended.

Appears in varied versions in Italian, French, and German.

WHAT TO DO /ĕ/

Tongue Position: Tip rests behind lower teeth. Front arched less and sides dropped lower than for /ā/. Sides at lowest point of contact with upper teeth of all four vowels /ē, /ĭ/, /ā/, /ĕ/.

Tongue now halfway down Vowel Ladder I to /ä/.

Lip Shape: Unrounded.

Mouth Opening: More open, released than /ā/.

WHAT NOT TO DO /ĕ/

Do *not* tense tongue, lips, or mouth (result: /ĕ/ moves toward /ā/).

Do *not* slacken jaw (result: /ĕ/ moves toward /ă/).

Do *not* glottalize /ĕ/ in first syllable of words like e*ffort*, e*lement*.

Speech Localisms to Avoid: Southern-style substitutions of /ĭ/ for /ĕ/ in words like *pencil* ⟶ pincil, *forget* ⟶ forgit.

Drawling this short vowel out of shape toward /ă/ and adding another vowel *met* ⟶ mă-uht.

Also heard, the bucolic *head* ⟶ haid, *egg* ⟶ aigg.

Nasalized twang in words like *many, tender,* etc.

PROGRESSIVE PRACTICE FOR /ĕ/

> Hear the sledges with the bells —
> Silver bells!
> What a world of merri*ment*
> their melody foretells!
>
> Poe

> He sett*eth* an end to dark*ness*
> and search*eth* out all perfection.
>
> Book of Job

First Say: Deliver spoken /ĕ/'s without tension, with brief, open quality and forward thrust.

Make the most of the lovely quality of /ĕ/ adjacent to /l/.

Be careful not to nasalize /ĕ/ adjacent to /m/ (*melody*) or /n/ (*end*).

Also make sure that *-ment, -eth, -ness* (weak syllables) are pronounced with schwa, [ə].

95

Then Sing: With your own tune, reproduce accurate /ĕ/'s in the poem and Biblical excerpt on different pitch levels.

Adhere to the contour of this distinctive English sound — a lovely color of vowel tone.

Note how the rhythm of the verse reflects weak and strong word-types of English (*near the sledges with the bells*)

SINGING /ĕ/

Distortions to Avoid: The unfortunate practice of speaking these short vowels /ĭ/ and /ĕ/ with throaty placement prompts singers to shun them altogether in song.

Also American performers frequently tend to replace the accurate English vowel, essential to intelligible song, with one of the foreign, more closed, and tense varieties.

Vocalize: Use any familiar vocalise to drill this English vowel.
Promote physical awareness of the differences between /ĕ/, a shorter, released vowel, and /ā/, a longer, extended vowel unit. While vocalizing, note the dissimilar sensations in tongue tension and lip contour. For Vowel Wheel, see p. 98.

Kinesthetics: Build the sensation of the released *and* sonorous character of the English /ĕ/. Feel the sides of the tongue in light contact with edges of upper molars, a slight arch at the front, and soft mouth shape.

Co-ordinate supportive breath.

Establish clear auditory feedback. Cultivate resonant responses on vault of hard palate in oral cavity and in the rest of resonating system.

MATCHING TO MUSIC /ĕ/ [ε]

In singing this excerpt work for accurate target vowel.

Heed the sense stress:
Yet slower yet; O faintly gentle springs List to the heavy part the music bears.

Yet slow-er yet;   O faint-ly gen-tle springs_ List_ to the

hea - vy part the mu - sic   bears.

Word and Setting	*Delivery*

yet   (slow.)

Do not stress /ĕ/ on upbeat to phrase

yet

Sustain vowel; keep stable on accented note

gen - tle   hea - vy

Use natural emphasis of downbeat and accents to stress strong syllable, and sing second note lightly in both words

bears

bâ-ərz

Divide half note:

Sing first syllable stressed and second weak; make sure active verb is strong

Final Note: The distinctive, common English vowel /ĕ/ becomes distorted frequently as sung. Singers either open too wide toward the "ah" position or they substitute a somewhat similar Italianate sound. The clear, unblurred English sound is essential in singing the language.

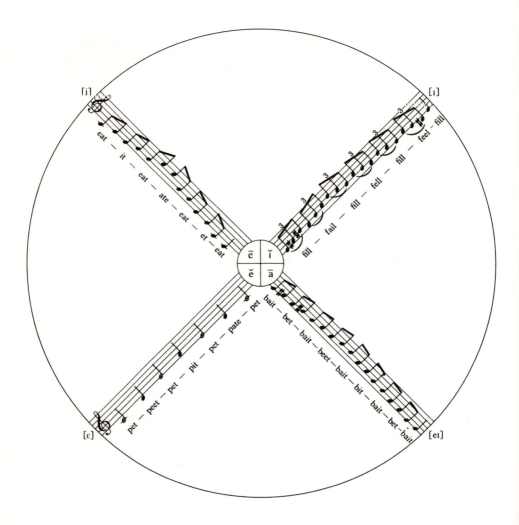

Vowel Wheel I: /ē/ĭ/ā/ĕ/

These vocalises are based on four vowels related to each other in the upper teeth area. In each of the four exercises the initial and final consonants remain the same; only the target vowel changes. Because of possible confusion among the vowels, practice them around the wheel, carefully distinguishing each vowel from the related ones.

Note: These vowels appear as Nos. 1, 2, 3, and 4 on Vowel Ladder I.

ă [æ]

act, man, black, smash, marry, anguish, charity, ask, laugh, grass

Distinctively English vowel; long released sound; most common stressed vowel.*

Usage: In Standard American, all /ă/ words are pronounced alike. Certain /ă/ words in New England and the South (*dance, ask, half,* etc.) are pronounced with /à/, a vowel midway between /ă/ and /ä/.

Does not appear in Italian, French, or German.

WHAT TO DO /ă/

Tongue Position: Tip securely down but relaxed. Front arched slightly forward, less than for /ĕ/. Sides aligned with lower teeth, touching lightly. No. 5 /ă/ is first vowel after /ĕ/, No. 4, to make contact with lower teeth.

Lip Shape: Unrounded, released, not spread.

Mouth Opening: More open than /ĕ/ but not all the way to /ä/. Jaw follows through untensed· Cheek area in repose.

WHAT NOT TO DO /ă/

Do *not* think of /ă/ as a short vowel.

Do *not* stretch lips tight against teeth.

Do *not* pull back corners of mouth.

Do *not* tighten muscles under chin.

Do *not* direct /ă/ through nose.

Do *not* open wide as for /ä/.

---

*The dictionary symbol *breve* (◡), used for short vowels, is misleading when applied to /ä/, since /ä/ is not short. In fact, the deceptive marking is probably in large part responsible for constricted and nasal production of this English sound.

Speech Localisms to Avoid: Spoken extensively in U.S. with flat, tense, nasal sound, especially when adjacent to /m/, /n/, or /ng/, *map, sang, dance (day-uhns,* or even *dee-uhns).*

Also heard, similar, substandard grating vowel in words like *after* ⟶ ayfter, *laugh* ⟶ lay-uff.

Marry, Mary, Merry. In areas from Pennsylvania westward the vowels in these words are often pronounced identically, all with a vowel more like /ĕ/ as in *merry.* However, in Standard American, these are three different vowel sounds: marry [mæri], Mary [mɛəri], merry [mɛri].

PROGRESSIVE PRACTICE FOR /ă/

> He clasps the crag with crooked hands
> Close to the sun in lonely lands
> Ringed with the azure world he stands.
>
> Tennyson

First Say: Follow directions in What to Do carefully. Remember to keep tongue down in contact with lower teeth.

Produce /ă/'s with long, level shape and over-all sense of ease.

Carefully match /ă/'s in verse, regardless of adjacent sounds.

Avoid tight /ă/ in proximity to /n/ in *hands, lands, stands.* Be sure to channel relaxed /ă/'s through mouth, then add hum of /n/.

Then Sing: Improvise, transferring spoken /ă/'s to song with meticulous care.

Do not broaden or narrow this characteristic English vowel. The eminently singable sound should be open and released.

SINGING /ă/

Distortions to Avoid: Traditional rules prescribing /ă/ for some words and proscribing it for others tend to befuddle American singers. From concert stages come words like *after* ⟶ ahfter (found in British dictionaries), but also *hand* ⟶ hahnd (found in no dictionary).

Often recommended by voice teachers as substitute for /ă/, the hybrid Italian *ah*-type sound strikes the listener as affected and "singerish."

100

Of course the nasalized /ă/ that carries over from speech is completely unacceptable.

The Standard-American vowel /ă/, mandatory for intelligible singing, makes a fine, sonorous vowel when properly produced. (See Vowel Ladder III for recommended modification to higher registers.)

Vocalize: Since the intrinsic quality of /ă/ cannot be blamed for its bad reputation, take pains to drill the authentic English sound. Use any one or several *ah* vocalises, replacing *ah* with /ă/ (potentially lyrical but rarely vocalized). For Vowel Wheel, see p. 117.

Kinesthetics: Because of problems associated with singing /ă/, meticulously build sensations of accurate contour of this vowel:

Feel the whole tongue without tension: tongue-tip at rest behind lower front teeth, front of tongue arching gently, and sides making contact with lower teeth.

Muscles under chin remain free and jaw follows through without tightness. Throat is open.

Develop in the resonating system specific responses to identity of English /ă/. Work for over-all resonance so as to incorporate the recognizable vowel with sonority essential to good tone. Establish a clear auditory feedback.

Compare with *ah* and feel the related as well as the different production. So as to keep identities distinct, measure the differences in boundaries and in resonant reflexes between the two English vowels.

MATCHING TO MUSIC /ă/ [æ]

In singing this excerpt work for accurate target vowel.
Heed the sense stress:

What passing bells for those who die as cattle? Only the monstrous

anger of the guns. Only the stutt 'ring rifles' rapid rattle

Owens   Britten: War Requiem

Allegro molto

What   pass-ing   bells___   for these who   die___   as

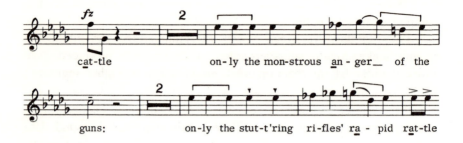

cat-tle   on-ly the mon-strous an-ger___ of the

guns: on-ly the stut-t'ring ri-fles' ra - pid rat-tle

Word and Setting	*Delivery*
 pass-ing	Stress first eighth-note to offset longer note value on weak syllable; sing *-ing* lightly, beginning *ng* ahead of time
ten. as	Sing weak conjunction lightly on high note; if necessary modify to more open sound (see Vowel Ladder III)
 *fz* cat - tle	Emphasize strong syllable by use of downbeat and sforzando
 an - ger ___ (of the)	Do not constrict or nasalize the vowel, keep open and released; do not accent second syllable despite ascent and tied notes
 ra - pid	Keep /ă/ stable on the two notes, modifying to more open sound
 rat - tle	Keep from accenting both syllables set on equal notes, while retaining percussive effect

102

Final Note: This English vowel, though often considered short, constricted, and nasal, can be a thoroughly singable sound.

The most common stressed vowel in English, /ă/ requires optimum production for best results in singing.

The substitution of the Italianate *ah* is to be avoided.

ī [aı̇]

I, lie, sky, eyes, buy, light, height, triumph, inspire, beguiling
Characteristic long English vowel, technically a diphthong.* (The sound is name of letter.)

Note: IPA symbol [aı] represents approximate sound [a] and final sound [ı] which form a blend in a single syllable. First element [a]†(dictionary symbol /à/), is midway vowel between /ă/ and /ä/. Appears in similar version in German.

WHAT TO DO /ī/

Tongue Position: Tip down. Front arched but less than for /ă/. Sides held, at first, at edge of lower teeth, then tongue moves upward and forward to upper teeth, toward /ĭ/ position.

Lip Shape: Released, unrounded. Does not pull back at corners.

Mouth Opening: Drops vertically from /ă/ but not as open as /ä/. Contour does not change as sound progresses.

Compound Vowel /ī/ [aı] in Slow Motion

Crest of sound

a a a **a aı** ı ı

The vowel elements gradually blend into a single unit — the first element

*See footnote p. 91 concerning diphthongs, traditionally treated separately. Here /ī/ is classified among the sixteen Standard American vowels.

†The vowel [a] is used generally throughout the United States as the first element in diphthong [aı]. As an individual vowel [a] is limited mainly to New England and is therefore not listed among the sixteen Standard American vowels.

longer and stressed, the second shorter and unstressed. Both sounds merge at the approximate crest of the diphthong pattern.

WHAT NOT TO DO /ī/

Do *not* add /ē/ after first element instead of moving toward short /ĭ/.

Do *not* round lips (result: vowel darkens to /ŏ/).

Do *not* hold first element /à/ too long.

Do *not* break /ī/ shape (keep level, with no perceptible point of separation).

Speech Localisms to Avoid: Heard mainly in the East: A distorted /ī/ sound caused by producing vowel back in the throat. *Sky* sounds more like *skoi.*

Heard mainly in the South: Drawled out of shape, with first element *ah* elongated, and second /ĭ/ dropped almost entirely (*spite*→ spah-uht).

All-American nasality heard in words like m*i*ne, t*i*me, etc.

PROGRESSIVE PRACTICE FOR /ī/

> Tiger, tiger, burning bright
> In the forest of the night...
> > William Blake

> She walks in beauty like the night
> Of cloudless climes and starry skies...
> > Byron

First Say: Hold to straight line in speaking /ī/. Be careful not to lose pitch within the sound unit. Hold to forward thrust so that the sound cannot fall back into throat.

Next Chant: As tempo slows and vowels stretch, intone long /ī/, maintaining as near as possible original shape as spoken.

Then Sing: Lending melody to verses, transfer to song the spoken and chanted /ī/ as faithfully as possible.

SINGING /ī/

Distortions to Avoid: Traditional manner of performing /ī/ as two detached sounds, the first extra long and the second added abruptly at the last instant (also wrong) vowel /ē/: *sight* ⟶ *sah-eet*.

Tendency to lose pitch during gliding action.

Vocalize: Drill /ī/ painstakingly to achieve level sound. Then contrast with *ah* in a vocalise and observe the difference between *ah* with tongue flat and /ī/ with tongue slightly arched in front, the arch increasing as tongue is raised toward /ǐ/ vowel.

Sing these words as a comparative vocalise:

wise ⟶ was		lock ⟶ like
write ⟶ rot		tar ⟶ tire

This drill should prove that target sound /ī/ is definitively one sound unit and not an artificial pattern of ä+ǐ. For Vowel Wheel, see p.117.

Kinesthetics: Feel distinct contour of longer first element /à/* with front of tongue arching slightly. Then the sides rise to make contact with upper back teeth toward the /ǐ/ position. The tongue-tip stays down, the unrounded lips do not move, and the relaxed jaw does not shift. There is very little movement throughout the production of this compound vowel.

Cultivate sensory responses in all resonating cavities, particularly the forward ring of bright sound on the vault of the hard palate.

MATCHING TO MUSIC /ī/ [aɪ]

In singing this excerpt work for accurate target vowel.
Heed the sense stress:

The branching tree stood dark a-light like willow in the wind,

so white Its unknown apples on the night. In space and time,

---

*Using this vowel rather than *ah* produces more satisfactory /ī/. *Ah* tends to be too wide and far back, necessitating a longer route to the second element of /ī/.

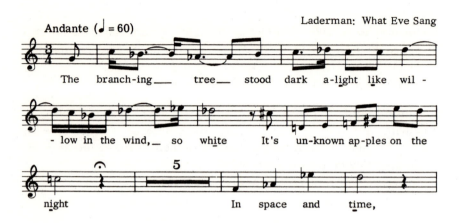

Andante ($\quarternote$ = 60)

The branch-ing___ tree__ stood dark a-light like wil - low in the wind,__ so white It's un-known ap-ples on the night In space and time,

Laderman: What Eve Sang

Word and Setting	*Delivery*
 dark a-light like	Sing both /ī/'s set to equal eighth notes clearly; the second /ī/, in *like*, receives less stress
 white	Sing an undivided vowel on long note without loss of pitch; use the breath sound of /hw/
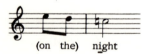 (on the) night	Sing preceding eighth notes on weak words lightly so as not to overshadow the strong word *night;* keep vowel secure on half note
 time	Watch nasality but make most of /m/; keep /ī/ firm on half note so that diphthong seems like an extension of one sound rather than two separate ones

106

Final Note: There must be no discernible shift from one vowel to the next in producing /ī/.

The traditional method in singing a diphthong of inserting another vowel at the last instant results in a wholly artificial sound, especially when that final sound is /ē/.

ä [ɑ]

ah, calm, God, heart, garden, sorrow, mirage, father, bother
Most open of all English vowels, long sound.*

Usage: Standard-American pronunciation consistent for words spelled with letter *a*, but variations occur with *o* spelling: **or**ange (**ah**-range or **aw**-range), horrid (**hah**rid or **haw**rid). In words such as these, *ah* is recommended for song.

Heard in New England and the South: a different vowel derived from the British, IPA [ɒ], a lip-rounded variety of *ah* (*Boston*, as pronounced in that city).

Appears in similar forms in Italian, French, German, Russian, etc.

Most favored vowel in song internationally.

WHAT TO DO /ä/

Tongue Position: Tip firm against bottom front teeth; body of tongue lying low in mouth (lowest, No. 7, on Vowel Ladder I). Front flattened (*no* arching). Back of middle somewhat raised.

Lip Shape: Released (not flaccid). Unrounded, untensed at corners.

Mouth Opening: Drop vertically to open, comfortable shape. Jaw descends, following through.

WHAT NOT TO DO /ä/

Do *not* arch tongue forward (result: vowel sound as in New England, *car* ⟶ kă).

Do *not* round mouth, tensing lips (result: *heart* ⟶ hurt).

Do *not* drawl, adding another vowel (result: *calm* ⟶ kahəm).

*This vowel is the one familiar to singers as *ah*.

Speech Localisms to Avoid: Substandard variations are not wide-spread. However, heard in New England: "părk the căr" and on the Eastern Seaboard: "gah-uht" (got), an excessively wide-mouthed, constricted production with slack jaw.

PROGRESSIVE PRACTICE FOR /ä/

> But all was locked and barred
> ....
> And dark in the dark old inn-yard
> A stable wicket creaked.
> Where Tim the ostler listened,
> His face was white and peaked,
> His eyes were hollows of madness...
> Alfred Noyes

First Say: Pay particular attention to the open character of /ä/, its size and length. Enunciate identical *ah*'s whether spelled with *a (dark)* or with *o (locked)*. Watch the /r/ after /ä/, making certain to add only a brief, forward /r/, more color than consonant. The vowel *ah* should retain its accurate shape, unhampered by the /r/.

Then Sing: Improvise melodic lines using two and three notes for some of the words. Observe what a stable sound *ah* represents, regardless of notation.

SINGING /ä/

Distortions to Avoid: Whatever difficulty singers may encounter with this vowel are so much part of vocal training that we need not dwell on them here. Performers have found the directions in What to Do useful in correcting or improving /ä/ as sung.

Vocalize: /ä/, the most vocalized vowel (though not the most common in English), is capable of maximum resonance and is often taught as basic to production of all other vowels. Use any of many standard vocalises.

The Italian /ä/ differs somewhat from the more open English equivalent (compare *caro* with *calm*).

For Vowel Wheel, see p. 117.

Kinesthetics: For /ä/ build sensation of tonal ease, of openness and freedom in mouth and throat.

Feel tongue relaxed on floor of mouth, and back of middle of tongue slightly elevated. Mouth is comfortably open.

Cultivate sympathetic resonance in all cavities to achieve ringing quality.

MATCHING TO MUSIC /ä/ [a]

In singing this excerpt work for accurate target vowel.
Heed the sense stress:

Dear March come in . . . Who knocks? that April? Lock the door

I will not be pursued. He stayed a-way a year to call when I am

occupied.

Dickinson   Copland: Dear March, Come In
With exuberance

Dear March, _ come in _____   Who knocks

that A-pril   Lock the   door _ I will not be pur-

sued _ He stayed a-way a year _ to call when I am oc-cu-pied _____

Word and Setting   *Delivery*

March _____

Sing a clear open /ä/ on long note for key word; the /r/ in that position is more color than consonant

109

knocks

Sing a bright /ä/ on downbeat for active verb; note different spelling for same vowel sound

Lock (the door)

Stress active verb strongly on low note; make use of percussive /k/; do not permit *door,* set an octave higher, to overshadow it

oc - cu - pied____

Accent the first syllable (*oc-*), helped by higher note and downbeat; sing the last syllable *(pied)* lightly to offset long note

Final Note: The /ä/, the classical vowel in vocalises, receives more practice than any other sound.

The Italian equivalent is less open than the English and should not be imitated.

Use the following excerpt for additional /ä/ and /ī/ practice.

Dello Joio: Bright Star

Andante semplice

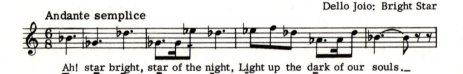
Ah! star bright, star of the night, Light up the dark of our souls._

ŭ [ʌ]

love, blood, does, judge, covet, humble, trouble, among, summer. Distinctively English vowel, neutral sound, stressed equivalent of unstressed /ə/.* *Note:* /ŭ/, always stressed, is heard only in strong word-types and syllables. (*Schwa* /ə/, the unstressed, weak form, is discussed on pp. 113-116).

*Often listed in textbooks as two separate vowels, /ŭ/ and /ə/ are here treated as the stressed and unstressed counterparts of the same vowel, No. 8 on Vowel Ladder I. (The word *above* illustrates both forms of this vowel.)

Technically known as a *middle* vowel, this sound comes between *ah* and a series of eight lip-rounded vowels (see Vowel Ladder I).

Does not appear in Italian, French, or German.

WHAT TO DO /ŭ/

Tongue Position: Central in mouth, neither high or low. Tip down and relaxed. Middle barely raised, hence called "middle" vowel. No rise in back or arch in front.

Lip Shape: Neutral, untensed, without a trace of rounding.

Mouth Opening: Released vertical drop, about midway between /ē/ and /ä/.

WHAT NOT TO DO /ŭ/

Do *not* permit /ŭ/ to lodge in throat.

Do *not* lip-round (result: non-English umlaut sound).

Do *not* tense mouth or facial muscles (result: poor tone and blemished vowel).

Do *not* shape energetically, but conform to neutral mold.

Speech Localisms to Avoid: Tendency in careless speech to execute /ŭ/ with hard attack and throaty, gruntlike sound. Also dialectal substitution of /ĕ/ or /ĭ/ for ŭ/ (*just* ⟶ jest or jist).

PROGRESSIVE PRACTICE FOR /ŭ/

> All lovers young, all lovers must
> Consign to thee, and come to dust.
> Shakespeare

First Say: /ŭ/ abounds in English poetry and occasions little trepidation when read aloud. (Singing is something else again.)

Give voice to the simple authentic quality in juxtaposition to more shapely sounds. Neutral color of /ŭ/ affords fine contrast with more brilliant vowels of the English galaxy.

Always deliver /ŭ/ with forward thrust. As with other vowels, use an initial consonant as a springboard (*lo*vers).

111

Next Chant: Hold lengthened, intoned /ŭ/ to same shape as when spoken, in preparation for sung sound. Observe how this non-pressured vowel can take on musical quality of its own, even within the monotone of chant.

Then Sing: With homemade melody, transfer /ŭ/ unimpaired to different pitch levels. Accurately produced, this middle vowel is entirely singable and resonant.

SINGING /ŭ/

Distortions to Avoid: Tendency to superimpose another shape on this simple vowel. Jaw opened too wide, almost to *ah:* I *lahv* you; or lip-rounded tensly to *aw:* I *lawv* you.

Vocalize: Take pains to locate vocally the precise shape of the target sound /ŭ/. Also alternate with *ah* and *aw*. For Vowel Wheel, see p. 117.

Kinesthetics: Methodically establish responses in resonating system to this all-English /ŭ/ sound. Feel "let-go" sensation in mouth and throat, cheek area in repose, and lips neither rounded nor spread but released and neutral.

This lip shape held unchanged is central to the character of /ŭ/.

Cultivate clear auditory feedback. Develop firm support on the breath for clear, not amorphous, contour and fully engage resonating cavities as with other vowels.

MATCHING TO MUSIC /ŭ/ [ʌ]

In singing this excerpt work for accurate target vowel.
Heed the sense stress:

Must the winter come so soon?

Menotti   Barber: Vanessa

Tranquil and sustained

Must the win - ter__ come   so   soon?

Accent the vowel in *must,* a neutral sound of relaxed quality. Note the unstressed counterpart /ə/ in the article *the* (and the /ər/ in winter).

Keep the vowel steady and neutral in contrast to the other vowels; make the most of /m/ on the active verb

Final Note: The vowel /ŭ/, a distinctive English sound, is a middle, released, but not shapeless vowel. (Familiar to singers as *uh*).

The quality of this vowel and its weak counterpart /ə/ afford contrast to the more brilliant ones.

Consonants take on special color with this vowel, especially the /l/ and /v/ in *love*, That Word in song.

/ə/ [ə]

A separate section is required for this weak counterpart of the stressed vowel /ŭ/ [ʌ]. The classic schwa /ə/ is the most common of English sounds. Because it is always unstressed, schwa performs a vital role in the contrasts within English word rhythms.

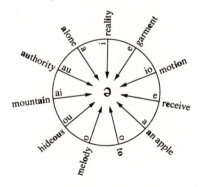

All Vowels Lead to Schwa /ə/

113

WHAT TO DO /ə/

Tongue Position: Lies at rest in central part of oral cavity. Middle rises slightly but not as high as for /ŭ/.

Lip Shape: Released, neutral.

Mouth Opening: Drops, relaxed. Smaller vertically than /ŭ/. Cheek area in repose. Jaw follows through as adjunct to mouth opening.

WHAT NOT TO DO /ə/

Do *not* open too wide toward *ah*.

Do *not* tighten muscles under chin.

Do *not* permit /ə/ to lodge in throat.

Do *not* shape tensely with tongue, lips, or jaw.

Speech Localisms to Avoid: National tendency to produce /ə/ with gruntlike, often glottalized effect, and also to pronounce /ər/ endings without /r/ (as in *sister* ⟶ sistuh, *labor* ⟶ labuh) with a throaty gulp.

The increasing use of strong /ā/ instead of weak /ə/ for the unstressed article (*ay* man) is destructive of English rhythms.

PROGRESSIVE PRACTICE FOR /ə/

> And his horse in the silence champed the grasses
> Of the forests ferny floor:
> And a bird flew up out of the turret
> Above the Traveller's head.
> Alfred Noyes

First Say: Become alert to the rhythmic effect of the neutral vowel juxtaposed to longer vowels. Note, too, how stress and sense correspond.

Produce *schwa* with as good speech tone as bestowed on other vowels. Carefully avoid glottal stroke on words with initial sound /ə/ (*of, above*) by linking the words in legato style.

Note: The weak vowel in several words (silence, etc.) may be either /ĭ/ or /ə/. See the Four Unstressed Vowels (pp. 118-120).

Next Chant: Prolong the short sound /ə/, trying to retain the cor-

114

rect proportion of weak to strong accents (as in song). Also guard the placement of this neutral sound by maintaining forward resonance throughout.

Then Sing: With your own notation, try to match short notes and longer notes to the syllables of the poetry. As you sing, feel the difference in dynamics, quality, and duration between weak and strong elements. How the neutral vowel functions in weak word-types (*of, the, and*) and in syllables (silence, grasses) determines the poem's clarity at the listening end.

SINGING /ə/

Distortions to Avoid: Widespread tendency to accentuate weak syllables and pronounce them as spelled: moun**tain,** child**ren,** na**ked.** This "hot potato" diction comes from exaggerating unstressed syllables and small filler words customarily soft-pedaled in idiomatic *correct* speech.

Vocalize: Use words to drill since isolated /ə/ is entirely unreal (**a** leaf, **a** laugh, **a** boy, **a** girl, **a** time, alone, alarm, among, afraid, attempt).
Now vocalize on these names with /ə/ in final position: Sylvia, Pamela, Sara, Bella, Eva, Flora. (Be careful not to stress the weak /ə/s.)
Keep vowel's neutral shape, and at all costs, avoid *ah.*

Kinesthetics: Build over-all sensation of ease with brief, uncolored vowel shape. Feel slight, gentle rise in middle of tongue. Also cultivate a mere touch of soft lip-rounding to bring /ə/ to forefront of mouth.
Keep working for a resonant, yet not diffused or unfocused, neutral sound. Establish resonant responses particularly in oral cavity, also breath support consistent with, and not apart from, other vowels.
Maintain quiet facial posture with teeth apart. Sense the subdued quality of *schwa* as compared with longer, brighter vowels.

MATCHING TO MUSIC /ə/ and /ŭ/

In singing this excerpt work for accurate target vowels.

Heed the sense stress:
The sun has fallen and it lies in blood. The moon is weaving bandages of gold.

115

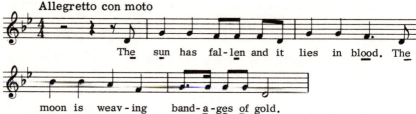

Allegretto con moto

The sun has fal-len and it lies in blood. The

moon is weav-ing band-a-ges of gold.

Word and Setting   *Delivery*

the   sun

Sing the article *the* lightly and stress the vowel in *sun*, its strong counterpart. Make the most of a distinct /ŭ/ to contrast with the previous /ə/; add a good resonant /n/ for the strong word

fal - len

Stress the first syllable, especially the vowel; subdue the second with a very short /ə/ between /l/ and /n/

blood

Stress this strong word, singing well-articulated /bl/ and a sustained /ŭ/ followed by a clear-cut /d/

band - a - ges   of

Subdue the weak syllables; add a voiced /z/ for the *s* at the end and link to the /ə/ in *of*

Final Note: Observe the vowel in *has* and in *and* may be weakened to /ə/ especially with *allegretto*. Since schwa /ə/ is indispensable as the weak beat in English word rhythms (the sense stress), singers must learn to handle this common, uncolored syllable skillfully.

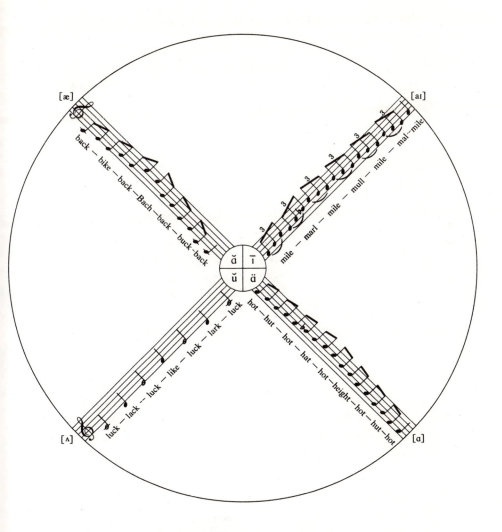

Vowel Wheel II: /ă/ī/ä/ŭ/

These vocalises are based on four vowels, produced with sides of the tongue making contact in the lower teeth area. In each of the four comparative exercises the initial and final consonants are always the same; only the target vowel changes. In drilling the groups around the wheel, carefully distinguish each vowel from the others.

Note: These vowels appear as Nos. 5, 6, 7, and 8 on Vowel Ladder I.

117

The Four Unstressed Vowels of English: /ə/ĭ/ĕ/ŏŏ/

Weak word-types and syllables have created these vowels of corresponding weakness vital to English speech rhythms. The following
listing is a summation.

1. /ə/

Most numerous by far is *schwa* /ə/ (familiar as *uh*) in unstressed
syllables:

adore	system
rumpus	occur
alone	**America**

/ə/ is also heard in weak word-types when unstressed within a phrase:

the	of	and	them
a	to	was	have

Note: The frequent weak syllable /ər/, as in *fath**er***, is related to
schwa and belongs in the constellation of unstressed English vowels.

2. /ĭ/

Second in importance is /ĭ/ (familiar as *ih*) interchangeable with /ə/.
For song, /ĭ/ makes the brighter sound and one less prone to throaty
placement. Slower tempo calls for an adjustment to a more neutralized
variant of /ĭ/ moving toward /ə/.

Sing /ĭ/ **(preferably)**

regret	minute	ment**ion**	patient
deny	beautiful	(and all -**tion**'s)	intimate
believe	loneliness	vi**sion**	separate
animal	mischi**evous**	(and all -**sion**'s)	graci**ous**
holiday	pitiful		artist

Note: In *slow tempo* prefixes *re-, de-, be-* move toward unaccented
/ē/.

Always /ĭ/ **(or nearly)** In weak syllables before *sh, j, v,* and voiced
-es and *-ed* endings:

118

| languish | cabbage | plaintive | roses | visited |
| cherish | package | motive | pleases | granted |

Note: In slow tempo, the vowel in these *-es* and *-ed* endings becomes more a blend of /ĭ/ and /ə/.

Once Again /ĭ/

> playing, startling, (and, of course, all **-ing** endings)

Note: -y and *-ly* as in *pretty, truly,* are spoken with /ĭ/ only in limited areas of the U.S. Recommended for song: the Standard-American pronunciation, an unstressed, diminished /ē/.

3. /ĕ/

Next comes /ĕ/ (familiar as *eh*). Found in stressed positions (bed, merry, weather), this vowel has only limited, unstressed use.

All Those "ex-" Words: Sing /ĕ/ in *ex-* prefixes (explain, excuse, experience) when tempo is slow to moderate. But make sure to decrescendo the *ex-*, always a weak syllable in these words. With lively tempo /ĭ/ is more suitable (*explain* ⟶ ixplain).

Sing /ĭ/ or a blend of /ĭ/ and /ə/, never /ĕ/, for all these and similar endings in moderate to fast tempi:

| sentiment | happiest | presence |
| wilderness | frequent | existence |

Note: For that too-frequent long note on the short ending, the best solution is a shaded sound of indefinite hue. Mix /ĕ/ with /ĭ/ and add /ə/. The mixture results in a toned down, blended effect to satisfy the demands of text and score.

Note also. To further reduce the weak syllable, add more duration to consonants (sentimen*t*). Also for balance highlight the stressed syllable, especially its vowel (*se*ntiment).

4. /ŏŏ/

Lastly there is /ŏŏ/ performing within unstressed syllables (the vowel in **put**).

thoughtful	rapture
joyful	pleasure
(all-**ful** endings)	(all-**ure** endings)

Note: -ure endings are spoken often with /ər/, but short /ŏŏ/ is preferable for song (*rapture* ⟶ rapchŏŏr): but *never* sing *rapchōōr* always shunning the long /ōō/ in these weak syllables.

/ŏŏ/ **or No Vowel.** The unstressed syllable in words like ev**il**, dev**il**, mart**ial**, is spoken with /ə/, /ĭ/, or /ŏŏ/ or very little vowel sound if any. Of these three brief vowels, lip-rounded /ŏŏ/ sounds most satisfactory in song with moderate to slow tempo. But regardless of the vowel chosen, make sure to linger longer on the sound of lyrical /l/.

Important. In a lively tempo, there need be no vowel at all, but merely the linked sound of the two consonants (*evil* ⟶ eevl).

Finally Remember

Correct stress demands contrasts between weak and strong vowels.

Weakened vowels cannot be reduced to a single exact sound.

Duration and tempo affect the choice of the weakened vowel.

As long as weak vowels receive no unnatural stress, the surrounding sounds will lead the singer (depending on the word) to /ə, ĭ, ĕ, ŏŏ/ or to a blend.

ûr [ɜ]

girl, **wor**d, **hear**d, **ver**se, **sur**ge, **jour**ney, rehe**ar**se, **vir**gin

Distinctively American-English vowel, lip-rounded with /r/ coloring, an American phoneme.

/ûr/, No. 9 on Vowel Ladder I, is first of eight lip-rounded shapes that follow.

Usage: /ûr/, always stressed, heard only in strong word-types and syllables. (/ər/ is unstressed, weak equivalent vowel discussed on pp. 124-127).*

Pronounced without /r/ mainly in Eastern and Southern areas: *burn* ⟶ bû(r)n [bɜːn].† Standard American is /ûr/ with /r/ intact.

Does not appear in Italian, French, German, or British English.

*Often listed in textbooks as two separate vowels, /ûr/ and /ər/ are here treated as the stressed and unstressed counterparts of the same vowel, No. 9 on Vowel Ladder I. (The word *murder* illustrates both forms of this vowel.)

†Note length sign in IPA (ː) to indicate longer, *r*-less vowel sound [ɜː].

WHAT TO DO /ûr/

Tongue Position: Whole tongue free from strain. Tip begins down behind lower teeth. Then rises gently, pointing *toward* gum-ridge for brief /r/ produced right behind upper teeth. Middle of tongue raised about halfway to hard palate.

Lip Shape: Definitely rounded. Firm but untensed lip protrusion, essential to accurate sound.

Mouth Opening: Drops slightly from /ŭ/, No. 8 on Vowel Ladder I, to somewhat larger vertical aperture. Relaxed but steady jaw, does *not* move during execution of /ûr/.

WHAT NOT TO DO /ûr/

Do *not* initiate vowel with tongue-tip already raised.

Do *not* permit tongue to curl backward or invert toward throat (result: mangled, gargled sound).

Do *not* hold tongue-tip down behind lower teeth without raising it for /r/ (result: danger of harsh /r/ sound).

Do *not* keep lips spread (result: strained, distorted sound).

Do *not* hold /r/ too long, but keep it brief with vibration forward.

Speech Localisms to Avoid: *r*-less, unlip-rounded variety, heard in New England and some Southern areas where, in addition, it is drawled: *bird* ⟶ bûəd.

Substandard Eastern seaboard sound, almost *oi*: *bird* ⟶ boid.

Throaty /ûr/ with retroflex excessive /r/ heard in Pennsylvania and points west: *girl* ⟶ girrl.

PROGRESSIVE PRACTICE FOR /ûr/

> Then to the lips of this poor **earthen urn,**
> I leaned, the secret of my life to **learn:**
> And lip to lip it **murmured,*** "While you live,
> Drink! for once dead you never shall re**turn**!"
>
> Omar Khayyám (Fitzgerald)

*Note: The word, m**ur**m**ur**ed, is an example of both the stressed and unstressed forms, /ûr/ and /ər/.

First Say: Try dropping the /r/'s in all /ûr/ words (earthen, urn). For most Americans this pronunciation sounds artificial.

Replace /r/'s and read again, *but* make sure to avoid the throaty variety.

Keep all /r/'s short and up front.

Next Chant: Intoning the lines, observe how /ûr/'s stretch to reveal their inner form, a resonant blend of vowel and /r/ coloring.

Then Sing: Improvise your own melodic line, trying with good tone to carry over the correct contour of /ûr/.

SINGING /ûr/

Distortions to Avoid: Insecurity persists concerning production of this distinctive American vowel. Singers flounder among affected British *r*-dropping, foreign rolled /r/ versions, and our regional twangy /r/.

Vocalize: Re-read What to Do. With your own vocalise, activate characteristic vowel shape. Feel the brief, soft murmur of /r/ right at the front of the rounded mouth. Note in the IPA symbol [ɝ] that the little *r* hook attached to the vowel symbol represents graphically the fragmentary duration of /r/, essentially a coloration of the vowel. For Vowel Wheel, see p. 138.

Kinesthetics: Build sensation for /ûr/ of unique shape responding throughout the resonating system. Lips purse in vertical contour. Become sensitive to gentle movement of tongue-tip from resting place behind lower teeth to behind upper teeth, not touching, but pointing high in the mouth toward gum-ridge. Establish brief /r/ more as a color than a consonant. The /ûr/ pattern functions as a continuous glide sustained sonorously in forward area.

Cultivate the easeful quality of this softly lip-rounding vowel with its touch of /r/.

MATCHING TO MUSIC /ûr/ [ɝ]

In singing this excerpt, work for accurate target vowel.

Heed the sense stress:

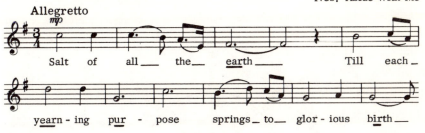

 glorious birth

Ives: Abide With Me

Word and Setting

earth ___

yearn - ing

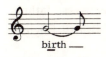

pur - pose

birth ___

Delivery

Keep lips rounded; raise tongue-tip; do not introduce /r/ too soon, and then only briefly; make sure to make the most of the voiceless /th/

Use good /y/ glide to the vowel and good /n/ hum after it; keep second, unstressed syllable subdued

Accent the first syllable, clear lip-rounded /ûr/; reduce the second, despite the ascent, using unstressed /ə/

Produce *birth* in the same manner as *earth;* articulate /b/ in /ûr/ shape in one movement

Final Note: Lip-rounding is essential to the production of this American phoneme and must be held consistent throughout.

The /r/ is not a separate consonant but an integral part of the vowel.

With the tongue-tip up, the /r/ resonance should be brief and produced directly behind the teeth to avoid a guttural sound.

ər [ə]

This weak, recurrent vowel is treated separately from its strong form, /ûr/.

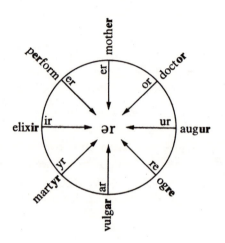

All-American /ər/'s

Distinctively American English vowel, lip-rounded with /r/ coloring. /ər/, unstressed equivalent of stressed /ûr/, bears same relationship to /ûr/ as /ə/ does to /ŭ/. It is heard only in unstressed syllables, most frequently at ends of words.

Usage: /ər/ pronounced with /r/ is Standard American. limited areas of the United States, /r/ is dropped, *father* ⟶ fathuh.

Does not appear in Italian, French, German, or British English.

WHAT TO DO /ər/

Tongue Position: Very like stressed vowel /ûr/, but more rapid. Whole tongue free from strain. Tip begins down and rises gently, pointing toward gum-ridge for very brief, de-emphasized /r/. Middle of tongue raised slightly, not as high as for /ûr/.

124

Lip Shape: Soft rounding, essential for /ər/ production. Lips not as protruded as for /ûr/.

Mouth Opening: /ər/ somewhat less open than /ûr/. Released jaw does *not* move as tongue-tip rises for very brief /r/ color.

WHAT NOT TO DO /ər/

> Do *not* tighten jaw, purse lips tensely, or curl tongue backward (result: unpleasant, unvocal /r/ growl).
>
> Do *not* hold on to /r/.
>
> Do *not* permit even a suggestion of nasality to creep into vowel (focus through mouth).

Speech Localisms to Avoid: Spoken without /r/ and with final sound dropped into throat (*number* ⟶ numb**uh**): extreme New Yorkese. /ər/, throaty with retracted prolonged /r/, widespread in U.S.

PROGRESSIVE PRACTICE FOR /ər/

> And down the other air and the blue altered sky
> Streamed again the wonder of summer
> with apples
> Pears and red currants
> Dylan Thomas

Note: The words *air* and *pears* are pronounced with two syllables. In each, /ər/ is the second and weak syllable. See pp. 153-55.

First Say: Read aloud, being conscious of the meter of the entire passage. Observe role of /ər/ in furnishing the weak beat:

And down the other air and the blue altered sky

Lean on accented vowels, then release pressure on weak beats by holding and letting go. To balance contrasting elements, be sensitive to the relative length and strength of /ər/ in *wonder, summer.* Its beat depends on the longer, stronger syllable, and vice versa. (Note that the accented vowel in *currants* is /ûr/.)

Next Chant: Stretch the sounds within the monotony of the exercise.

Keep the relationship of strong to weak vowels, particularly the balance with the target sound /ər/. Slow the tempo without distorting the rhythm.

Then Sing: Improvise, setting appropriate notation to fit the weak syllable /ər/ in the poetry. The effort to find correct rhythms will develop greater sensitivity to the built-in beat within English words.

SINGING /ər/ [ə]

Distortions to Avoid: Fancy and ludicrously accented diction:
actor ⟶ act**awr**, *monarch* ⟶ mon**ahck**.
Gargled, over-extended /r/ especially noticeable in American singers whose native speech features the same unvocal noise.

Vocalize: Use words for this unstressed vowel since it does not occur in isolation. Vocalize on broth**er**, sist**er**, eith**er**, mot**or**, lat**er**, murm**ur**, rememb**er**. Also Arth**ur**, Pet**er**, Hect**or**, Rob**er**t, Herb**er**t. (Be sure not to stress the /ər/s.)
Many singers now favor this soft, lip-rounded, so singable vowel with the merest fragment of /r/. Its effect resembles somewhat the French mute *e* used in poetry and song *(triste)*, also lip-rounded but lacking /r/.

Kinesthetics: For this shorter, unstressed equivalent build sensation similar to /ûr/. Feel lips round softly.
Establish rhythmic contrast in dynamics between brighter, accented vowels and subdued, non-accented /ər/'s. Feel how the *r* element vibrates fleetingly right behind teeth, as tongue-tip tilts upward. Supply supportive breath as with other vowels. Incorporate small /ər/ as *single* unit of resonant sound, sustained softly in forward area.

MATCHING TO MUSIC /ər/ [ə]

In singing this excerpt work for accurate target vowel.

Heed the sense stress:

I do not grudge thy splendour Bid souls of eager men awake

Be kind and bright and tender Give day to other worlds

126

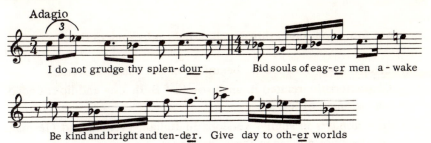

I do not grudge thy splen-dour___   Bid souls of eag-er men a - wake

Be kind and bright and ten-der.   Give day to oth-er worlds

Word and Setting	*Delivery*

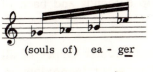

splen - dour ___

Reduce stress conflict between the word and music by making the most of the first syllable, especially /l/ and the vowel; -dour (dər) on the long note (tempo adagio) calls for diminuendo

(souls of)   ea - ger

Accent the first syllable, to offset equal notes and ascent

ten - der   (give)

Stress first syllable *ten-*, especially the vowel; begin crescendo on first syllable toward the *a* flat; second syllable requires subdued, lip-rounded /ər/

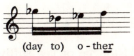

(day to)   o - ther

Handle the same as word *ea-ger* above

Final Note: This short /ər/, the weak counterpart of /ûr/, occurs very frequently in English.

It is important to produce it correctly to make the most of its pleasant quality.

The /ər/ should be lip-rounded, with the /r/ more color than consonant, and always subdued to provide contrast, so essential in English, with the brighter accented syllables.

127

o͞o [u] and ū [ju]

o͞o: **too, soon, blue, threw, rule, tomb, juice, uncouth**

ū: ·**cue, few, view, music, beautiful, usual, value, universe**
Characteristic, related English vowels.* Both long and lip-rounded.
(/ū/ is name of letter.)
/o͞o/ appears in similar versions in Italian, French, and German.
/ū/ does not appear in these languages.

WHAT TO DO /o͞o/ AND /ū/

Tongue Position: /o͞o/ Tip firmly down. Back arched toward soft
palate in highest arch of all lip-rounding vowels.
/ū/ Consonant /y/, a semi-vowel, blends with /o͞o/ to form /ū/,
as in *you*. Tongue movement begins at /y/ position* with sides in
contact at inner surfaces of upper teeth, then glides forward to central
point in mouth as /y/ merges with /o͞o/. Tip descends and back of
tongue rises.

Lip Shape: /o͞o/ and /ū/ Rounded, smallest circular shapes of all
English vowels. Firm lip-rounding essential to accurate production.
See position of both on Vowel Ladder I.

Mouth Opening: /o͞o/ and /ū/ Small vertically. Wide opening in
center of mouth between tongue and hard palate.

WHAT NOT TO DO /o͞o/ AND /ū/
Do *not* permit lip shape to sag (result: sound lowers to short /o̯o̯/
as in *school* ——➤ sko̯o̯l).
Do *not* arch tongue too high in back or hold tongue or jaw stiffly
(result: muffled, swallowed sounds).
Do *not* nasalize words like *moon, fume*.

*/o͞o/ and /ū/ are presented together, since they are closely allied in production and
sometimes interchangeable in pronunciation.
  Traditionally listed separately as a consonant and vowel combination, /ū/ is
included here as a common English vowel, one of the sixteen on Vowel Ladder I.

†For a discussion of /y/, see pp. 173-76.

Speech Localisms to Avoid: Cutting down long /ō͞o/ contour to short /o͝o/: ro͝om, ro͝of, ro͝ot, even *spo͝on* instead of spo͞on!

A "diphthongized" /ō͞o/, caused by the tongue sliding instead of holding still, especially before /l/ (*fool* ⟶ foo*uhl*).

Unlip-rounded, tight-mouthed /ō͞o/ and /ū/.

Constant confusion in use of /ō͞o/ and /ū/. (Is it Toosday or Tyoosday?)

PROGRESSIVE PRACTICE FOR /ō͞o/ AND /ū/

> She left the web, she left the loom,
> She made three paces through the room,
> She saw the water lily bloom,
> She saw the helmet and the plume,
> She looked down to Camelot.
> > Tennyson
>
> Then gods, to reverent youth grant purity...
> > Horace
>
>
> Beautiful for situation, the joy of the
> whole earth is Mount Zion...
> > Psalm XLVIII

First Say: Keep all the /ō͞o/ sounds level. Link all words in a legato flow, making sure that small connective words remain weak and relatively short and the vowels lucid and long in the main thought-carrying words.

Lean on /ū/'s in you*th*, *purity*, and *beautiful*. Feel the full level length of this sound. Note how /ū/ in the word *situation* is shorter because unstressed.

Next Chant: Intoning the lines, observe how, when both /ō͞o/ and /ū/ are lengthened, the similarity and difference between them is revealed. Firm breath support keeps both these vowels stable.

Then Sing: Improvise, trying different tempi. Song is speech intensified, the spoken form providing the basis for faithful reproduction in song. Adjust the vowels as spoken, carrying over the two recognizable lip shapes /ō͞o/ and /ū/.

129

SINGING /o͞o/ AND /ū/

Distortions to Avoid: The European variety of /o͞o/ is more tense than this typical released English vowel.

Failure to keep back of tongue up and steady slackens the clear-cut contour of /o͞o/.

Forming either vowel back in throat results in squeezed, guttural sounds.

Teaching techniques that shun lip-rounding for vowels result in unintelligible /o͞o/'s. Both vowels require accurate lip-shaping for listening recognition.

Neither the affected *t-yune* nor the colloquial *toon* (and similar "tune" words) is recommended for song.

Vocalize: Drill each vowel /o͞o/ and /ū/ separately and then in comparison with the other. Their definitive molds include essential lip-rounding.

Note: The lips should never initiate any vowel but merely follow through the inner shaping begun at the vocal cords. As vowels move forward toward the mouth opening, the lips contribute a final shaping to form the recognizable sound. However, dispensing with lip aid can only mean singing English the hard way.

For Vowel Wheel, see p. 138.

Kinesthetics: Keeping a clear tone image of the long /o͞o/ vowel, build articulatory action very carefully: lips protrude with sides narrowed in circular formation, back of tongue is up and tip down securely until ready to move to next sound. Feel how rounding of lips aids projection of forward tone. (*Note:* The rounder the lip contour, the higher the back arch.)

Cultivate ease and resonant responses in reactive cavities. Establish clear auditory feedback.

/ū/: Feel lips and tongue glide from closed position of /y/ to circular contour of /o͞o/.

Incorporate sense of added length of /ū/ as compared with /o͞o/, especially as sung. Also co-ordinate /y/ with /o͞o/ so that /ū/ emerges as an inseparable compound unit.

WHICH? /ū/ OR /o͞o/

Among performers in general and singers in particular, the shape of the vowel in words like *new* or *tune* appears to be constantly shifting. What rules exist are complex and unstable. Therefore the following presents no infallible guide but rather a preferred listing.

Always /ū/: All words beginning with the letter *u: use, universe, unique,* etc. Also the following mixed grouping:

huc	amuse
few	beauty
pure	cupid
huge	fury
view	value

Never /ū/, Always /ōo/:

blue	suit	lucid
flute	slew	tumult
include	cruel	rumor
luminous		

Avoid either a flat and lax or constricted and squeezed /ōo/. Cultivate a really "forward" sound focused right behind the teeth in the forefront of the mouth.

Spoken Either with /ū/ or /ōo/:

new	consume	gratitude
dew	tulip	numerous
duty	duel	enthusiasm
stupid		

But Sung like this:

Recommended for singing — a compromise. Since *new* as *nyoo* tends toward affectation, and as *noo* toward grossness, use neither. Instead substitute a blend of brief /ē/ and long /ōo/, resulting in *neoo* [niu]. To produce the desired effect, /ē/ should merge into accented /ōo/ and be pronounced simultaneously. The blend (more like miewing than mooing) omits the /y/ consonant glide in /ū/, replacing it with a short version of the vowel /ē/. This compromise provides a recognizable and sonorous solution to the quandary.

Interpretive note: The performer, of course, should choose the form which best serves the song.

MATCHING TO MUSIC /ōo/ [u]

In singing this excerpt work for accurate target vowel.

131

Heed the sense stress:

Yés, fools yŏu aŕe, and will bĕ...Until yŏu leáŕn whát wómĕn áre

And knŏw thĕm throúgh and throúgh...óne dáy you'll ăwáken

With faith thăt's rúdely̆ shákĕn

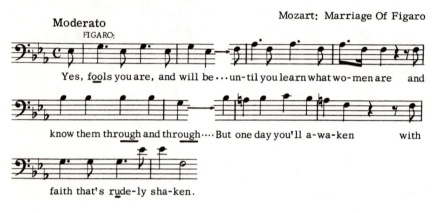

Moderato

Mozart: Marriage Of Figaro

FIGARO:

Yes, fools you are, and will be···un-til you learn what wo-men are   and

know them through and through····But one day you'll a-wa-ken   with

faith that's rude-ly sha-ken.

Word and Setting

Delivery

fools

Be sure to lip-round and not insert a second syllable (foo-uhlz)

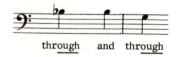

through   and   through

Keep both /oo/ vowels stable

rude - ly

Do not permit upward leap to give weak -*ly* undue emphasis; hold lip-rounded /oo/ shape; do not permit lips to grow slack

Final Note: The /oo/ is the most closely lip-rounded of all English vowels, although less tense than in the European languages.

132

MATCHING TO MUSIC /ū/ [ju]

In singing this excerpt work for accurate target vowel.

Heed the sense stress:

Oh what's the use There's no excuse For all this anger and a-buse

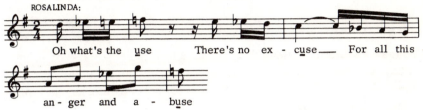

Dietz

Strauss: Dic Fledermaus

Allegretto moderato (meno mosso)

ROSALINDA:

Oh what's the use   There's no ex - cuse___ For all this

an - ger   and   a - buse

Word and Setting

Delivery

use

Make certain of well-produced /y/ glide blended into long /ōo/; be sure to round lips firmly

ex - cuse___

Sing a stressed /ū/ on downbeat; sustain until brief /s/

a - buse

Use natural emphasis of downbeat for strong syllable; a well-produced /y/ *abyus* will help on the high note; make sure to sing first weak syllable lightly on the rise

Final Note: This vowel, actually a combination (a blend of the /y/ glide and the long /ōo/ vowel), requires secure lip-rounding.

Use the /ū/ where appropriate and not where /ōo/ is called for, since this substitution sounds affected in American English.

A compromise sound, (ĕ ōo) works very well in song (p. 131).

133

o͝o [ʊ]

good, book, could, full, bosom, cushion.

Also found in unstressed syllables: pleasure, fulfill, joyful, supreme

Characteristic English vowel; short, rounded sound.

Note: /o͝o/ bears same relation to /o͞o/ as /ĭ/ does to /ē/.

Appears in German, not in Italian or French.

WHAT TO DO /o͝o/

Tongue Position: Released tip behind lower teeth, back of tongue raised, but lower than for /o͞o/. Place finger behind chin, say /o͞o/ then /o͝o/ and feel relaxation of tension for second, shorter, and more released English vowel.

Lip Shape: Definitely rounded but not as firm as for /o͞o/, significantly less tension in lip muscles.

Mouth Opening: More open than /o͞o/ but still comparatively small. Jaw follows through by dropping slightly from /o͞o/ position.

WHAT NOT TO DO /o͝o/

Do *not* push from throat with guttural sound.

Do *not* permit mouth or jaw to sag (result: amorphous sound).

Do *not* round lips too small or open too large (result: sound moves to constricted /o͞o/ or gross /ŭ/).

Speech Localisms to Avoid: /o͝o/ un-rounded and pronounced tight-mouthed (*put* ⟶ puht).

Drawled out-of-shape, adding another vowel (put ⟶ po͝ouht).

PROGRESSIVE PRACTICE FOR /o͝o/

> And this our life, exempt from public haunt,
> Finds tongues in trees, books in the running brooks,
> Sermons in stones, and good in everything.
>
> Shakespeare

First Say: Practice the lines to achieve the correct vowel sound of /o͝o/. It is a mistake to think of /o͝o/ as just a short /o͞o/; it has a distinct individual character. Compare these pairs: *pull—pool, full—fool, could—cooed, would—wooed.*

Next Chant: Try to lengthen /o͝o/ without drawling by holding to the short character on the extended note. This will help meet the challenge of lengthening an essentially short sound when required by the score.

Then Sing: Let your speech ear lead to a recognizable reproduction of lip-rounded /o͝o/ in song. Work to achieve this regardless of varied pitches or duration.

SINGING /o͝o/

Distortions to Avoid: The substitution of long /o͞o/ sound, indulged in habitually by American singers, gives a foreign, accented delivery to such simple words as put ⟶ poot; pull ⟶ pool; look ⟶ Luke. The released "short" vowels of English, /ĭ/, /ĕ/, /ə/, and /o͝o/, demand complete ease in production or their distinctive shapes become indistinct.

Vocalize: /o͝o/ is another one of those seldom vocalized, non-Italian vowels. To drill this typically English sound, build its specific shape into the voice mechanism by pronouncing it in words (took, put, should), then removing to drill separately. Also vocalize short /o͝o/ and long /o͞o/ together for comparison. For Vowel Wheel, see p. 138.

Kinesthetics: Build over-all sense of ease. Establish clear auditory feedback and specific responses in resonating system to /o͝o/ contour.

    Feel character of its brief shaping, the back of tongue high in the mouth, its unpressured, essential lip-rounding, more open than /o͞o/.

MATCHING TO MUSIC /o͝o/ [ʊ]

In singing these excerpts work for accurate target vowel.

Heed the sense stress:
Why can't you be good? And do just as you should?

and when you leaped so quick from the bush Betty took fright

135

Porter

Why can't you be good?___ And do

just as you should?___

Stambler

Ward: The Crucible

and when you leaped so quick from the bush Bet - ty took fright

Word and Setting

good ___

should ___

Delivery

To prolong the /o͝o/ on the long notes it may be necessary to add a brief off-glide by holding the vowel firm until just before the consonant, and then adding a short *ih*

Produce clear-cut /b/ in shape of rounded vowel joined to /sh/, also rounded

Stress this active verb to give the illusion of a longer note

Final Note: The /o͝o/, a characteristic English vowel, causes problems because singers frequently distort its short, lip-rounded shape. It should be drilled in words until the sound corresponds with the accurate spoken vowel.

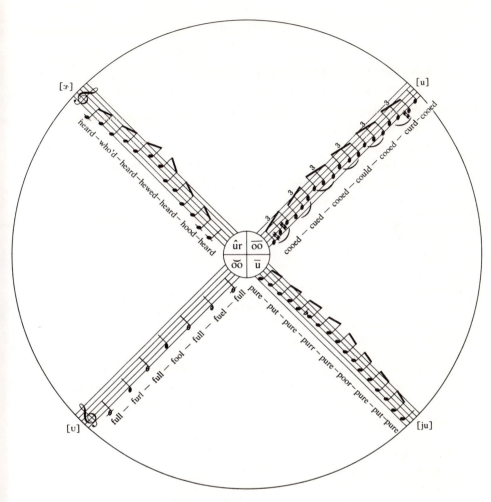

Vowel Wheel III: /ûr/o͞o/ū/o͝o/

These vocalises are designed for comparison of four lip-rounded vowels. In each of the four exercises the initial and final consonants remain the same;* only the target vowel changes. Where similarities in vowels can cause confusion, practice them around the wheel to establish the distinguishing features of each vowel.

Note: These four lip-rounded vowels appear as Nos. 9, 10, 11 and 12 on Vowel Ladder I.

*The word *put* is the exception.

role, ode, roam, grow, though, reproach, shoulder

Characteristic English vowel unit; rounded, long, technically a diphthong.* (Sound is name of letter.)

Note: IPA symbol [oʊ] clarifies the diphthong pattern.

Usage: relatively long /ō/ sound is Standard American even in unstressed syllables: obey, piano, sorrow, fellow, window, etc. Appears in short, tense version (so-called pure vowel) in Italian, French, and German.

WHAT TO DO /ō/

Tongue Position: Compound formation begins with tip behind lower teeth and back of tongue raised halfway between /o͞o/ and /ô/. Then in limited movement toward position of /o͝o/ as in *good*, back of tongue moves upward slightly as tip releases.

Lip Shape: Definitely round, with larger circle than for /o͝o/. Outer lip contour should change little if at all, during scarcely perceptible glide within /ō/ shaping. Keep shape as stable as possible with slight inner movement.

Mouth Opening: Larger than for /o͝o/, quite open. Jaw is released but does not move during production of /ō/.

Compound Vowel /ō/ [oʊ] in Slow Motion

Crest of sound

oooo O OUuu

Two vowel elements gradually blend into a single unit — the first element longer and stressed, the second shorter and unstressed. Both sounds merge at the approximate crest of the diphthong pattern.

*Usually listed separately as a diphthong, /ō/ is here included among the sixteen representative American English vowels.

138

WHAT NOT TO DO /ō/

Do *not* raise tongue too high in back of mouth (result: /ō/ moves to *aw* sound).

Do *not* open lips and then narrow them abruptly.

Do *not* slacken the rounded lip-shaped unit (result: vowel tends to lose pitch).

Do *not* add another vowel after /ō/ before /l/ (result: *old* becomes *o-uhld*).

Speech Localisms to Avoid: Country-wide lack of lip-rounding responsible for misshapen, flat /ō/. In rural areas this chronically tight lip downgrades /ō/ to /ŭ/ *(hole* ⟶ hull, *home* ⟶ hum).

PROGRESSIVE PRACTICE FOR /ō/

> ...All day the wind breathes l**ow** with mell**ow**er t**o**ne:
> Thro' every holl**ow** cave and alley l**o**ne
> R**ou**nd and r**ou**nd the spicy d**ow**ns the yell**ow**
>   Lotus-dust is bl**ow**n.
>   Tennyson

First Say: Use good speech tone with particular attention to how English /ō/ feels and sounds in all bold type /ō/'s of the poetry.

Next Chant! Hold fast to the single unit of sound without losing pitch on /ō/, however prolonged. Does the outline of /ō/ begin to droop as you protract it? Combat the tendency to decrease the breath pressure on the transition to the second element /o͝o/.

Then Sing: Provide /ō/ with favorable notation.
  Stressed /ō/ should always be highlighted.
  Preserve the integrity of the spoken form when sung.

SINGING /ō/

Distortions to Avoid: Widespread use of an Italian-English hybrid "*o*" transforms *no* to *naw*, *behold* to *behawld*, and so on and on.

  Pseudo-British elegance accounts for a variety of /o/ quite unlike the American vowel (*boast* ⟶ bû-o͝ost [bɜ ust]).

  Singing /ō/, as frequently taught, by forming larger circle first and then closing to a second, tight one produces an artificial "singerish" sound.

Vocalize: Singers who drill Italian /ô/ instead of /ō/ are advised to save that for their Italian diction. Practice the necessary English /ō/ holding to the good and true sound with well-supported, stable production to build it into the voice mechanism.

Use vocalise that repeats /ō/ on single notes.

For Vowel Wheel, see p. 153.

Kinesthetics: Establish sensation of stabilized extension of one given sound rather than the gliding together of two different vowels. Keep "one-ness" not "two-ness" in mind to develop accurate English /ō/. Feel how this vowel unit begins to modify almost immediately, forming its distinctive blend as body of tongue moves up slightly and tip stays down.

MATCHING TO MUSIC /ō/ [oʊ]

In singing these excerpts work for accurate target vowel.

Heed the sense stress:

without you no rose can grow

And ev-ry stone that was thrown Spoke for the whole of Rome

Rorem: Little Elegy

Andante (♩ = 66)

With - out you no— rose can grow——

Word and Setting   *Delivery*

no —

Keep vowel stable on moving eighth notes; avoid separating into two distinct elements

rose

Emphasize vowel on short eighth note for key word

140

grow ___

Produce a clear /g/ in shape of lip-rounded /r/ to initiate vowel as a stable blend of sound; avoid narrow constricted /ʊ̆/ at the end

Duncan   Britten: The Rape Of Lucretia

MEN'S CHORUS *pp*

And ev-ry st<u>o</u>ne   that was thr<u>ow</u>n Sp<u>o</u>ke for the wh<u>o</u>le of R<u>o</u>me.

Word and Setting   *Delivery*

st<u>o</u>ne

In this recitative produce /ō/ to resemble the accurate speech sound, lip-rounded and not tense

thr<u>ow</u>n

Stress active verb with clear, round, stable vowel, avoiding any vestige of nasality

Sp<u>o</u>ke

Produces a relaxed vowel in the same manner as above

wh<u>o</u>le

Accent /ō/ on downbeat with bright sound; the /h/ (not an /hw/) is produced in the shape of the vowel; do not permit an extra syllable before the /l/

R<u>o</u>me

Add sonorous /m/ to key word after /r/ glide to lip-rounded /ō/

Final Note: The American English /ō/ is less closed than its British counterpart and less open than the Italian short "aw" sound.

Lip-rounding is an essential feature of this sound and the lip shape remains fixed during production except for a slight narrowing at the end.

141

ô [ɔ]

saw, dawn, caught, all, thought, broad, mourn, office, morning, walking

Characteristic English vowel; long, rounded (more oval than circular).

Spoken both as firmly *aw*-shaped, long vowel (recommended for song): *daughter* —→ dawter; or shorter, less rounded, closer to *ah: daughter* —→ dahter.

Appears, in assorted short versions, in Italian, French, and German.

WHAT TO DO /ô/

Tongue Position: Tip securely behind lower teeth. Back of tongue raised, slightly lower than for /ō/. Lowest arch in back of all lip-rounded shapes (see Vowel Ladder I).

Lip Shape: Elliptical, firm at the sides, higher than wide.

Mouth Opening: Vertically almost as large as for *ah*.

WHAT NOT TO DO /ô/

Do *not* change lip shape during production.

Do *not* tense back of tongue.

Do *not* blend into *ah*.

Speech Localisms to Avoid: These two sub-standard examples: in the Middle and Far West, *water* —→ wahter, *thought* —→ thahght; in New York, *office* —→ aw-uhfice, *dog* —→ daw-uhg.

Also, New England lip-rounded *ah* sound in words like *soft, often, moss.*

PROGRESSIVE PRACTICE FOR /ô/

Sometimes whoever seeks abroad may find
Thee sitting careless on a granary floor,
. . . .
Then in a wailful choir the small gnats mourn
Among the river sallows, borne aloft...

Keats

First Say: Check What to Do step-by-step, particularly the required lip-rounding. With good speech tone, carefully match all /ô/ sounds.

Keep all /ô/'s consistent and stable. In *floor*, as in *more*, the /ô/ is followed in Standard American by a second syllable /ər/ *(floor ——➤ flôər)*. See pages 155-56 for this diphthong pattern, actually two syllables.

Watch /ô/ before /l/ *(small)*. Keep vowel intact; do not glide, injecting another sound *(small ——➤ smaw-uhl)*.

Then Sing: Base sung vowel on speech sound. Reproduce faithfully the distinctive "dark" /ô/.

SINGING /ô/

Distortions to Avoid: Abbreviated foreign version of long English vowel sound.

Also prevalent, an unlip-rounded, wider *ah*-type sound, carried over from speech (or merely an excuse to sing *ah*?).

Vocalize: Essential for distinct production are a secure oval contour and long, sustained sound. Carefully drill this characteristic English /ô/, based on correct speech model transferred to song.

Compare in vocalise /ô/ (oval) with *ah* (unrounded), using consonants: *taw — tah, kaw — kah, daw — dah, baw — bah*; and using words: *yon — yawn, don — dawn, farm — form, bard — bored.*

For Vowel Wheel, see p. 153.

Kinesthetics: Establish clear auditory feedback. Feel resonating system respond to specific identity of English /ô/. Develop sensation of well-apart and well-protruded lips, slightly drawn in at corners. Feel tongue low in mouth with slight elevation at the back.

Co-ordinate supportive breath.

To prevent /ô/ from slipping back and becoming too dark and throaty, cultivate sensation of forward "ring" on vault of hard palate.

MATCHING TO MUSIC /ô/ [ɔ]

In singing this excerpt work for accurate target vowel.
Heed the sense stress:

Where the ships of youth are running close hauled on the edge

of the wind with all adventure before them.

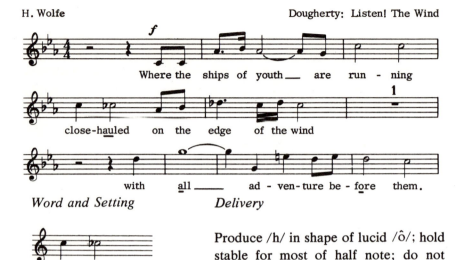

Word and Setting   *Delivery*

close-hauled

Produce /h/ in shape of lucid /ô/; hold stable for most of half note; do not permit vowel to sag; keep lip-rounded

all ——

Make clean attack on high note; do not permit sound to waver in the five beats; do not glide to /l/ adding another vowel; articulate /l/ clearly with deft movement of tongue-tip to gum-ridge

be - fore

Sing a good recognizable /ô/ on accented syllable on downbeat; perform *fore* as two syllables like this: fôər, the /r/ belongs to the weak syllable, /ər/ more color than consonant

Final Note: The /ô/, a characteristic English vowel, though dark should not lodge in the throat.

The mouth should have an elliptical shape which should not alter during the production of the sound.

In the United States, the /ô/ is produced in two versions, the darker vowel and the more open one closer to "ah." Recommended for song: the darker variety which is more readily understandable throughout the country.

oi [ɔɪ]

joy, voice, noise, toil, loyal, poignant, annoy, avoid, boisterous
Characteristic English compound vowel unit.* Long, mainly rounded. Technically a diphthong.

Note: Both sets of symbols clarify the diphthong pattern.

Appears in similar version in German.

WHAT TO DO /oi/

Tongue Position: Approximately same as /ô/ for the initial and longer portion of sound. Tip down behind lower front teeth with back slightly arched toward soft palate. Then as /ô/-like sound blends toward /ĭ/, front of tongue arches gradually toward hard palate, approaching the tongue position for /ĭ/.

Lip Shape: Mainly oval as for /ô/, then corners of lips release toward /ĭ/ shape, with minimal movement to form vocalic unit /oi/.

Mouth Opening: Quite open vertically, then retracts slightly. Jaw remains flexible and steady throughout.

Compound Vowel /oi/ [ɔɪ] in Slow Motion

Crest of sound

ɔɔɔɔ ɔɪ ɪ ɪ ɪ

Two vowel elements gradually blend into a single unit — the first element longer and stressed, the second shorter and unstressed. Both sounds merge at the approximate crest of the diphthong pattern.

WHAT NOT TO DO /oi/

Do *not* mouthe the shape with excessive lip protrusion followed by spreading at the sides.

Do *not* enunciate long /ē/ as second element in /oi/ instead of short /ĭ/ blend.

Do *not* disjoint the two elements so that a slide between them becomes audible.

*Generally listed separately as a diphthong, /oi/ is here included among the sixteen basic vowels.

Speech Localisms to Avoid: Few with /oi/, except some flagrant examples *(boil* ⟶ berl, and vice versa, *early* ⟶ oily). Also extreme Southern localisms *(boil* ⟶ bawl).

PROGRESSIVE PRACTICE FOR /oi/

> Recoiling, türmoiling and toiling and boiling.
> > Robert Southey

> Nor brighter was his eye, nor moister
> Than a too long opened oyster.
> > Robert Browning

First Say: Read aloud with well-supported tone, and note how uncomplicated /oi/ comes across as spoken. Most important: keep lips firmly rounded, releasing rounding briefly at end.

Next Chant : Protract /oi/ words to reveal in slow motion the process of longer /ô/ quality merging with shorter / ǐ/. Both sounds lose their identity within the blend, becoming a third sound.

Then Sing: Improvise with different melodies for each excerpt. Keep the musical line slow and legato, and then change to light and quick. In either case establish the individuality of /oi/ as sung.

SINGING /oi/

Distortions to Avoid: Separatist approach to diphthongs destroys authentic shape of /oi/, functionally a single unit. An attenuated effect, ending in long /ē/, produces a synthetic pattern heard too often in art songs or arias *(joy* ⟶ jôee).

Vocalize: Most important is to maintain the stability of this compound unit. Give it length but do not drop pitch, particularly as the long sound modifies to /ǐ/ position.

> Firmly support a level tone through the whole diphthong pattern.
> Use vocalise that repeats /oi/ on single notes.
> For Vowel Wheel, see p. 153.

Kinesthetics: Establish over-all sensation for oval-shaped /oi/ with firmly supported breath. Feel tongue related to bottom teeth at the beginning and briefly held, and then rising to upper teeth in approximate /ĭ/ position as lips unround. Throughout this action, the tongue moves smoothly without disturbing other articulators.

Cultivate clear auditory feedback and specific responses in resonating system.

MATCHING TO MUSIC /oi/ [ɔɪ]

In singing this excerpt work for accurate target vowel.
Heed the sense stress:

My heart unfolds with joy when I hear your sweet voice

Oh, speak to me, my love, that still I may rejoice

Saint-Saëns: My Heart At Thy Sweet Voice from "Samson and Delilah"

DELILAH:

My heart un folds with joy when I hear your sweet voice_

Oh, speak to me, my love that still I may re - joice_

Word and Setting	*Delivery*
joy	Combine voiced /j/ with long compound vowel on half note; maintain secure pitch throughout
 voice_	Avoid artificial separation on interval; keep cohesive vowel blend
 re - joice _	Use same appraoch as with *voice* above

Final Note: This vowel unit, along with /ou/ (*house*), comes closer than other diphthongs to revealing two blended sounds. The result, however, should be an imperceptible glide between them. (See Vowel Ladder II, p. 76.)

The two elements are neither /ô/ nor /ĭ/ but an approximation of each to form a distinctive third sound /oi/, with lips forming a firm oval and then releasing briefly.

ou [ɑʊ]

out, **now**, **doubt**, **down**, **found**, **coward**, **pronounce**, **hour**, **flower**, **howling**, **plough**

Characteristic English compound vowel unit; long, partially rounded. Technically a diphthong,* /ou/ is last sound, No. 16, on Vowel Ladder I.

Note: Both sets of symbols clarify the diphthong pattern.

Usage: /ou/ is pronounced in two somewhat different ways in U.S. More prevalent is blend of /å/ and /o͝o/ (first element, /å/ is midway between /ă/ and /ä/. The second pronunciation, a blend of /ä/ and /o͝o/ has as first element the more open sound *ah*. Recommended for song is this open pattern, familiar to singers.

Appears in German, not in French or Italian.

WHAT TO DO /ou/

Tongue Position: Whole tongue flat in mouth. Slightly raised at the back in approximate /ä/ position for longer first element. Then as sound moves toward /o͝o/, the back rises a little higher. Tongue movement requires small adjustment and should be held to a minimum.

Lip Shape: Unrounded, open, then rounds gently for /o͝o/. Lip-rounding as part of /ou/ contour is essential for accurate production.

Mouth Opening: Begins almost as large as for /ä/, then closes smoothly toward /o͝o/, but not as closed. Released jaw follows through with very little movement, if any.

---

*Generally listed separately as a diphthong, /ou/ is included here among the basic sixteen vowels. Do not confuse this dictionary symbol as in *out* with IPA [ou] for diphthong /ō/ as in *go*.

Compound Vowel /ou/ [au] in Slow Motion

Crest of sound

αααɑ ɑUᴜᴜ

Two vowel elements gradually blend into a single unit — the first element longer and stressed, the second shorter and unstressed. Both sounds merge at the approximate crest of the diphthong pattern.

WHAT NOT TO DO /ou/

Do *not* mouthe with exaggeratedly wide opening and tight closing action.

Do *not* arch front of tongue during formation.

Do *not* disjoint the blend into two parts.

Do *not* permit transition within /ou/ to become an audible slide.

Speech Localisms to Avoid: Substandard, nasalized, so-called Yankee version which is actually heard country-wide (*downtown* ⟶ dayoon-tayoon).

Southern style *ah-uh* for *our*, and many other /ou/ words.

PROGRESSIVE PRACTICE FOR /ou/

> Speak the speech, I pray you, as I pronounc'd
> it to you, trippingly on the tongue; but if
> you mouthe it, as many of your players do, I
> had as lief the town-crier spoke my lines.
>
> Shakespeare

First Say: Make certain that no nasality is permitted to impair the /ou/ words. Always channel this long compound sound through the mouth. Observe that when spoken, /ou/ falls into shape quite naturally as a single entity.

Hold on to this cohesive pattern in preparation for singing it.

There are four compound vowel units (diphthongs) in this famous selection: **pray**, **pronounced**, **crier**, **spoke** (with only /oi/ missing). Note that of the four, /ou/ is the longest vowel pattern.

Next Chant : Prolong the /ou/'s to reveal the anatomy of the compound unit without altering its fundamental shape. As the two elements closely combine in the chant, observe how a third, /ou/, emerges, which is neither /ä/ nor /ŏŏ/.

Then Sing: Improvise as recitative since Hamlet's words lend themselves very well to such delivery. Transfer as intact as possible the integrated /ou/ shape. This selection encourages skillful use of weak and strong word-types. Follow their lead:
"Speak the speech, ⁄ pray you, ⁄s ⁄ pronounc'd ⁄t ⁄o you..."

SINGING /ou/

Distortions to Avoid: Traditional miscasting as two segmented vowels with resultant synthetic acoustical effect.
Performing long /ōō/ instead of short /ŏŏ/ with pedantic exaggeration (*mountain* ⟶ mah-ōō-tain). This comes perhaps from the influence of Italian *ah* plus /ōō/ as in *paura* (pah-oo-rah) with three syllables.

Vocalize: Drill, comparing *ah* and /ou/ to point up the difference between the single sustained vowel and the unique blend. Be careful not to drop pitch during production.
Use vocalise that repeats /ou/ on single notes. Also fashion a vocalise on single notes with all five compound vowel units (diphthongs) based on these words beginning with *s*: *say, sigh, so, soy, sow* (the pig, that is).
For Vowel Wheel, see p. 153.

Kinesthetics: Establish the boundaries of movement for clear auditory feedback to avoid the exaggeration so common with this sound. Build painstakingly the resonant responses in sympathetic cavities.
Co-ordinate supportive breath.
Feel how the first element, approximately *ah,* is held briefly prior to modifying forward *toward* lip-rounded /ŏŏ/ (*not* so far as /ōō/).
Cultivate the sensation of one sound and keep refining it until the unifying, combining action becomes the remembered reflex for singing the identifiable compound vowel.

MATCHING TO MUSIC /ou/ [ɑu]

In singing this excerpt work for accurate target vowel.

Heed the sense stress:

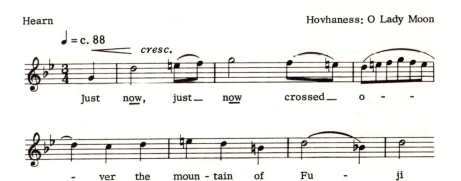

Just now, just now crossed over the mountain of Fuji.

Hearn   Hovhaness: O Lady Moon

Word and Setting

now

now

moun - tain

Delivery

Sing a relaxed /ou/ with no trace of nasality nor separation into two distinct vowels

Modify on high note (See Vowel Ladder III, p. 77)

Use natural emphasis to stress syllable *moun-* on downbeat; avoid nasality which often occurs with this word; use unstressed vowel /ə/ in final syllable (-tain).

Final Note: Singing this sound with an audible transition between two segments (ah-oo) reveals a lack of skill in enunciation.

The tendency to substitute a long /ōō/ sound instead of the /o͝o/ as the second element of the diphthong, so widespread among singers, should be abandoned.

It is important to lip-round the last element, but not tensely.

MATCHING TO MUSIC /oi/ AND /ou/

In singing this excerpt work for accurate target vowels.
Heed the sense stress:

Háve, gét, befóre ĭt clŏy Befóre ĭt clóud, Chríst Lórd, Aňd

sóur wĭth sínnĭng ínnŏcěnt mínd aňd Máy-dáy ĭn gírl aňd bóy.

Hopkins

Rorem: Spring

Have, get, be-fore it cloy_ Be-fore it cloud, Christ

Lord, And sour with sin-ning in-no-cent mind and

May-day in girl and boy.

Word and Setting	*Delivery*
 (-fore it) cloy_	Do not permit descent to blur active verb; keep vowel unit stable
 (it) cloud	Adhere to natural stress on upward leap; produce well-defined /kl/ and brief, voiced /d/ along with /ou/
 sour	Modify /ou/ on high note closer to /ŭo͝o/. Drop the /r/ in that elevated position, substituting /ə/

152

boy

Do not lose important key word on lowest note of phrase and diminuendo; note the fermata and keep compound vowel from losing pitch

Final Note: In both these vowel units, the word *unit* is the key to their production.

Though two blended elements are involved, the first longer, there must be no perceptible point of union, and no slackening of pitch.

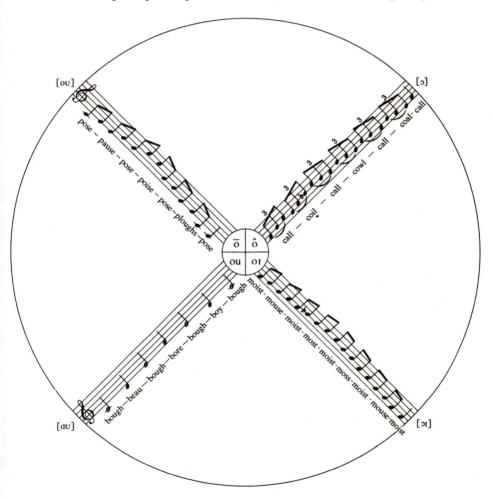

Vowel Wheel IV: /ō/ô/oi/ou/

153

Vocalises, p. 153, are designed for comparison of four lip-rounded vowels; the compound units /oi/ and /ou/ are lip-rounded only in part. In each of the four exercises initial final consonants remain the same;* only the target vowel changes. In drilling the group around the wheel, it is important to establish the distinguishing features of each vowel.

Note: These four lip-rounded vowels appear as Nos. 13, 14, 15, and 16 on Vowel Ladder 1.

Two Syllables, Not Diphthongs

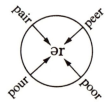

The four words pointing to /ər/ represent four similar patterns conventionally classified as *centering diphthongs with r.* As spoken in most of the country, however, these are not diphthongs but actually heard as two distinct segments, the first stressed and the second, /ər/, always weak. Only in New England and in Southern *r*-dropping speech do we hear the diphthongized enunciation with the two syllables compressed into one.

Delivered "*r*-less" in song as a diphthong of one syllable the words become artificial and, worse, most difficult to understand. Clarity comes with the recognizable two-syllable American pattern which, with the prolonged vowels of song, is entirely congenial to singing.

THE "AIR" PATTERN

Words like *care, despair,* etc. turn up so repeatedly in song as to require added comment. While the stressed vowels in *peer, pour,* and

---

*Although the four target vowels remain consistent in sequence, some consonants of necessity alter in these drills.

154

poor do not alter and the sound /ĕ/, /ô/ and /o͞o/ remain intact, the stressed vowel in *pair** is not identical with the /ĕ/ sound or IPA [ɛ ɚ].
Contrast these words: *errand — airing, cherry — chairing, very — vary, ferry — fairy.*

Try this somewhat roundabout route to the correct vowel sound. Say "yeah" nicely (!) without nasality or lip-spreading and then add a brief /r/. This exercise helps to reveal the two essential cohesive segments and the more accurate vowel sound.

Often set to one note, this "air" pattern (and the three others) should nonetheless be sung in two linked segments by dividing the given note:

♩   ♪ ♪

pair   pâ - ər

Some additional word examples of all four related patterns:

/âər/*	/ēər/	/o͞oər/ †	/ôər/
fare	dear	poor	more
there	cheer	tour	soar
e'er	mere	sure	door
despair	appear	allure	before

Three musical excerpts demonstrate these recurrent word patterns.
Remember to sing the two syllable formation: the first one strong and stressed, and the *second weak, brief and unstressed.* (Note: All four patterns are underlined.)

Symonds   Dello Joio: Farewell

*The specific symbol, /â/ for the "air" pattern is customary in American dictionaries. A second pronunciation /ă/ as in cat, heard in some sections of the country, is not recommended for song.

†In the r-dropping areas, the vowels in *peer* and *poor* are spoken with a short /ĭ/ and /o͝o/ instead of long /ē/ and /o͞o/ as in the rest of the country (pĭə, po͝oə).

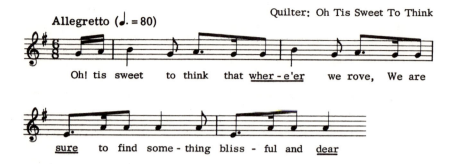

Oh! tis sweet to think that wher - e'er we rove, We are sure to find some - thing bliss - ful and dear

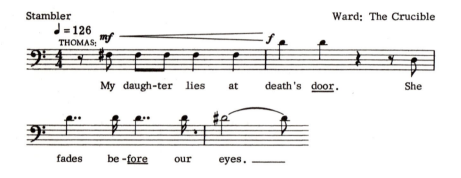

Stambler

Ward: The Crucible

♩ = 126
THOMAS:

My daugh-ter lies at death's door. She fades be -fore our eyes.

Summary Guidelines for Vowels

1. The sixteen. Do not confuse the innate quality of our sonorous sixteen vowels with the slipshod variety heard in daily chatter. The most flagrant national flaw is the pervasive nasality of American vowels. Remain ever alert to these distortions creeping into song.

2. Short Vowels. English short vowels (**pit-pet-putt-put**) frequently have to be held to unnatural length. Regardless of notation the short vowel, more open than the long one, should retain its original character.

3. Kinesthetics. The definition: sensation of correct movement of articulators and other responsive areas of the voice mechanism. When piano or orchestra competes with the voice, the ear can be only a partial monitor of the singer's production. Kinesthetic sensation, or the feel of the sound, is an additional guide to the accurate vowel.

4. Feedback.   The definition: the flow-back of information in a self-regulating system. To fortify fidelity to the sounds of English, singers need to develop consistent auditory feedback (inner hearing based on learned sensation) of authentic vowels as sung.

5. Discipline.   Mystiques abound. The "think" school never mentions tongue or lips (*just think!*). The study of diction in depth contributes a much-needed objective approach to a too subjective field. For an artist, instinct is not enough.

6. Vocalises.   A vocalise doth not a song make! When most needed, the best-drilled vowels may crumble before the challenge of performance.

7. The model.   Use the sustained, level vowels of good speech as phonemic models. Discover how much more released American English vowels are than foreign ones, including those of British English.

8. Practice big.   Like the actor whose voice must reach the balcony, practice as though before an audience. Maintain muscular tonus for more vitalized articulators for singing than for speech. Singers early in their training should become accustomed to the enlarged size of vowels as sung.

9. Modification.   When notation places the voice at its highest or lowest tessitura, it may often be impossible to produce even a reasonable facsimile of the required vowel. At such times use the voice like an instrument, but make every effort to form the vowel before "signing off." Consult Vowel Ladder III, p. 77, for all *possible* moves.

10. Presto.   When extra rapid tempo (à la Gilbert and Sullivan) pressures the text into unintelligibility, the answer is to *lean on the vowels*. Let the consonants ride along. The reverse would result in breathless haste and little clarity. The vowel anchors the word to stabilize the phrase.

11. Lip-rounding.   Never begin a vowel at the mouth. The lips follow through as final shaping after the sound, begun at the cords, has traveled through the pharynx and oral cavity.

12. Uniformity.   Perform vowels within the phrase as if they belonged together in tonal uniformity. Guard against cutting off prematurely or allowing vowels to fade before the onset of a consonant.

13. Sixteen different.   Avoid the trap of imagining a given vowel as merely a shorter or longer version of another. Preserve the maximum difference between them and do justice to the rich variety of color inherent in English vowels. (Drill all four Vowel Wheels.)

14. Not alike.   Especially seductive are those foreign vowels which sound somewhat similar to English but are not the same. Watch out for these "sound-alike" vowels which lead singers down the road to distortion.

15. Typically English.   Not surprisingly, English vowels not found in Italian or French cause problems when isolated in vocalises. Overcome this by vocalizing these vowels within words. Sing *fill, fill, fill,* etc., and then extract the vowel to develop the accurate English phoneme /ĭ/. Do the same with *full, fell, fun,* etc.

16. Stability.   Vowels and consonants modify each other. Though this interdependence makes sense acoustically at the listening end, remember to sustain the recognizable vowel for the allotted duration before it joins the next sound.

17. Downbeat directive.   Singing the vowel on the downbeat of each measure should not permit the abbreviation of consonants to non-recognition. Incorporate consonant and vowel so that both retain their identities. Learn the different duration of consonants to determine which ones can be begun ahead of time and which can be produced in a single action with the vowel on the downbeat.

18. Unlearning.   The mastery of vowels requires the learning of new co-ordinations to counteract faulty patterns acquired in speaking. Develop new responses to replace the old conditioned reflexes which inhibit the tonal ease and resonance essential to singing accurate American English vowels.

CHAPTER FIVE

THE SHAPES AND SOUNDS
OF THE CONSONANTS

Reiterating that consonants make words intelligible gives these vital shapes only half their due. Along with their clarifying role in song, consonants lyrical, vibratory, or percussive can sing or whisper, soothe or shatter. American singers need to take the strength and beauty of these virtuoso sounds for their own. How better to keep live and communicative the two-way current that always travels between artist and listener!

There are no ugly consonants, only inept execution. Profuse sibilant-percussive combinations in German certainly present no hindrance to beautiful singing of lieder or arias. And Italian consonants (neither less plentiful nor intrinsically more beautiful) frequently occur at the beginning of words (*sgridare*) whereas ours can be found clustered at the end and between words (mum*bled sl*owly — *mbldsl*). The telling difference, of course, is the care with which Italians have traditionally spoken and sung their language.

The trilled Italian *r*, evolved through centuries, is homebred as pasta; the British tap or flip as national and exemplary as Sir Lawrence Olivier. But to American ears, a superimposed trill or flip impresses as affected if not outlandish. It would seem to be a patriotic duty to rescue the American-English /r/, a fine sound when well made. Of course unvocal native /r/'s, particularly tenacious, call for all-out resistance.

Note: The Chapter *English, a Legato Language* includes a discussion of the salient function of consonants as linking elements in the flow of song. Pages 59 to 62 should be reviewed in conjunction with the detailed study of individual consonants which follows these guidelines.

Consonant Guidelines

NO NAME CALLING

The malpractice of downgrading consonants as troublesome interruptions of the vocal line to be disposed of swiftly still works considerable mischief. As a result these English tongue, lip, and teeth shapes tend to suffer neglect and even total obscurity while singers hurry on to the next vowel.

Hold consonants long enough to establish their individual identity. Bring consonant dynamics into balance with vowels.

NO MARGIN FOR ERROR

While the production of vowels permits a certain latitude in forming clear and recognizable sounds, consonants demand precise execution. Deviation from the prescribed pattern can only result in deviant sounds — inaccurate and often unintelligible.

Guard against too much jaw action. For precision, train the tongue and lips to move independently of the jaw.

THE BIG SIX

The consonants /t/d/n/s/r/l/ recur most frequently in English; three /n/r/l/ lead in sonority, two /t/ and /d/ add percussive character, and one /s/ supplies sibilance. So much for the allegation that English is all sibilant.

Four of these most common consonants, /t/d/n/ and /l/, are pro-

160

duced with the tongue-tip at the gum-ridge,* and for the other two, /r/ and /s/, the tongue-tip points toward it.

Make certain to develop quick, skillful response to these ever-recurring consonants.

FREEDOM AND EQUALITY

The low abdominal support needed for sustained vowels belongs equally to well-executed consonants. The tendency to drop body and breath support and merely tack these sounds on with tongue and lips accounts for flabby delivery of murky words.

Sing consonants and vowels with the same firm, supported breath impulse.

NO DROP-OUTS

The same singer who hesitates to drop a note often thinks little of dropping a consonant. Yet this language element is as indispensable to meaning as the note is to music.

Put all consonants to work! The only non-operative ones are mere spelling forms (psalm, wreck, etc.), or one of doubles within words (calling, marry, etc.).

VOICING AND UNVOICING

Unvoicing of even one of the fifteen voiced consonants, which contribute immeasurably to the effect of continuous tone in legato, causes a needless loss of tonal continuity and intelligibility.

Commit to memory and have at fingertips (tonguetip!) all fifteen voiced consonants. Distinguish between them and the ten voiceless ones.

VOICE IMMEDIATELY

Many singers have the bad habit of beginning a consonant as unvoiced and then easing gradually into voicing it (a holdover from careless and breathy speech). Delay in phonation arrests the flow of tone, weakening the non-stop movement of song.

Learn how to produce prompt vibration of the vocal cords for all voiced consonants.

*The most important place in the mouth for the articulation of English consonants is the gum-ridge at the front part of the hard palate above and behind the upper teeth.

NOT IN LIMBO

The time value of a word in music must be distributed equitably among the sounds in that word. The greatest portion of time goes to the vowels, but the consonants deserve their just if minor share. Time should be taken from the vowel when necessary to satisfy the consonant; however, do not lengthen the vowel in compensation or the tempo will falter.

Learn to share the time value of notation among these sounds. But stay with the beat.

GUESSING GAME

When consonants are inaudible, the ticket-buyer out front tries vainly to fill in the gaps between vowels. Soon he tires, gives up on the words, and has to content himself with the accompaniment and the voice. (It had better be a good one!) Audiences grasp meaning acoustically only in continuity of linked consonants and vowels.

Deliver the message of song in linked form so it can be understood.

PREHEARING

What singers refer to as "prehearing" is technically *auditory feedback,* a self-monitoring system based on learned responses to the accurate vowel. Consonants such as /t/d/p/b/k/g/ with hold-and-release action should be produced in the shape of the oncoming vowel.

To preserve unbroken legato, prehear the vowel, form a clear-cut consonant and articulate both in a single pattern.

FIRST AND LAST

In flawless legato, all consonants within a phrase link with vowels or with other consonants. Therefore, within the sung line let us regard the first consonant as initial and the last as final.

Incorporate this "one long word" approach to phrasing, the essence of legato singing.

PRECARIOUS AREAS

Legato is most apt to break down at those white spaces between words (really an optical illusion). Lyric linkage means closing the white spaces, especially where consonant clusters form between words.

Connect these sounds, singing right through the bar line to the end of the phrase.

HIGHER OR LOWER — WHICH?

Musical intervals between words or syllables often present the problem of whether to sing the consonant on the lower or higher note. The choice (never scooping or sliding) depends on various factors: notation, tempo, word-type, stress pattern, and, of course, interpretation.

Preserve the legato, the main objective, whether the consonant is on a higher or lower note.

ACCEPT NO SUBSTITUTES

The vowel-like nature of American singable /r/ acts as an embellishment to song texts. In speaking, *r*-dropping is entirely legitimate when confined to its natural habitat (New England, the South, and most of the Eastern Seaboard). Singers, however, should use standard American English without local persuasion and not trill, flip, tap or drop the /r/.

Sing the American /r/ correctly and on pitch wherever it occurs.

HAVE THE LAST WORD

The disappearance of that final consonant in song can probably be blamed on the familiar all-American decrescendo at the end of every spoken phrase.

To keep the sung line solid, and the sense of the phrase intact, hold on to the very last sound of the very last word.

YOU FEEL IT ⟶ THEY HEAR IT

In the production of accurate consonants the feel of vibration, hum, or voicelessness, of tongue movements and the action of lips and teeth — all of these sensations become kinesthetic responses.

Sing with precise, built-in sensory cues so listening ears will register the meaning.

IN UNION — STRENGTH

We investigate consonants in isolation, the better to combine them. Only skillful linkage of segments into phrases can produce intelligible and beautiful singing in English.

Bind consonants to vowels and to each other in syllables and words along with their built-in stress and non-stress.

163

Consonant Articulation Chart

Voiced	**Voiceless**

With Both Lips

b as in **b**eauty	**p** as in **p**iano
w as in **w**ord	**hw** as in **wh**isper
m as in **m**usic	

With Upper Teeth and Lower Lip

v as in **v**ibration	**f** as in **f**unction

With Tongue Pressed Against Upper Teeth

<u>th</u> as in brea<u>th</u>ing [ð]	**th** as in **th**eme [θ]

With Tip of Tongue on Gum Ridge Behind Upper Teeth

d as in **d**rill	**t** as in **t**ongue
n as in **n**asal	
l as in **l**ink	
j as in **j**aw [dʒ]	**ch** as in **ch**ant [tʃ]

With Tip of Tongue Curled Up

z as in **z**eal	**s** as in **s**ound, dance
s as in measure [ʒ]	**sh** as in **sh**ape, motion [ʃ]
r as in **r**hythm	

With Middle of Tongue on Hard Palate

g as in **g**lide	**k** as in **k**ey
y as in **y**awn [j]	
ng as in si**ng** [ŋ]	

With a Breath

h as in **h**ear

Some consonant combinations: qu [kw] as in **qu**ality; ex [eks] as in **ex**ercise; ex [egz] as in **ex**act.

This chart* represents a modified version of the conventional listing of consonants in speech texts. Consonants are divided first as to their production with voice (vibration of vocal cords) and without voice (breath alone) and second as to the articulatory organs involved (lips, teeth, tongue, and palate). Consonants appearing opposite each other on the chart are cognates (voiced and voiceless counterparts).

*Adapted from *Everybody's Book of Better Speaking* by Dorothy Uris, McKay Co., New York, 1960, p. 189.

The *Consonant Sonority Table*, geared to singing the language, lists the order of study to be followed.

The following table shows the relative sonority of consonant groups arranged in the descending order to be studied with the most sonorous first and the least sonorous, the breath called h, *last.*

Consonant Sonority Table

Semi-vowels: /r/w/y/ [j]
All-tone Shapes: the humming /m/n/ng/ [ŋ] and lyrical /l/
Buzz Sounds Plus Voice: z/zh/ [ʒ] /v/<u>th</u>/ [ð]
Percussives Plus Pitch: /d/b/g/j/ [dʒ]
Sibilant and Rustling Sounds Minus Voice: /s/sh/ [ʃ] /f/th/ [θ]
Percussives Minus Pitch: /t/p/k/ch/ [tʃ]
Breath Shapes: /hw/h/

Note: IPA symbols, in brackets, are indicated only when different from the corresponding dictionary markings in slashes.

Study Plan for Consonants

TWENTY-FIVE IN ALL

Sonority — the quality of full, resonant sound, often with clear or rich tone — is inherent in all vowels and certain consonants. The friction-free, sonorous consonants, those with buzzing sound, and the voiced percussives (when correctly produced) add greatly to the carrying power and uninterrupted legato of the vocal line. In contrast to the fifteen voiced consonants, the ten voiceless ones contribute a variety of toneless sound effects.

This approach which focuses on the relative resonance of consonant groups and their characteristic sounds proves valuable in singing the language. Singers benefit from an analysis of consonants in the order of comparative sonority, a sequence of study which implants an awareness of the distinctive sound value of individual consonants along with precise execution.

THE STUDY PLAN FROM SPEECH TO SONG

Introductory Discussion of Groups: A poetry selection exemplifying the group of related consonants to be analyzed; description of production and character of their sounds and special quality as sung.

Individual Consonants Introduced: A list of word examples, voiced or voiceless counterpart when indicated, technical description, the absence of certain English consonants in foreign languages.

OPERATION

Speech analysis of target sounds; when necessary more extensive discussion for selected consonants.*

Place and Action.   A precise description of the production of individual consonants within the designated groups. *Acoustic Result:* description of the recognizable sound.

PRACTICE PERIOD

Test the Action.   Target consonant practiced in isolation to develop feeling (kinesthetic sensation) of specific movements of articulators and inherent quality of sounds.

Sample the Verse.   Several examples of target consonant in context of short poetry selection to be spoken.

Remedies for Faulty Consonant.   Common problems pinpointed and specific remedies prescribed.

HOW TO SING AND LINK

Special character and problems of consonants analyzed, by groups and individually, in relation to singing. Recommended practice and techniques for effective articulation in flow of song.

TESTING WITH TEXT AND MUSIC

Finally, a musical excerpt selected from repertoire materials demonstrating several examples of the target group or individual consonant as required.

*The consonants /r/l/t/s/, among others, are singled out for more detailed treatment on the basis of their frequency in the language and special problems or unusual resonance.

166

Working Method: Step-by-step guide with key "shorthand" drawings; consonant combinations and clusters from the text practiced in isolation for smooth linking and then replaced in the phrase; the achievement of an improved level of legato with correct stress patterns.

The Twenty-Five Consonants

Dictionary	IPA	Key Word
r		red
w		wet
y	[j]	yet
m		met
n		net
ng	[ŋ]	sing
l		let
z		zeal
zh	[ʒ]	beige
v		vim
<u>th</u>	[ð]	then
d		debt
b		bet
g		get
j	[dʒ]	jet
s		set
sh	[ʃ]	shin
f		fit
th	[θ]	thin
t		ten
p		pet
k		kin
ch	[tʃ]	chin
hw	[hw]	when
h		hen

Note: IPA symbols, in brackets, are indicated only when different from dictionary markings.

The Twenty-five English Consonants

Half Consonant, Half Vowel: /r/w/y/

We in thought would join your throng,
Ye that pipe and ye that play,
Ye that through your hearts today
Feel the gladness of the May!

Wordsworth

THE GROUP

These consonants, related organically to three vowels, /ûr/ [ɝ], /ōo/ [u], and /ĕ/ [i], are known as semi-vowel glides.* From the position of these three vowel shapes, /r/,† /w/, and /y/ move quickly to the next sound, always a vowel and always stressed. The gliding action gives these sounds their consonant character while the initial vowel formation invests them with vowel-like nature.

On the borderline between vowels and consonants, /r/, /w/, and /y/ add distinctive resonance in transit, setting off and enhancing the main vowel in words. First on our Consonant Sonority Table (p. 165), these English semi-vowel glides, produced without friction or breathiness, are very congenial to song texts.

*Glide: A consonant produced in movement from its initial articulatory position to another position formed by the oncoming vowel.

†Unlike /w/ and /y/ which are always followed by a vowel, /r/ is found frequently before consonants. Only when preceding a vowel can /r/ be considered a semi-vowel glide.

Note: A separate analysis of /r/, a common, many faceted sound, follows. Less frequent in the language, /w/ and /y/ are then studied together.

r [r]

rose, rhyme, wrong, heart, born, bird, word, mother, fear, caress, hurry, borrow

Technical description: Voiced gum-ridge/palate/tongue-tip continuant* and semi-vowel glide. (Distinctively American English common consonant.)

Appears in diverse versions: Italian (trill or roll), French (uvular or trill), German (trill or uvular-guttural), British (flipped).

OPERATION /r/

Place: Tongue-tip and area just behind gum-ridge.

Action: Body of tongue released. Tongue-tip reaches toward back edge of gum-ridge. Tongue somewhat hollowed behind firmly up-tilted tip. Sides in light contact with edge of upper back teeth. Lips pursed slightly. As vocal cords vibrate, brief resonance is focused forward over tip. /r/ functions as a glide in pre-vocalic position.

Acoustic Result: Characteristic resonant, vowel-like sound.

PRACTICE PERIOD

Test the Action. Isolate and enunciate vowel /ûr/ as in *sir*, observing how vowel sound blends into /r/. Sustain isolated /r/ sound, keeping tongue-tip resolutely up. Continue with series of brief resonant /r/'s. With jaw and throat relaxed, and position of tongue-tip stationary, feel soft murmur in front of gently rounded mouth.

Continuant: A speech sound that may be voluntarily continued as long as breath supply permits. All the consonants except the *plosives* are *continuants.*

Sample the Verse

> The rainbow comes and goes,
> And lovely is the rose,
> The moon doth with delight
> Look round her when the heavens are bare;
> Waters on a starry night
> Are beautiful and fair;
>
> Wordsworth

Remedies for Faulty /r/'s

Fault: The Amurrucan /r/ reverberates gutturally, with tongue tensely inverted backward toward throat.

Remedy: Sonorous /r/ depends on forward production, and relaxation of all of tongue except the pointed tip. Try this daily drill to keep /r/'s resonant and up front:

> no-no-no
> toe-toe-toe
> low-low-low
> *row-row-row*

Fault: The intrusive /r/, originating in the East, keeps spreading its sphere of influence. The sound is gratuitously inserted to facilitate linking two words, one ending and the next beginning with a vowel. This /r/, as in "the idea-r is good," often adheres to words even in the absence of linking, "I'll take vaniller."*

Remedy: Practice linking two vowels by keeping the tongue-tip down behind lower teeth, then merely shifting gently from one vowel to the next. Try these phrases:

> I saw Albert. (*Not:* I sawr Albert.)
> The Sonata in B Flat. (*Not:* The Sonater in B Flat.)

Fault: "Wed, Wed, Wose" comes from an indolent tongue, literally at the bottom of it all. Considered "so cute" in little children's chatter, even a touch of /w/ substitution for /r/ in adults cries for correction.

Remedy: To drive home the essential difference between these two consonants, use a mirror to observe that: For /w/ lips move back as the tongue lies at bottom of mouth with *the tongue-tip inactive.* For /r/ lips hold still with *the tongue-tip up.* Compare these pairs: *reap-weep, red-wed, rage-wage, run-won.*

---

*Curiously enough, *r*-adders are often *r*-droppers ("more and more ideas"——➤ "mōuh and mōuh idea*r*s").

170

HOW TO SING AND LINK /r/

Because It Is There! This most distinctive, abundant, and abused American consonant demands no less than an analysis in depth. Continuing to provoke controversy and confusion, /r/ as presently sung calls for suitable standards of usage and production.

Once and for all, there is nothing inherently unpleasant about /r/, just as there is nothing inherently agreeable about r-dropping. Produced without friction or constriction, softly pursed American English /r/ is all voice and eminently singable. After years of trilling and flipping, singers turn to this resonant /r/ with relief.

To Each His Own. Non-native rolls, trills, or taps, executed by rapidly interrupted contact of the tongue and hard palate, are all consonant. The semi-vowel /r/ points the tongue toward the very same area of activity, but refrains from touching the palate. Instead, the tip holds still as vowel-like resonance passes over it.

Effective Corrective. For r-dropping singers, eager to pry loose clinging Southern, New England, or New York dialects, there is no more specific remedy than adopting the good /r/ for speech and song wherever it occurs.

False Homonyms. When singers pronounce *caught* for *court*, *laud* for *Lord*, *God* for *guard*, *alms* for *arms*, the resulting confusion could be banished by inclusion of fleeting /r/ in these words.

Adaptable in All Situations. Though relatively short, and sung on the same pitch as the adjacent vowel, /r/ can have the duration of an accented semi-vowel or of a mere touch of color. Within words /r/ performs consistently in varied positions that dictate the dynamics:

1. *Initial position in words* (rose) is the strongest. Here /r/ functions as a semi-vowel glide moving quickly to the next sound, always a vowel.

2. *Initial in a stressed syllable* (arise), the /r/ performs in the same manner.

3. *Before an unstressed syllable* (merrily, forest), /r/ still glides to the vowel but with its intensity reduced.

4. *The linking /r/ between words* (roar of welcome) aids legato flow as it blends softly into the following word. This /r/ should never be stressed.

5. *Initial consonants followed by* /r/ are strewn throughout the language (**cry**, **breath**, **grow**, etc.). Consonants preceding /r/ serve to modify the /r/, which then joins the vowel.

6. *The vowel* /ûr/ (**burn**, **learn**) absorbs a reduced version of /r/ as an integral, lesser element. (See /ûr/ in Chapter IV.)

7. *The weak counterpart* /ər/ (**father**, **honor**) requires an even briefer /r/, a sound more color than consonant.

8. *After vowels and before consonants* (darling, mortal) the /r/ consists of a brief insertion of /r/ color to link with the following consonant. The stressed vowel (**ah** in darling) must be held the full length. Over-long /r/'s must not be permitted to muddy these vowels.

9. *Pair, peer, pour, poor,* and words like these, so copious in song, are correctly sung as two syllables. With the second, unstressed syllable pronounced as /ər/ (a mere touch of /r/), these words are readily comprehended.

Omission and Commission (A Summation). When instructed to omit an /r/, the American performer will often retain in the attempt just enough /r/ quantity. While this may work as a device, it is better to strive for a correct /r/ than to depend on psychology.

Rather than sing that folksy growl, the unsingable Amurrucan /r/, omit it, especially before a consonant (for *start*, better *staht* than *starrt*; for *Lord*, better *Laud* than *Lorrd*). The trilled /r/ before a consonant sounds grotesque, and only before a vowel is it defensible at all.

Of course, the most suitable /r/ is a singable American sound:

tongue-tip pointing very close to the gum-ridge.

sides of tongue in relaxed contact with upper teeth.

lips pursed softly (before vowels).

over-all sensation of lack of tension in open throat, released jaw, and facial muscles.

Practice these /r/s in different positions.

Wolfe   Hoiby: The Tides Of Sleep

Andante con moto

The hooves of night, the hors-es of great

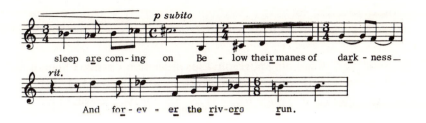

sleep are com-ing on Be - low their manes of dark - ness—

And for - ev - er the riv-ers run.

w [w]
y [j]

weep, once, dwell, beware, **qu**iet (kw), languish

your, **y**ear, **u**se, m**u**te, be**y**ond, milli**o**n, **beau**ty, halleluj**a**h

Technical description /w/: voiced bi-labial semi-vowel glide.

Technical description /y/: voiced tongue/palate semi-vowel glide.

Voiceless counterpart of /w/: /hw/* [hw] (pp. 252-54).

Note: /w/ and /y/ are never found in final positions in words.

/w/ is silent in words like *sorrow, window.*

/y/ is a vowel (an unaccented *ĕ*) in words like *happy, fury.*

/w/ appears commonly in French, briefly in Italian, and not at all in German.

/y/ appears commonly in German and briefly in French and Italian. The /w/ and /y/ sounds in the foreign languages are spelled differently than in English.

OPERATION /w/ and /y/

Place /w/: Lips.

Place /y/: Sides of tongue and palate.

Action /w/: Beginning position: Tongue-tip down and back up, lips

---

*With reduced usage, there has been a gradual loss of voiceless /hw/ in American speech. In song, however, the distinctive color of this voiceless sound should be retained, particularly in poetic context.

closely rounded for /ōo/. Position immediately changes as lips open, moving back in a glide to shape next sound, always a vowel (w e).

Action /y/: Beginning position: Lips unrounded, tongue high in mouth with sides at hard palate and tip down as for /e/ vowel. Tongue moves forward quickly in a glide for next sound, always a vowel (y ou).

Acoustic Result /w/ and /y/: The lip-shaped and the palatal glides both have characteristic vowel-like resonance.

PRACTICE PERIOD

Test the Action. Feel the gliding sensation from /w/ or /y/ into the shapes of the vowels in these words:

> woo we war woe
> you ye yawn yoke

Sample the Verses

> For some must watch while* some must weep.
> so runs the world away.
> > Shakespeare

> Lift up your heads O ye gates;
> And be ye lifted up ye everlasting doors:
> > Psalms

Remedies for Faulty /w/ and /y/

Fault: Lazy lips and sluggish tongues are responsible for the neglect of these attractive sounds. When their inherent gliding movement is bypassed, /w/ and /y/ become shapeless and dull.

Remedy: To take advantage of these unique semi-vowels, study carefully *Operation of /w/ and /y/* and then put the sounds to use in daily speech.

Fault: Intrusive glides, as in "I yam go-wing," are further examples of careless speaking habits.

Remedy: Say these phrases, taking care to link both vowels between words without adding glides.

*In *while* /hw/ is the voiceless counterpart of /w/.

How often (*not* how woften)
So eager (*not* so weager)
She isn't (*not* she yisn't)

Fault: Flowwer powwer! Many speakers (and singers), misled by the spelling, are apparently unaware that there are no /w/'s in such words.

Remedy: Sustain the stressed compound vowel /ou/, as in *out*, then add, with no glide between, the weak ending /ər/ (*power* ⟶ pouər [pɑuə]).

HOW TO SING AND LINK /w/ and /y/

The beauty of these glides often goes unrealized in singing. By bringing vowels to the forward area in the mouth. /w/ and /y/ friction-free, offer resonant support to vowels and clarity to words.

Practice these two excerpts for /w/ and /y/.

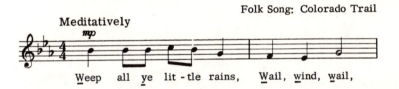

Folk Song: Colorado Trail

Meditatively

Weep all ye lit - tle rains, Wail, wind, wail,

Villon   Peter Pindar Stearns

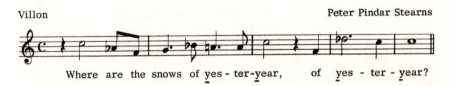

Where are the snows of yes - ter-year, of yes - ter - year?

Do's and Don't's. Sing /w/ and /y/ on the same pitch as the more prominent stressed vowel that follows. Never carry the glides in a scoop, as with a *glissando,* from one note to another.

be - ware   this   year

Begin /w/ on *e* note   Begin /y/ on *g* note

Shun all /y/ substitutions. Sing *can't you* (*not* canchew), *beside your* (*not* besijawr).

Do not linger on the brief vowel shapings that initiate /w/ and /y/.

175

Never sing *wander* as *ooahnder*, *yesterday* as *ee-esterday*.

Between words, link a final consonant to the /w/ or /y/ beginning the next word: *golden yellow*, *fervent wish*.

Do not use voiced /w/ for voiceless /hw/. Make the most in song, wherever it occurs, of the distinctive /hw/ sound, sing *which* not *witch*, *whither* not *wither*.

Testing with Text and Music /r/w/y/

Duncan

Britten: Rape Of Lucretia
poco a poco cresc.

LUCRETIA:

They wake us from the sleep of youth   In-to the   dream ——— of

pas - sion___   Then   ride   a - way, then ride   a - way, then

ride   a way,   While we still   yearn

The Method (Removing and Replacing). The target consonants /r/w/y/ have been removed from the text of the music excerpt. Practice them as marked, in combinations with vowels and in clusters with other consonants between words. Apply the KEY on next page to follow the "shorthand" drawings below which guide the movements of articulators. Continue until all sounds within the isolated segments are smoothly linked.

176

KEY:

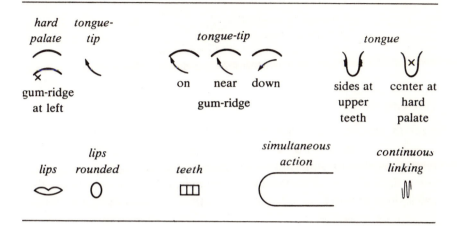

hard palate / tongue-tip / gum-ridge at left

tongue-tip — on / near / down — gum-ridge

tongue — sides at upper teeth / center at hard palate

lips / lips rounded / teeth / simultaneous action / continuous linking

Target Consonant with Vowel:

wa (wake) w ⌒0 ⫴ /ā/

dre (dream) dr ⫴ /ē/
dr

Consonant Clusters Between Words:

sfr (us from) s ⫴ f ⫴ r ⌒0 ⫴ glides to /ə/

vy (of youth) v ⫴ y ⫴ glides to /ōo/

nr (then ride) n ⫴ r ⌒0 ⫴ glides to /ī/

lw (while we) l ⫴ w ⌒0 glides to /ē/

ly (still yearn) l ⫴ y ⫴ glides to /ûr/

For Legato: Replace within the phrase all the practiced combinations and clusters with /r/w/y/. Now sing the entire excerpt. Take note of the improved level of lucid legato, which always includes correct stress on syllable and word as follows:
Thĕy wáke ŭs frŏm thĕ sleép ŏf yoúth...

177

All Tone: /m/n/ng/l/

I sway outside **myself**
Into the darkening currents,
Into the **small** spillage of driftwood,
The waters swirling past the tiny headlands.

Roethke

THE GROUP

Next in line on our sonority table, three humming consonants and lyrical /l/ compete with the semi-vowel glides for first place. By sustained vocal cord vibration and sympathetic resonance of all cavities, /m/n/ng/l/ demonstrate vowel-like attributes. But unlike vowels, they are fashioned into four different articulation patterns of lip and tongue to become consonants.

The technical classification of sonorous /m/n/ng/ as *nasal consonants* seems inappropriate. While these consonants do produce resonance in the naso-pharynx (and other areas), the quality is not "nasal" as the term implies. All tone, /m/n/ng/ endow speech and song with humming vibrance.

English /l/ sheds its luster upon all adjacent sounds. A boon to interpreters, no consonant performs better in legato singing. Happily, the **members** of this **singable** foursome are found extensively in the language.

Note: Next is an analysis of /m/n/ng/ studied together; /l/ follows in a separate section.

m   [m]

n   [n]

ng*   [ŋ]

me, **m**irth, e**m**pty, la**m**ent, sche**m**ing, autu**m**n, cal**m**

no, k**n**eel, mour**n**, sin**n**er, an**n**oy, ame**n**

so**ng**, ki**ng**, year**ning**, stro**ng**ly, amo**ng**, li**ng**er, sa**nk**, twi**nk**le

Note: Words like *linger, finger,* etc., are pronounced *ling-ger;*

---

*Note that /ng/ is not *n* plus *g*, but a third distinctive consonant.

n before *k* is always pronounced /ng/. Also /ng/ never initiates a word or syllable.

Technical description /m/: Bi-labial, *nasal.*

/n/: Tongue-tip/gum-ridge *nasal.*

/ng/: Tongue/soft palate *nasal.* (Distinctive English consonant.)

/ng/ appears frequently in German, infrequently in Italian, and not at all in French.

OPERATION /m/n/ng/

Place /m/: Lips.

Place /n/: Tongue-tip and gum-ridge.

Place /ng/: Middle tongue and back area of hard palate. (Soft palate position not recommended for singing.)

Action /m/n/ng/: *Common Velar-Valve Reflex:* Relaxed velum (soft palate, especially its lowest section), drops like a valve enabling these sounds along with the breath to enter nasal passages.

Action /m/: Lips lightly together, leaving small space between teeth. Tongue lies flat in mouth as for *ah.* Jaw released. Action is completed when lips open softly to join next vowel or to link with next consonant.

Action /n/: Tip against gum-ridge not pointed rigidly, but slightly flattened. Lips either open or closed. Jaw released. Action is completed when tip descends in quick movement to join next vowel or link with next consonant.

Action /ng/: Middle tongue raised toward back area of hard palate touching lightly. Tip down behind or below lower teeth. Sides of tongue in contact with back teeth. Action is completed when tongue-tip, already down, stays down, merely shifting slightly to accommodate the next vowel, or rises quickly to link with next consonant.

Acoustic Result /m/n/ng/: Characteristic continuant humming sound common to all three, with individual features identifying each.

PRACTICE PERIOD

Test the Action.   Keep the continuity of resonance from /m/ to /n/ to /ng/ without any break. Begin with lips softly together for /m/. Sustain /m/. Then tongue-tip rises for /n/. Sustain /n/. Tongue-tip goes down for /ng/ as middle tongue rises. Sustain /ng/. Observe the similarity of quality and the difference in resonance.

Sample the Verses

> We are the music-makers,
>   And we are the dreamers of dreams.
>
>   O'Shaughnessy

> And the night shall be filled with music,
>   And the cares, that infest the day,
> Shall fold their tents, like the Arabs,
>   And as silently steal away.
>
>   Longfellow

> Deep in that darkness peering, long
>   I stood there, wondering, fearing,
> Doubting, dreaming dreams no mortal
>   Ever dared to dream before.
>
>   Poe

Remedies for Faulty /m/n/ng/

Fault: General neglect, countrywide, of all these sonorous gifts to English shows up in flat speaking voices.

Remedy: Practice all three sample verses until the hum permeates the three consonant sounds to add resonance to the speaking voice.

Fault: The nasal spillover into constricted vowels adjacent to /m/n/ng/ is a national blight. Four vowels suffer most from this contagion, /ă/, /ou/, /ī/, and /ā/, in that order (man, down, time, same).

Remedy: Make the nose test. Hold nostrils closed. Say the word *man* very slowly, separating the sounds: *m - a - n.* Is there a vibration in the nose on /m/? *And none on* /ă/? And then another vibration on /n/? If so, all's well!

Try the same procedure for *down* (d-ow-n), *time* (t-i-m-e), *same* (s-a-me).

Remedy: If there is even a slight nasal vibration on the vowels, try this sequence:

After vowel, raise tongue-tip for /n/ hum.

> add-add-a⟶ nd
> doubt-doubt-dow⟶n

After vowel, bring lips together for /m/ hum.

> tie-tie-ti⟶me
> say-say-sa⟶me

After vowel, tongue-tip stays down as middle of tongue rises to center of hard palate.

> sit-sit-si⟶ng

Fault: The so-called /ng/ click plagues Americans, especially in Eastern urban areas. Many factors, including spelling, account for the persistence of this problem. On guard against the guttural intrusion, speakers mistakenly omit the legitimate /g/ in words like *English* (ĭng-glĭsh) a reverse problem.

Note: For rules covering /ng/ plus /g/ words, see p. 211.

Remedy: With hands on ears, say *ring*. Feel the hum as you hold the final /ng/ sound. This is the accurate sensation of /ng/ resonance, not to be confused with the percussive fragmentary voicing of /g/.

With hands on ears, say *ring*. Feel the hum in your head as you hold the final /ng/ sound. This is the accurate sensation of /ng/ resonance, not to be confused with the percussive fragmentary voicing of /g/.

For the precarious two-syllable pattern, such as *singer*, to avoid inserting *guh*, make sure that the first syllable *sing* is strongly stressed. Some /ng/ resonance should then carry over to unstressed /ər/. Without any tension whatsoever, make an effortless transition from *sing* to *er*. As the tongue sides drop adjusting gently, the tongue-tip stays down.

Compare these pairs: *hug-hung, rag-rang, wig-wing, brig-bring, hag-hang, rug-rung.* Keep at this until transition is smooth from vowel to /ng/ hum.

Go on to phrases: *singing it, going out, wrong answer, gang up.* (Remember — if you feel it, they hear it.)

Fault: "Strenth" and "lenth." The substitution of /n/ for /ng/ in words like *strength* and *length* has become so widespread as to seem almost normal. No dictionary, however, sanctions this trend which should be equally ignored in song.

Remedy: After the vowel /ĕ/ the tongue-tip *stays down* behind lower teeth for /ng/, *then* moves up to make contact behind upper teeth for /th/ (le-ng-th).

HOW TO SING AND LINK /m/n/ng/

Give Them Time.   To do justice to the ringing tone and mellow resonance implicit in these consonants means to accord them commensurate duration. Time value may be taken at the expense of an adjacent vowel (see p. 60f). Of course, the exaggerated effects in popular music are ruled out ("over the mmmountainnn"). But remember, underdoing — not over doing — is the general problem.

Attention: /ng/!   While /m/ and /n/ enjoy an international reputation, /ng/, typically English, is not sufficiently understood or utilized. Also rich in timbre, /ng/* merits similar recognition. Because of their insecurity with this consonant, singers tend to accord it perfunctory treatment.

  The solution: Sing this consonant in a more forward position than in its spoken form. Elevate the middle of the tongue — *not the back* — to touch the hard palate — *not the soft*. In that corrected position, cultivate a feeling of relaxation in the tongue, palate, and above all, jaw, as well as openness in the throat. Now feel /ng/ resound vowel-like *on the hard palate*.

Devices to Keep /ng/ from Back-sliding.   *Onion drill.* The first /n/ in combination with vowel /ĭ/ (o*n*ion), when enunciated slowly, produces a pleasant quality, not too far from that of /ng/. Compare *onion* with *young'un*. Feel how the /ng/ now resounds up front.

  From /n/ to /ng/. The most common of the sonorous threesome, /n/ usually fares the best. Compare these pairs: *kin-king, sin-sing, run-rung, clan-clang, gone-gong*. Feel how /ng/ benefits from this juxtaposition with /n/.

> *Italian /gn/ and English /ng/ are first cousins. *Signor:* /gn/ is produced with tongue-tip behind lower teeth and front of tongue at area behind gum-ridge on hard palate. *Singer:* /ng/ is produced with tongue-tip behind lower teeth and middle of tongue at back area of hard palate. The resonance in cavities is similar in both consonants; but the English /ng/ is a more open sound, especially when produced as recommended on hard palate.

Hidden hum-power. Make the most in song of words spelled with *n* before *k* (always pronounced /ng/). IPA [ŋ] makes clear that /n/ becomes /ng/ before /k/: drink ⟶ [drɪŋk].

Drill these words with clear /ng/ leading /k/ forward on to the hard palate: think, sank, trunk, crank, brink.

All-Important /m/n/ng/ Arch. The soft palate should be stretched in a tension-free arch at the same time that its lower edge drops to permit characteristic resonance for each consonant to pass through the cavity above the soft palate. The naso-pharynx, including the nasal passages, vibrates along with the other responsive cavities. (Once again, *if you feel it, they hear it.*)

Caution: Three "If's." If the soft palate is pulled down too far, the tone will remain pinched in the nose shutting off the flow of resonance.

If the arching is too tense, the path to the nasal passages will be blocked.

If the tongue is bunched, a throaty sound will cut off the ring.

Barber: Knoxville: Summer of 1915

One is a mu-si - cian, she is liv-ing at home.

Andante moderato   Purcell: I Attempt From Love's Sickness To Fly

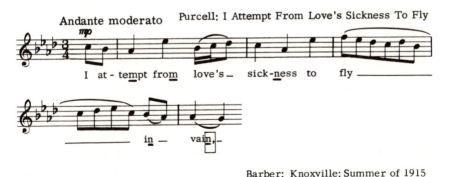

I at - tempt from love's — sick-ness to fly _____

_____ in — vain, —

Barber: Knoxville: Summer of 1915

Allegro

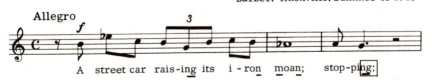

A street car rais-ing its i - ron moan; stop-ping;

183

Shun the Off-glide. *The rule:* Resonance must cease before articulators move to avoid "home-uh," "vain-uh," and "stopping-uh." (p. 183).

Before a rest: /m/ — Lips remain together with the tongue uninvolved.

/n/ — Tongue-tip holds on the gum-ridge.

/ng/ — Tip stays down, middle up against the hard palate.

For all three: Maintain these positions as long as called for by the notation. Only when the voice ceases, do the articulators release silently. Try this technique on the last words of the previous excerpts.

Testing with Text and Music /m/n/ng [ŋ]

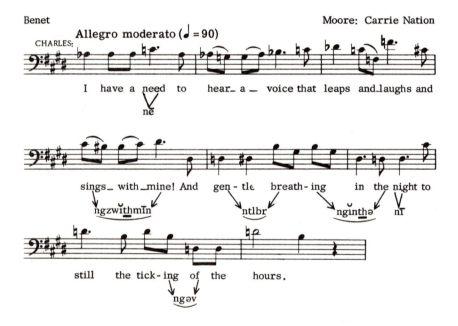

Benet

Moore: Carrie Nation

The Method (Removing and Replacing). The target consonants /m/n/ng/ have been removed from the text of the music excerpt. Practice them as marked, in combinations with vowels and in clusters with other consonants between words. Apply the KEY on the next page to follow the "shorthand" drawings below which guide the movements of articulators. Continue until all sounds within the isolated segments are smoothly linked.

184

KEY:

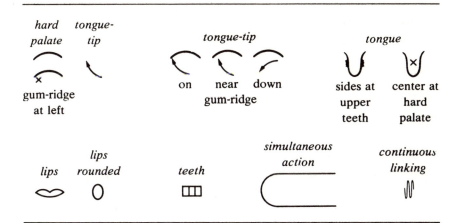

hard tongue-
palate tip

tongue-tip

tongue

gum-ridge
at left

on near down
gum-ridge

sides at center at
upper hard
teeth palate

lips
lips rounded teeth

simultaneous
action

continuous
linking

Target Consonant with Vowel:

ne (need)
ni (night)

Consonant Clusters Between Words:

ngzw...thm...n (sings with mine)

ntlbr (gentle breathing)

ng...nth (breathing in the)

ngəv (ticking of)

For Legato. Replace within the phrase all the practiced combinations and clusters with /m/n/ng/. Now sing the entire excerpt. Take note of the improved level of lucid legato, which always includes correct stress on syllable and word as follows:

I have a need to hear a voice...

1 [l]

low, love, light, play, blue, soul, self, alive, holy, battle

Technical description: Voiced tongue-tip/gum-ridge *lateral.*

OPERATION /l/

Place: Tongue-tip and gum-ridge.

Action: Voiced breath flows laterally around sides of tongue as tip presses lightly but firmly against gum-ridge directly above upper teeth. Released tongue does not touch at side teeth. Back of tongue low and free of tension. Teeth slightly apart. Resonance comes through without any sensation of pressure.

Acoustic Result: Characteristic lateral, entirely vocal consonant, clear or dark. The terms *clear* and *dark* refer to two different resonances, depending on the position of /l/ in words.

PRACTICE PERIOD

Test the Action. *Clear* /l/ appears in initial position in words or syllables:* lead, love, lid, led, laid, allow, lonely.

   Without any sensation of pressure, and with the tongue-tip securely on the gum-ridge, feel the forward clear resonance of initial /l/'s in these words.

   Dark /l/ (not a disparaging term) appears *after* vowels (call, I'll, fell), or before consonants (cold, help, silk). For dark /l/, the back of the tongue rises slightly to accommodate the preceding vowel or next consonant.

   Whether articulating a clear or a dark /l/, the tongue-tip remains on the gum-ridge with the back of the tongue unconstricted. The quality of resonance alters, consistent with the shape and color of adjacent sounds. The acoustic effect of these fraternal /l/'s varies, but their resonant nature does not. Compare these pairs: si*l*k-ki*ll*s, *l*ied-dia*l*, f*l*esh-se*l*f, *L*uke-coo*l*, *l*aw-a*ll*.

*Serviceable /l/ may precede any English vowel.

Sample the Verses

Glory be to God for dappled things —
For skies of couple-colour as a brindled cow;
For rose-moles all in stipple upon trout that swim....

Gerard Manley Hopkins

I hear lake water lapping with low sounds by the shore....

William Butler Yeats

Remedies for Faulty /l/'s. Too few Americans receive anything like true value from the resonant wealth reposited in /l/'s. Undermined, brushed off, often omitted entirely, ailing /l/'s stand in need of therapeutic measures.

Fault: Retroflex /l/. Only muffled /l/'s can result from retracted, curled back tongue-tips. Worse, all surrounding sounds are contaminated.

Remedy: Make sure the tongue-tip adheres to that crucial area, the gum-ridge. To check accurate position: Compare /l/ with another gum-ridge consonant, /n/. Raise tip to ridge and hum the sound of /n/. Feel flattened tip, then adjust for /l/ with a pointed tip. The rest of the tongue should remain untensed and free.

Compare these pairs: *knit-lit*, *net-let*, *neigh-lay*, *not-lot*.

Fault: Nasalized /l/. A lowered soft palate and tense throat deform musical /l/ into a most unmusical sound. Funneled through the nose, words like *lie*, *long*, *lazy* account for some typical American twang.

Remedy: Massage throat and jaw with fingers, loosening tightness. Yawn, opening the throat. Feel the palate arch without any constriction in back of tongue. Now whisper: *sly*, *ply*, *flow* (initial voiceless consonants help to combat nasality). Add voice, still speaking softly.

Fault: Infantile /l/. The speech term *lalling* includes the familiar baby talk /l/ which unfortunately differs little from adult patterns. A substitute sound resembling /y/ (I *y*ove you) is one infantile form; another drops /l/ altogether, substituting a vowel (*little* ⟶ ittl, *battle* ⟶ battoo, *milk* ⟶ miook).

Remedy: The only corrective therapy is to discipline the tongue. Re-educated lingual muscular response will come from diligent practice of the distinct movements involved. To sharpen the tongue-tip, chant: la-la-la, lo-lo-lo, lay-lay-lay.

Continue with /l/ spoken in context: *I love milk, **till the soil, tell** the lady.* Feel a new sense of strength develop in that flabby old tip.

Fault: Dental /l/. Executed with a limp tongue leaning on the teeth, the dental /l/ sounds thick and dull.

Remedy: Put tongue-tip on the gum-ridge and *keep it there*! Return to the list of words, p. 186, and practice *and practice*.

Fault: Missing /l/. "Hep me!" This localism peculiar to the South clings to Southerners up north.

Remedy: Of course, articulate all /l/'s wherever found. No /l/'s are dispensable except those in words like *calm, psalm,** salmon, folk, talk, half*. Also watch for the more elusive /l/'s slurred in unstressed syllables: *relevant, challenge, quality*, etc.

HOW TO SING AND LINK /l/

A Rose by Any Other Name. Some phoneticians label /l/ a semi-vowel for its tonal quality, or a glide for its smooth linking to other sounds. What matters most is to cherish this lyrical sound. Singers who barely brush past /l/ are the losers, along with the text.

If there is trouble with any vowel before or after /l/, look to the /l/. Feeble /l/'s will devitalize vowels, just as solid /l/'s will strengthen them.

Clear or Dark? When perplexed about which variety of /l/ to sing, scrutinize the position of /l/ in the word. The /l/ in *leap* and that in *peal* illustrates the two varieties of /l/, the first clear, the second dark. Try this: sing *leap* and superimpose the identical /l/ into *peal* and observe how odd the transferred /l/ sounds. Now sing the dark, resonant, and correct /l/ in *peal*.

Adjustment to the adjacent sound takes care of which /l/ to use. With tip safely anchored, the rest of the tongue (untensed, of course) goes about the business of co-ordination with the vowel or consonant.

Sing English /l/'s. Some singers make the mistake of embracing the Italian /l/ exclusively. Produced with tongue-tip on the teeth, *bel canto* /l/ resembles our clear /l/ but has a different "liquid" tongued sound.

---

*Americans, of late, have been incorrectly sounding these traditionally silent /l/'s. This practice is not sanctioned by any English dictionary.

Italian has no other /l/, only this unvaried consonant (appropriate for *Italian* song).

Do not color English with this foreign brush: "I hear you calling (kaulyeeng) me."

Prepare in Advance. For /l/'s that follow consonants (**blame, glory, hopeless**), bring the tongue-tip to the gum-ridge in advance of /l/. Thus, in one co-ordinated move, articulate the percussive along with the following /l/.

Share the Beat. Make sure to accord this pellucid sound a portion of the count. "Don't come in too soon with /l/." "Don't hold too long," These admonitions, while occasionally valid, often succeed in lopping off the /l/'s (a serious loss to song). Prolonged /l/ is rarely a problem, adequate duration is!

Voice Immediately. Do not delay phonation of /l/ with a breathy initiation.

Vowel-like Function of /l/n/m/. In certain positions these sounds become so-called *syllable consonants* [l̩ n̩ m̩],* a pattern consisting of two consonants which, when linked, give the impression of a syllable unit minus a vowel. The language is replete with examples: *battle, mortal, cradle, sudden, garden, brighten, chasm, prism.*

Sing this with a fairly brisk tempo:

Here, the sixteenth note over *-tle* makes possible a speech-like tempo and eliminates the vowel. When sustained slightly, /l/ absorbs a portion of the time value of the consonant syllable.

The same words in slow tempo:

*In IPA, l, n, and m appear with a dot beneath to signify the syllabic consonant.

189

There, a quarter-note over *-tle* calls for a vowel sung in that syllable. But hold the vowel down to a brief *schwa* /ə/ and sing on /l/.

No Stru-guh-ling, Please!   Refrain from adding an extra syllable to *struggling, babbling, settling,* and similar words. Two will do.

Testing with Text and Music /l/

Hopkins   Barber: A Nun Takes The Veil

The Method (Removing and Replacing).   The target consonant /l/ has been removed from the text of the music excerpt. Practice it as marked, in combinations with vowels and in clusters with other consonants between words. Apply the KEY on the next page to follow the "shorthand" drawings below which guide the movements of articulators. Continue until all sounds within the isolated segments are smoothly linked.

190

KEY:

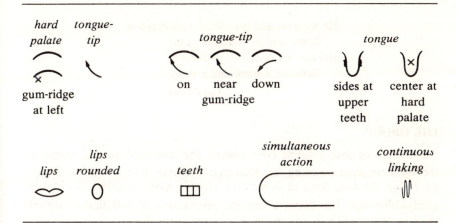

hard palate	tongue-tip		tongue-tip			tongue	
gum-ridge at left			on	near	down	sides at upper teeth	center at hard palate
				gum-ridge			

lips	lips rounded	teeth	simultaneous action	continuous linking

Target Consonant with Vowel:

al (fail, hail) /ā/ ∭ l ⊂

fli (flies) f ⌒⊞ ∭ l ⊂ ∭ /ī/

li ⎱
le ⎰ (lilies) l ⊂ ∭ /ĭ/ /ĕ/ ∭ z ⊂∪

blo (blow) bl ⌒⊂ ∭ /ō/

Consonant Clusters Between Words:

ldzhw (fields where) l ⊂ ∭ dz ⊂ ∭ hw ⌒O ∭ /âər/

For Legato. Replace within the phrase all the practiced combinations and clusters with /l/. Now sing the entire excerpt. Take note of the improved level of lucid legato, which always includes correct stress on syllable and words as follows:

Ĭ háve desirĕd tŏ gó...

191

Sound Effects Plus Voice: /z/zh/v/<u>th</u>/

> He weaves, and is clothed with derision;
>   Sows, and he shall not reap;
> His life is a watch or a vision
>   Between a sleep and a sleep.
>   Swinburne

THE GROUP

This group of four related consonants, the so-called voiced *fricatives* (an acoustic term meaning "friction-like"), is next in order on the Sonority Table. All four have in common a characteristic rustling sound mingled with voice. For each, a specific interaction of articulators diverts the breath which, focused through a restricted passage, sets up a typical buzzing vibration.

To describe /z/zh/v/<u>th</u>/ technically as fricative "noise elements," as many speech and voice textbooks do, is to downgrade these vivid consonants. Their variety of buzzing sound effects invest song literature with striking dramatic color.

z [z]

zeal, Zion, breeze, rose, zephyr, lazy, music, loses, birds, (and most plurals); common words like is, has, these, etc.

Technical description: Tongue-tip/gum-ridge voiced *fricative.*

Voiceless counterpart: /s/, p. 219.

OPERATION /z/

Place: Tongue-tip and gum-ridge.

Action: Front of upper and lower teeth touch lightly or are a little apart. Sides of tongue press against inside of upper back teeth sealing off breath which then moves forward along groove of tongue toward

192

center of upper teeth. Vibration is set off between tip of upraised tongue and gum-ridge. Teeth and hard palate act as sounding board.

Acoustic result: Characteristic voiced, high frequency, sibilant sound.
   Note: /z/ and /s/ are sometimes produced with tongue-tip down behind lower teeth. Though acceptable, this tends to dull the sound.

PRACTICE PERIOD

Test the Action.   Imitating a bumblebee up and down a scale makes a good /z/ exercise. Feel the sensation of buzz on the front teeth and try to direct the sound right through the center of the mouth. Keep the bee sound from spilling from the sides of the teeth.

Sample the Verses

>   There were three buzzing bumblebees;
>   Three buzzing bumblebees;
>   They swept the garden all the day,
>   With their zoom, zoom, zoom, zoom, zoom....
> Anonymous

>   Of his bones are coral made,
>   Those are pearls that were his eyes....
> Shakespeare

Remedies for Faulty /z/'s*

Fault: Neither /s/ nor /z/. Due to habitual eye-mindedness we tend to downgrade the many /z/'s spelled /s/. *Soundz, voicez, vowelz* are misspelled, yes, but correctly pronounced. The sole addition of a quick, positive /z/ buzz (not an unvocal "between" sound) guarantees instantly improved communication.

Remedy: Place fingers on vocal cords and imitate the noise of a leaking tire, "ssssssssss." You feel no response in the throat. Next produce "zzzzzzzzzz" like that of a buzz saw. Now your cords respond by vibrating. (Use no pressure.) Keep /z/ quite short but truly vibrating. Voicing all /z/'s reduces excessive sibilance in speech and song.

---

*Along with /s/, /z/ is one of the lisped sibilants, though lisped /z/'s are less frequent. Recommended remedies for lisped /s/ (p. 222), can be adapted as well for /z/.

The Over-all Rule. The sound /s/ follows the sound of *unvoiced* consonants; /z/ follows *voiced* consonants and vowels.

In Plurals. When the preceding consonant is *voiced*, pronounce *s* as /z/; so**ngs**(z), musicia**ns**(z), playe**rs**(z). When preceded by a vowel, *s* is always pronounced /z/: sk**ies**(z), tr**ees**(z), cr**ows**(z).

When the preceding consonant is *voiceless*, pronounce *s* as /s/: ships, streets, tracks.

In Verbs. To form the *third person singular* the rule is the same as for noun plurals. If the preceding sound is *voiceless*, use /s/; if *voiced*, use /z/: lau**ghs**, ta**kes**, belie**ves**(z), moa**ns**(z).

Possessives take the same endings: Phili**p's**, Be**th's**, John**'s**(z), thei**rs**(z).

When es Is Added. Always pronounce *ez:* kiss**es**(əz), choos**es**(əz), blush**es**(əz), mirag**es**(əz); or use vowel /ĭ/ kiss**es**(ĭz), etc.

What Is X? Again, spelling is deceptive: few recognize the two x's, one pronounced *eks* as in express, the other *egz* as in *exalt*. Since no rules exist to guide pronunciation, when in doubt consult the dictionary.

Purcell: Nymphs And Shepherds

If *egz* is called for, link /g/ to /z/ making sure to voice a vibrant /z/, ("Every valley shall be exalted" ⟶ **egz**alted).

Attention: /z/ continued on pp. 199-201

zh [ʒ]

azure, illusion, pleasure, rouge, prestige, Asia, visual, persuasion
Note: /zh/ never begins a word in English.
Technical description: Tongue blade behind gum-ridge, voiced *fricative.*
Voiceless counterpart: /sh/, p. 222.
Appears in French, but not in Italian or German.

OPERATION /zh/

Place: Back of gum-ridge and tongue blade (area directly behind tip).

Action: Entire tongue farther back than for /z/. Tongue surface is flat from side to side and ungrooved, middle tongue arched close to hard palate. Breath (very little required) moves forward toward broader channel formed between upraised front of tongue and hard palate. Vibration set off in this area. Teeth and hard palate act as sounding board. Lips round slightly.

Acoustic Result: Characteristic voiced, buzzing, sibilant sound.

PRACTICE PERIOD

Test the Action. For students of French, /zh/, as in "je," is familiar. Although relatively uncommon in English, the sound does appear in

195

some common words: vision, leisure, measure, etc. To insure the correct shape of /zh/, practice the hushing sound of /sh/, then add voice for /zh/. Feel the sensation of buzzing.

Sample the Verse

Rich the treasure
Sweet the pleasure
Sweet is pleasure after pain.

Dryden

Remedies for Faulty /zh/'s

Fault: Mushy /zh/. A lax-tongued, "shushing" sound (*treasure* ⟶ trea*shr*) is decidedly unpleasant. This lateral lisping spills from the sides of the tongue and may even whistle.

Remedy: Keep the sides of the tongue pressed against the inside of upper back teeth. Feel the tongue center arched against the hard palate as vocal cords vibrate. Channel the /zh/ buzz right down the middle of the mouth through rounded lips. Compare these pairs: *Confucian-confusion, ruching-rouging, glacier-glazier.*

Attention: /zh/ continued on pp. 199-202.

v [v]

vow, view, of, I've, love, saved, moves, revive, devil
Technical description: Lip/teeth voiced *fricative.*
Voiceless counterpart: /f/, p. 222.

OPERATION /v/

Place: Upper teeth and lower lip.

Action: Cutting edge of upper teeth rests lightly on inside of lower lip. Lips relaxed and apart. Relaxed tongue remains in low position in mouth without touching lower teeth. Very little breath is required. Cords vibrate as voiced sound passes through barrier of teeth against lip. Teeth act as sounding board.

Acoustic Result: Characteristic voiced, lip/teeth, buzzing sound.

PRACTICE PERIOD

Test the Action. Isolate sound of /v/, sustaining buzz. Feel the sensation of tingle inside the lower lip. Repeat until the buzz flows freely.

Sample the Verse

> Music, when soft voices die,
> Vibrates in the memory;
> Odours, when sweet violets sicken,
> Live within the sense they quicken.
> Shelley

Remedies for Faulty /v/'s

Fault: /w/ for /v/. Lingering baby talk accounts for a variety of /v/ that resembles /w/ and is "wery bad!"

Remedy: Check the correct articulation of the semi-vowel, friction-free, lip-rounded glide /w/ (p. 173). Compare it to the action of /v/ described above and *feel* the difference. Compare these pairs: *woo-view, wane-vane, west-vest.*

Fault: /f/ for /v/. "Hafta," following *I, you, we,* etc., is so commonplace as to be almost acceptable. Even a moment's thought will reveal that voiceless /f/ has been carelessly substituted for voiced /v/. Good speech and song, of course, favor "have to."

Remedy: Practice slipping in a brief, vibrating /v/ to link with /t/ (have to).

Fault: Mispronounced little word "of." Since the /f/ is really /v/, this prolific preposition suffers from spelling. In lickety-split talk, correct sound of /v/ either reverts to /f/ or is dropped completely ("mosta the time").

Remedy: Insert the quick buzz of /v/ in all *of*'s (ov's) and add its vibration throughout speech and song. Note the improvement, with this small correction, in continuity of tone and intelligibility of text.

Attention: /v/ continued on pp. 199-201.

<u>th</u> [ð]

thy, breathe, smoothed, southern, mother, clothing, withered

And: **the, these, they, there, though,** etc.

Technical description: Tongue/teeth voiced *fricative*. (Distinctive English consonant.)

Voiceless counterpart: /th/, p. 225.

Does not appear in Italian, French, or German.

(*Note:* Underlined symbol /<u>th</u>/ for voiced **th**, and IPA [ð].)

OPERATION /<u>th</u>/

Place: Tongue-tip and upper teeth.

Action: Tongue-tip makes light but firm contact with back of upper teeth, close to cutting edge. Lips relaxed and apart. Very little breath required. Cords vibrate as voiced sound passes through barrier of tongue-tip against upper teeth. There is tingling sensation in tip. Teeth act as sounding board.

Acoustic Result: Characteristic voiced, tongue/teeth, buzzing sound.

PRACTICE PERIOD

Test the Action.   Isolate the sound of /<u>th</u>/, sustaining the buzz. Feel a tingle on tongue-tip. Repeat until the buzz flows freely.

Sample the Verse

> Though thou the waters warp
> Thy sting is not so sharp
> As friend remembered not.
>   Shakespeare

Remedies for Faulty /<u>th</u>/'s

Fault: Dees, Dem, and Dose. Substituting /d/ for /<u>th</u>/ is flagrantly substandard, forever scorned by educated speakers. A flaccid tongue,

198

however, in rapid speech, often slips dangerously close to the /d/ position, and at best manages a very weak /th/.

Remedy: Avoid any contact of the tongue with the gum-ridge area. Produce a clear /th/ by pressing the tip firmly against the back of upper teeth. Establish the sensation of buzz in contrast to the sensation for /d/, a hold/release action of the tongue-tip at the gum-ridge. Compare these pairs: *dine-thine, doze-those, dare-there, den-then.*

Fault: The missing /th/. Watch out for slangy "what's 'at." Also beware of *sooz* for *soothes, breeze* for *breathes,* etc. Such truncated words, deprived of th, sound illiterate.

Remedy: Co-ordination of /thz/ (brea*thes*) may be somewhat difficult. When analyzed, however, these two buzzing sounds can blend with ease. First, voice the /th/ and feel the vibration on the tongue-tip, then for /z/, raise the tip that very small distance just short of the gum-ridge, as teeth come together for the vibration of /z/. All insecurity evaporates when this /th/ to /z/ linking is achieved.

HOW TO SING AND LINK /z/zh/v/th/

Misleading Labels: To think of these vibrant consonants as friction sounds suggests harsh and abrasive effects. Singers do *not* produce friction when performing these consonants. The focusing of small amount of voiced breath through narrowed channels, specific for each shape, produces the vibratory sound effects listeners recognize as /z/zh/v/th/. *Important:* Always keep the exterior muscles of face and throat uninvolved so as not to impede the vocal line.

Tone Not Air: Never blow or push breath. There should be no sensation of air, only resonant buzzes on pitch. Many words in song call for two or more of these kindred sounds in sequence. Prime example: /v/z/th/ (belie*ves* **th**em) when delivered as linked, assorted, mellow buzzes, have a cello-like sound effect.

Immediate Voicing: A common flaw in speech turns up in song: delayed phonation. When *divine* is sung as *difvine, lazy* as *laszy,* the effect cuts fuzzily through the vocal line. Do not initiate these consonants with their voiceless counterparts, but work for prompt vocal cord vibration. The beauty of *bel canto* singing springs from this very principle.

A functional first aid: Sustain the neutral vowel /ə/, and without cessation of voicing, merge directly into the voiced consonants. Repeat: əz/əzh/əv/əth. Build in sensation of instant vibration of consonants after neutral vowels, then drop the vowel.

The Long and Short of It: Constant admonitions against holding on to these and other consonants have made singers jumpy. They may rest assured that only adequate duration, however brief, conveys /z/zh/v/th/ to listeners in audible and intelligible form. Audience recognition of language sounds should always be the goal and gauge of duration.

Reminder: Keep time value consistent with English stress patterns. In *vivid*, for example, /v/ in the first, stressed syllable demands longer and stronger execution than /v/ in the second. Consonants beginning weak syllables are never accented.

Take care not to exaggerate the voiced /th/ in the article *the*, since this small word must be kept subordinate at all times. The same care not to exaggerate applies to other weak word-types such as *is* (iz), *of* (əv), and *with* (with).

The "Uh" Appendage: *Love-uh, breathe-uh, daze-uh, mirage-uh.* To prevent these obtrusive off-glides that often surface before a rest, hold the lip-teeth-tongue pattern of each of these consonants. Wait for the vibration to cease, and only then release the articulators. Exception: With rapid tempo, to keep words intelligible before rests, it may sometimes be necessary to permit a short off-glide.

In final position (seize, liege, grieve, wreathe), these consonants should not simply be tacked on, but supported with the same breath impulse as the vowels to the last instant of vibration at the end of a phrase.

At Change Points: *Live vitally, breathe the perfume, his(z) zeal* (not possible with /zh/ which never initiates a word).

Meeting between words, /z/v/th/ follow the rule of holding the first consonant briefly and executing the second, identical consonant firmly. The resultant slightly prolonged buzzes on pitch are a source of color and drama.

Share the Count: These reverberating sounds do not exist in limbo (as some would have it) but form integral elements of words in time and

200

space. Sing /z/zh/v/<u>th</u>/ with due duration, taken, if necessary, at the expense of the preceding or following vowel.

ESPECIALLY FOR /z/

Small Clarifier: Take advantage of all /z/'s deceptively spelled *s*. The brief buzz of /z/ on pitch is an unparalleled aid to lucid singing. Compare *stormz* with *stormss* (actually neither /s/ nor /z/, but an unvoiced sibilant). When all the voiced /z/'s in plurals and verbs found in song texts are added, the result is sheer gain in clarity and resonance.

Because of the pervasive, unfortunate unvoicing of final /z/ in speech, performers find difficulty in mastering its urgent voicing. No effort will prove more rewarding than the acquisition of the /z/ buzz. A handy drill: sing the following list adding a vowel off-glide in each case: *comes(z)-uh, tells(z)-uh, please(z)-uh, cheers(z)-uh, vines(z)-uh*. Here purposely use the off-glide. After articulating final /z/, continue voicing through the vowel. Repeat several times. Next, lop off the vowel, but retain the vibration of /z/, a short sound, perfectly voiced.

Practice for /z/ Spelled s:

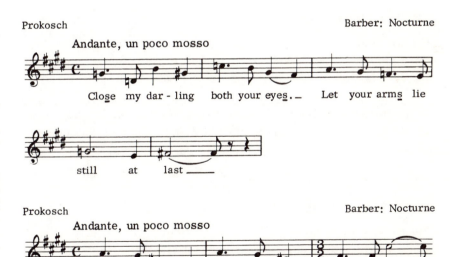

Prokosch   Barber: Nocturne

Andante, un poco mosso

Close my dar - ling both your eye<u>s</u>. _ Let your arm<u>s</u> lie

still at last ___

Prokosch   Barber: Nocturne

Andante, un poco mosso

Wave<u>s</u> a-cross the<u>s</u>e hope - less sand<u>s</u> Fill my heart _

201

ESPECIALLY FOR /zh/

Lips Forward: The consonant /zh/, of lower frequency than /z/, benefits from lip-rounding which reinforces its sound. Of course the degree of lip rounding varies with individuals. At most, lips need be only lightly pursed.

Comparatively uncommon in English and very congenial to song, /zh/ should be performed as expertly as possible.

Practice For /zh/ (and th)

Nicolas Flagello

Andantino

Soft - ly sweet in Ly - di - an mea - sures

Soon he sooth-ed his soul to plea - sures.

ESPECIALLY FOR /v/

Do Not Bite: When teeth bear down heavily on the inside of the lower lip, a muffled (if not bloody) /v/ emerges. For optimum vibration, find the most favorable place to rest the teeth inside the lower lip.

Make the Most of Love: The most sung word in the language boasts the built-in advantage of both /l/ and /v/. To the ineffable quality of /l/, vibrant /v/ adds fervor. Link the /v/ buzz closely: *love you... v me...v him...v them...v John.* (No song excerpt needed here!)

ESPECIALLY FOR /th/

Most Economical Route: While an acceptable voiced /th/ sound can be produced with tongue-tip showing between the teeth,* the effect is neither attractive nor desirable. (To be convinced, check with a mirror.)

*Foreigners having difficulty with this typically English consonant may find tongue protrusion an aid in mastering the action. Once learned, however, the intradental co-ordination is difficult to unlearn.

The sound of /th/ is better with the tongue-tip held back of the teeth, more mobile and closer to the position for all other sounds.

The tongue moves from its position behind the upper teeth toward the next sound, with the buzz of /th/ conveyed *on the move*. This nimble action reinforces the legato of the phrase. In singing the word *though*, for example, /th/ vibrates as the tongue deftly moves back for the vowel /ō/.

Little Word "With": Voiceless /th/ instead of voiced /th/ as final sound in *with* has grown so usual in American speech that the dictionary now lists voiceless /th/ as a second pronunciation.

Faced with a choice, singers should voice the *th*. Establish the feel of fleeting, vibrant spillover of voiced /th/ (*with all, with love, with anger, with joy*).

S or Z for /th/: A corrective for non-natives who switch to /s/ or /z/ when /th/ is called for (*this* ⟶ sis or zis): Keep the teeth and lips apart while the tongue adheres resolutely to the upper teeth and voice the /th/ feeling the tingle on the tip. For practice compare these pairs: *so-though, sigh-thy, see-thē, seize-these, sows-those.*

Practice For /th/:

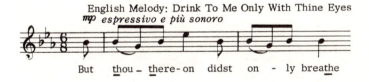

English Melody: Drink To Me Only With Thine Eyes

mp espressivo e più sonoro

But thou — there-on didst on - ly breathe

Testing with Text and Music /z/zh/v/<u>th</u>/

Folk Song: The Passionate Shepherd

The Method (Removing and Replacing) The target consonants /z/zh/v/<u>th</u>/ have been removed from the text of the music excerpt. Practice them as marked, in combinations with vowels and in clusters with the consonants between words. Apply the KEY on next page to follow the "shorthand" drawings below which guide the movements of articulators. Continue until all sounds within the isolated segments are smoothly linked.

KEY:

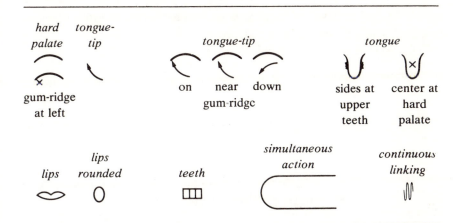

hard palate	tongue-tip		tongue-tip			tongue	
gum-ridge at left			on	near	down	sides at upper teeth	center at hard palate
				gum-ridge			

	lips			simultaneous action	continuous linking
lips	lips rounded	teeth			

Target Consonant with Vowel:

beds of
roses and
thousand
posies

Brief /z/s (spelled s) link to next vowels.

Consonant Clusters Between Words:

vw...thm (live with me) v 🔲 w /ĭ/ th

m /ĕ/

lth (all the) l th /ə/

zh...rzpr...v (pleasures prove)

zh /o͞o/ rz /o͞o/ pr /o͞o/ v

kth (make thee) k th /ē/

dz...vr (beds of roses)

dz /ə/ v r /ŏ/ z /ĭ/ z

205

For Legato. Replace within the phrase all the practiced combinations and clusters with /z/zh/v/<u>th</u>/. Now sing the entire excerpt. Take note of the improved level of lucid legato, which always includes correct stress on syllable and word as follows:

Cóme lĭve wĭth mĕ aňd bé mў lóve...

Percussives Plus Pitch: /d/b/g/j/

To be**h**ol**d** the **j**unipers sha**gg**ed with ice
The spruces rough in the **d**istant **g**litter
        of the **J**anuary sun.
                                    Wallace Stevens

THE GROUP

These consonants with fragmentary pitch appear next in order after the voiced fricatives on our table of sonority. Included in this listing is /j/, a so-called voiced affricate, defined as a plosive plus a fricative articulated as the single sound /j/. The IPA symbol [dʒ] makes clear this blended consonant. The acoustic impression of /j/ is mainly percussive /d/ mingled with the buzz sound of /zh/.

Technically classified as *plosives* or *stop-plosives*, /d/b/g/ are defined as consonants produced by explosive emissions of air. We must consider the designation *plosive* as misleading particularly when applied to singing. The precise hold-and-release muscular actions give these consonants their distinctive pattern, but do *not* result in a built-up explosion of air. Each consonant, /d/b/g/j/, employs a different form of closure followed by rapid separation* of the articulators involved. Abundant in English, these crisp sounds underscore the flow of song with characteristic pulsation.

*For the affricate /j/, the separation is not quite so rapid as for /d/b/g/.

206

d [d]

do, day, dead, produce, medal, sadder, throbbed, ended
Technical description: Voiced tongue-tip/gum-ridge *stop-plosive*.
Voiceless counterpart: /t/, p. 234.

OPERATION /d/

Place: Tongue-tip at gum-ridge.

Action: Sides of tongue in close contact with upper back teeth and gums. Action begins with tongue-tip securely placed on gum-ridge behind upper teeth at center. Tip releases with springlike movement to below bottom teeth as cords vibrate briefly. During this rapid action, tongue adjusts to the position of next sound.

Acoustic Result: Characteristic voiced, tongue-tipped percussive sound.
Note: As tongue descends, there is no sudden rush of air or "explosion."

PRACTICE PERIOD

Test the Action. Say in succession t-d-t-d-t-d. Then change to *to do- to do- to do.* Feel the impact of /d/ on the gum-ridge as the vocal cords respond to the rapid voicing.

Sample the Verse

> I walk down the patterned garden paths
> In my stiff brocaded gown.
>
> Amy Lowell

Remedies for Faulty /d/'s

Fault: The dental /d/. Heard frequently in everyday speech is a variety of /d/ produced with the tip or blade of the tongue flattened against the teeth. The effect is slovenly and substandard. Since /d/ and its voiceless counterpart /t/ are so numerous, the accumulative effect of these toothy sounds infects the whole speech pattern.

Fault: The slack /d/. A flaccid tongue tends to slip. When the broader areas of the tongue beyond the tip land on the gum-ridge, /d/ is no longer a clear click but comes through as thick and dull.

Remedy: For all deviant /d/'s the first step is to establish the feel of the gum-ridge. With the tip of the tongue held firmly on the ridge for /l/n/d/t/, repeat: **lah-nah-dah-tah**. The tip descends to behind lower teeth each time for the vowel. With the mouth ajar and the jaw not moving, all the action is accomplished by the tongue muscles. Use other vowels in the same manner (**l**ay, **n**ay, **l**o, **n**o, etc.).

Once the tongue-tip has been energized, the clarity of countless English words will improve immeasurably.

Fault: The dropped /d/. The final /d/ in di**d**, cleare**d**, crie**d**, etc. should still be heard, however briefly.

Remedy: "I di**d** so." Slip in that final /d/ before /s/. "I di**d** go." Insert /d/ very lightly in a double drumbeat effect of "**d**go." Be repaid in dividends of clear speech by cultivating the /d/ click.

Fault: Didint, wouldint, and shouldint. These babytalk carry-overs are indulged in by far too many adults.

Remedy: Co-ordinate linking of all three consonants /d/n/t/ on the gum-ridge: pronounce *did* and feel the tongue securely on the ridge for the final /d/. Next, *without disengaging the tip*, voice the hum of /n/. Then with the tongue still holding its position, articulate the voiceless /t/ by releasing the tongue-tip rapidly. Thus, correctly, "di**dnt**, woul**dnt**, shoul**dnt**," minus the intrusive second vowel.

Fault: Didjoo or didn'tchoo? Slipshod substitutions of /j/'s and /ch/'s in the expressions *did you? would you? didn't you?* and *wouldn't you?* etc., are so commonplace that the practice begins to seem normal.

Remedy: Carefully link /d/ or /t/, the percussives, to the continuant /y/ (p. 123). Remember the semi-vowel quality of /y/ is also the more sonorous (di**d y**ou).

Fault: Troublet or troubled, missed /t/ or missed? The past tense, always spelled *-ed* but sometimes correctly pronounced /t/ and other times /d/, often causes errors.

Remedy: Learn the rules:

When preceded by a voiced consonant, *-ed* is pronounced /d/, troubl**e̸d**, crown**e̸d**.

When preceded by a voiceless consonant, -ed is pronounced /t/, miss*ed*/st/, talk*ed*/kt/.

When preceded by a verb ending in *t* or *d*, -ed becomes a separate syllable with the vowel pronounced before /d/, ha**ted**(ĭd), plea**ded**(ĭd). (The suffix -ed is never the accented syllable.)

When the verb preceding -ed ends with a vowel, the -ed becomes simply /d/, pray*ed*, echo*ed*.

Whether pronouncing voiced /d/ or voiceless /t/, make certain the articulation is crisp and clear.

Attention: /d/ continued on pp. 213-15.

b [b]

beat, **b**loom, ro**b**e, Septem**b**er, so**bb**ed, re**b**el, pro**b**a**b**ly

Technical description: Bi-labial voiced *stop-plosive*.

Voiceless counterpart, p. 240.

OPERATION /b/

Place: The lips.

Action: Tongue is inactive. Lips come together (not pressed together) then spring apart energetically as vocal cords vibrate briefly. During this rapid action, lips adjust to position of following vowel or consonant.

Acoustic Result: Characteristic voiced, percussive, lip-formed sound.

Note: No explosion results, nor is there air compression behind the lips. Specific muscular lip action produces the shape of /b/. Only in final position before a pause is there a slight "pop."

PRACTICE PERIOD

Test the Action.   Feel the sensation of firm lip contact and quick bounce of the release. Listen for the feedback of percussive /b/. The "buh, buh, buh" sequence should be clear and sharp.

Sample the Verse

> Bright before it beat the water,
> Beat the clear and sunny water,
> Beat the shiny big-sea water.
>
> Longfellow

Remedies for Faulty /b/'s

Fault: Lazy lips cause sloughed-off /b/'s that sound more like /p/'s.

Remedy: To counteract, try this: with finger at vocal cords, distinguish between the vibrating /b/ and the voiceless /p/. Compare these pairs: *path-bath, peat-beat, pump-bump, lap-lab, rip-rib, hop-hob, rapid-rabid, ripping-ribbing, popping-bobbing.*

Attention: /b/ continued on pp. 213-15.

g [g]

gay, guide, green, sprig, rogue, regret, beggar, struggle

Technical description: Voiced, tongue back/velar* *stop-plosive.*

Voiceless counterpart: /k/ p. 243.

OPERATION /g/

Place: Middle of tongue and hard palate.

Action: Mouth is open. Tip of tongue rests behind bottom teeth. Middle of tongue placed in contact, not with soft palate, but with hard palate,† a little behind center. Tongue springs away from this position as vocal cords vibrate briefly and adjusts to oncoming sound.

Acoustic Result: Characteristic palatal percussive sound.

Note: As with /d/ and /b/, there should be no explosive release of air from behind the tongue.

---

* *Velar:* from velum, the soft palate.

†This action is recommended for song in contrast to the conventional classification of /g/ as a soft palate consonant.

PRACTICE PERIOD

Test the Action. Isolate /g/ and articulate in a series. Feel the sensation of the percussive bounce from off the hard palate.

Sample the Verse

> And you may gather garlands there
> Would grace a summer's queen.
>
> Sir Walter Scott

Remedies for Faulty /g/'s

Fault: The frog-like gulp. Producing /g/ gutturally back in the throat creates the danger of pulling all other sounds along into the throaty regions. With *girl*, for example, the entire word tends to lodge back of the tongue.

Remedy: The procedure that recommends a hammer stroke against the soft palate causes some of the mischief. Study Action for more precise, favorable placement.

Try this: Because the so-called front vowels like /ē/ are enunciated in a more forward position, a word like *geese* will encourage a favorable placement. Keep the tongue's middle firmly placed on the hard palate for all the /g/'s regardless of the vowels that follow: **geese, gay, goose.**

When /g/ follows the vowel, try for the same front placement: **league, sprig, hag.**

The tongue-tipped /l/ also brings the vowel forward: **gleam, glimpse, glade.**

Fault: That confusing "guh." Fearful of inserting an "*ng* click" (p. 181), even when /g/ after /ng/ is correctly called for, many stumble over such words as *finger, younger, anguish.*

Some rules to help clear the confusion:

Use only /ng/ [ŋ] within words formed from verbs: *singer, longing.*

If the first syllable does *not* form a word, add /g/ to /ng/. Thus *finger* ⟶ fing-ger, *anguish* ⟶ ang-guish. Exceptions: Three common adjectives *long, strong, young* need /g/ plus /ng/ only before *-er* and *-est*: long, longer (long-ger), longest (long-gest).*

Attention: /g/ continued on pp. 213-16.

---

*IPA symbols are clarifying: singer ⟶ [sɪŋə], finger ⟶ [fɪŋgə]; adjectives *long, strong,* and *young,* add /g/ in their comparative and superlative forms: thus, [lɔŋ] but [lɔŋgə] and [lɔŋgəst].

j [dʒ]

joy, gem, judge, huge, image, aged, agitate, soldier, injure
Technical description: Voiced tongue-tip/gum-ridge/palate
*affricate.**
Note: The IPA symbol [dʒ] makes clear the two components of
/j/, plosive /d/ plus fricative [ʒ].
Voiceless counterpart: /ch/ p. 247.
Appears in Italian, not in French or German.

OPERATION /j/

Place: Tongue-tip, gum-ridge, and palate.

Action: Sides of tongue in close contact with upper back teeth. Action begins with flattened tongue-tip, including blade, securely placed on gum-ridge and front section of hard palate (further back than for /d/). Lips round slightly as for /zh/. Tip releases with spring-like movement as /d/ and /zh/ simultaneously blend into single entity, /j/. Because of buzz-pitch of /zh/, however, release for /j/ is not as rapid as for percussive /d/ alone. Tongue adjusts to position of oncoming sound.

Acoustic Result: Characteristic voiced, percussive buzz sound.
Note: As with /d/b/g/ there is no explosive release of compressed air.

PRACTICE PERIOD

Test the Action. Articulate a series of staccato /j/'s (j-j-j-j-j). Feel the quick thrust of tongue downward and vibration on teeth acting as sounding board.

Sample the Verse
> Angels fall, they are towers, from heaven — a story
> Of just, majestical, and giant groans.
> Gerard Manley Hopkins

Affricate: Combined plosive-fricative forming a single sound.

Remedies for Faulty /j/'s

Fault: The slack /j/. The brisk hold-release quality of /j/ is often lost in slipshod speech. A mushy sound invades words like *orange* or *jolly*, and names like *George* and *Jim*. Mainly responsible is a sluggish tongue lying prone below the back teeth.

Remedy: Make sure that the sides of the tongue are in close contact with upper back teeth. Feel the muscular response of /j/ as a result of correct placement.

Fault: Disappearing /j/. The final /j/ in words like *page* and *hodgepodge* tends to disappear when pronounced more like a misshapen /ch/ or some vague sibilant.

Remedy: Develop the habit of voicing a clear-cut /j/ [dʒ]. Though the final consonant in words is correctly less emphatic than the initial, it is there to be spoken and sung. Bring the tongue-tip up to the gum-ridge and feel the percussive buzz-blend.

Compare these pairs: *perch-purge, batch-badge, etch-edge.*

HOW TO SING AND LINK /d/b/g/j/

Precise, Unpressured Production: Articulate separately and energetically *bah, dah, gah, jah.* Throat, facial muscles, and jaw are free of tension. Feel a distinct tug at the low abdominal muscles for each hold-and-release action. These fragmentary sounds require the same bodily support as do vowels. The common fallacy of performing plosives superficially with just lips or tongue makes them flabby and inaudible.

Shun Non-English Sounds: Italian /d/, /t/, and /j/ are correctly articulated against the top of the upper teeth. When introduced into English song, however, these dentalized consonants sound foreign. Remember that in English *only* the *th*, voiced and voiceless, involves the tongue at the teeth.

Percussive into Vowel: Brisk /d/, /b/, /g/ and /j/ are sung on the pitch of the adjacent vowel.

Make sure, also, of immediate voicing. Easing into these sounds makes them fuzzy and unclear.

A good exercise to develop prompt voicing:

for /d/ — warm up with *n* (nnn-*d*).

213

for /b/ — warm up with *m* (mmm-*b*).

for /g/ — warm up with *ng*, as in *sing*

for /j/ — use an *n* then blend with *zh*.

Controlled Off-glide: Before a rest or pause for breath these consonants in final position in words (hea*d*, so*b*, do*g*, ra*ge*) may be said to be truly stop-plosives.* In other positions they combine with oncoming sounds, while before a pause they "pop."

An off-glide, while unavoidable in the very nature of hold-release action, can be skillfully reduced. When a word ends in /d/b/g/ or /j/, begin voicing the consonant, then immediately change to its voiceless counterpart.

For example, sing the word "hea*d*." After the vowel /ĕ/, the vocal cords continue vibrating for /d/. Then immediately unvoice /d/ to /t/. This action cuts "uh" sound to a minimum. (Of course /t/ is never heard, becoming simply a silent shape.) The same technique works with *b* ⟶ *p, g* ⟶ *k, j* ⟶ *ch*.

Varying Intensities: Different positions of percussive consonants within words affect their dynamics. Compare first and last sounds in *dead, bob, grog, judge*. The degree of intensity of a given consonant must be consistent with correct English stress. If singers, striving for clarity, accentuate the consonant beginning a weak syllable, they distort the stress pattern of the word (**num**ber *not* num**ber**, **win**dow *not* win**dow**).

No Compression, No Explosion: The numerous /d/b/g/j/'s in the language require careful handling since excessive air works havoc with a vocal line. A notorious enemy of legato is the blast of air which cuts through non-stop tonal continuity.

Herewith a demonstration to prove the essential airlessness of the hold-release action common to all these consonants:

Breathe out, emptying the lungs of air. Hold tongue-tip on the gum-ridge; then release with a bounce to produce /d/.

Repeat: Breathe out, then bring the lips together, letting them spring apart to produce a clean /b/.

*The affricate /j/ in final position functions like a plosive although the release is slower.

Repeat: Breathe out, raise the middle of the tongue to the hard palate; release energetically to produce /g/.

Repeat: Breathe out, raise the flattened tongue-tip to gum-ridge and border of hard palate; release tongue slightly slower to produce blended clear sound of /j/.

Proof: Clearly, an explosive spurt of air does not produce these percussive shapes. Muscular action does, along with the breath used in the support of the whole phrase.

The Vowel Role: The vowel is the main body of tone which carries these consonants to the listener. The preceding or following vowel should be sustained fully, all the better to convey concise voiced percussives.

Use the following excerpt to practice sustaining the vowels before and after the underlined percussives.

Frost   Reif: Birches

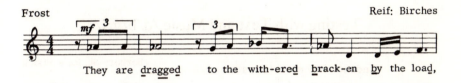

They are dragged   to the with-ered brack-en by the load,

Especially for /d/: The double drumbeat of combined percussives is extremely effective: stab*bed,* lag*ged,* a*ged.* The hold-release action of the first consonant (*b, g,* and *j*) links in rapid percussive action without air spill to the final *(d).* In the previous musical excerpt note this effect in the words *dragged,* and *withered bracken.*

Especially for /g/: For song it is urgent to produce /g/ with the middle of the tongue on the hard palate and to sing the sound as far forward as possible.

Suggested practice: Vocalize this entire word sequence by keeping all vowels in the favorable front positions as with /ē/, /ĭ/, and /ā/ in the first three words. Sing *geese, give, gave,* then *guile, gab, girl, ghoul, goal, gall, gown.*

The French /g/ is always produced on the hard palate, running no risk of slipping back. A good practice consists of intoning a series of French words to establish the feeling of proper placement: *gaffe, gai, guerre, gagnier, garcon, glasse, gloire.*

215

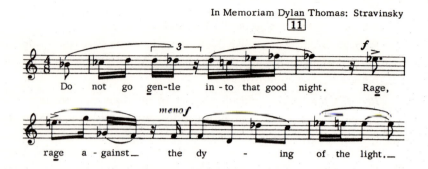

Especially for /j/ [dʒ]: This consonant functions somewhat differently. The release is slower than for /d/b/g/. The lips round slightly; the tongue-tip is further back than for /d/ to accommodate the /zh/ component. When /j/ meets /j/ between words, both are pronounced (large gem, orange juice, huge jet).

Testing with Text and Music /d/b/g/j/

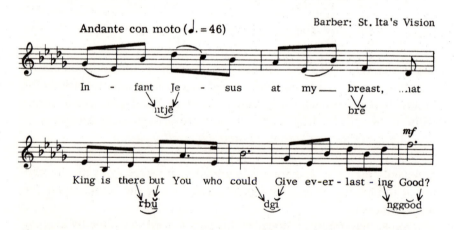

The Method (Removing and Replacing)   The target consonants /d/b/g/j/ have been removed from the text of the music excerpt. Practice them as marked, in combinations with vowels and in clusters with other consonants between words. Apply the KEY on the next page to follow the "shorthand" drawings below which guide the movements of articulators. Continue until all sounds within the isolated segments are smoothly linked.

KEY:

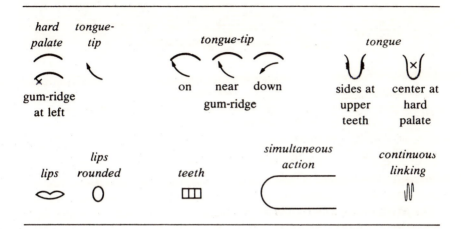

hard palate | tongue-tip | tongue-tip — on, near, down gum-ridge | tongue — sides at upper teeth, center at hard palate

gum-ridge at left

lips | lips rounded | teeth | simultaneous action | continuous linking

Target Consonant with Vowel:

bre (**bre**ast) **br** ⌣⌒O ‖ /ĕ/

rbu (the**re** **bu**t) r ⌒O bu ⌣ /ŭ/

Consonant Clusters Between Words:

ntj (Infa**nt** **J**esus) **nt** ⌒ ‖ **j** ⌒∪O /ĕ/

dg (coul**d** **g**ive) **d** ⌒ ‖ **g** ⌒ᵛ /ĭ/

ngg...d (everlasti**ng** **G**oo**d**) **ng** ⌒ᵛ ‖ **g** ⌒ᵛ /ōō/ ‖ **d** ⌒

For Legato: Replace within the phrase all the practiced combinations and clusters with /d/b/g/j/. Now sing the entire excerpt. Take note of the improved level of lucid legato, which always includes correct stress on syllable and word as follows:

Infant Jésus at my bréast...

217

Sondheim

Bernstein: Maria

I've just kissed a girl named Ma - ri - a _____ and
vjŭ

sud-den-ly I've found how won-der-ful a sound can be
dnlē   ndhou   nbē

The Method (Removing and Replacing): For this added /d/b/g/j/ song excerpt, follow the same procedure as on pages 216-17.

Consonant Clusters Between Words:

vj (I've just)   **v** ⌒ 🙼 **j** ⌒ O /ŭ/

dnl (suddenly)   **dn** ⌒ 🙼 **l** ⌒ 🙼 /ĕ/
                     d n

ndh (found how)   **nd** ⌒ 🙼 **h** /ou/
                      n d

nb (can be)   **n** ⌒ 🙼 **b** ⌒ /ĕ/

Sound Effects Minus Voice: /s/sh/f/th/

> Is this the face that launched a **thousand ships**
> And burnt the topless towers of Ilium?
>
> Marlowe

THE GROUP

The voiced plosives, the last group of voiced consonants, are followed on the Sonority Table by ten voiceless consonants, of which these fricatives are the first group to be discussed. The vocal cords remain at rest as the articulators mold all ten on breath alone. Voiceless but not soundless, each creates a distinctive sound effect.

218

For /s/sh/f/th/ the individual impression is created by breath diverted around a specific barrier within the mouth (teeth, lips, tongue). The narrowed channels thus formed, focus and shape outgoing breath into speech sounds.

To dismiss these consonants as necessary nuisances (a notion unfortunately popular in some singing circles) derogates their vital contribution and invites error in execution. Why should any student seriously study impugned "noise" elements?

Appearing with great frequency in speech and song, these expressionistic "sound effects minus voice" offer a variety of contrast to all vowels and the fifteen voiced consonants. Indeed, one of the features of contemporary music is a sibilant-frictional texture similar to the unique instruments /s/sh/f/th/ in the orchestra of language sounds.

s [s]

say, cease, spring, scent, us, talks, once, bounced, waltz, lasts
Technical description: Tongue/gum-ridge, voiceless *fricative*, also referred to as a *sibilant*.
Voiced counterpart: /z/, p. 192.

OPERATION /s/

Place: Tongue-tip and gum-ridge.

Action: Tip of tongue near but not touching gum-ridge.* Sides of tongue in close contact with inside upper back teeth /ē/ vowel position. Tongue slightly grooved. Teeth should occlude (or almost). Mouth nearly closed. A narrow channel is formed between tongue-tip and gum-ridge and teeth. As small quantity of breath passes through barrier of upper teeth and across cutting edge, a slight hissing sound ensues.

Acoustic Result: Characteristic voiceless, high frequency sibilant sound.

> *It is possible to produce a satisfactory s with tongue-tip behind lower teeth. However, this s tends to be dull, not as sharp as when the tongue points up toward gum-ridge.

PRACTICE PERIOD

Test the Action. Articulate series of /s/'s in sequence. *Feel* sides of tongue close to back teeth or gums. There should be no spilling of air but merely a soft hissing which seems to come through an imaginary small hole at center of teeth.

Sample the Verse

> How sweet the moonlight sleeps upon this bank...
> Soft stillness and the night
> Become the touches of sweet harmony. Sit, Jessica.
>
> Shakespeare

Note: The /s/ in touches is pronounced /z/.

Remedies for Faulty /s/'s

Fault: The Copious Lisps. The most obtrusive speech defects (for men as well as women) are the variety of lisps, partial or severe, usually carry-overs from infantile speech. Babytalk substitutions of /th/ or /f/ for /s/ persist to become established habits. The removal of this flaw is simple enough in theory, but the fine muscular adjustments require persistent practice.

Singers who consider only extreme speech defects to be lisps and assume that their impaired /s/'s need no remedial attention are mistaken. (Technically, all deficient /s/'s are lisps.) For them, as well, the following drills are urgently recommended.

1. Remedy: The /z/ approach (to the *dental lisp* with tongue on teeth). Since not everyone lisps both /s/ and /z/, first look to /z/.* If the /z/ proves clear, remember that it is the voiced counterpart of /s/. Begin with /z/ words, switch to /s/ words: *zoo-sue, zip-sip, zeal-seal, zinc-sink, his-hiss, buzz-bus, prize-price, rise-rice.* Work to develop the same mechanical action for both. Having removed the voice from /z/, discover a correct /s/.

2. Remedy: The /t/ approach. Articulate t-t-t-t with precision on the gum-ridge, and keep at it. A thereby strengthened tongue-tip pointing toward the gum-ridge is vital for the objective of a good /s/. Now graduate to words. Compare these pairs: *teem-steam, tick-stick, tag-stag, take-stake, tone-stone, two-stew, till-still.*

---

*For those who lisp both /s/ and /z/, the other recommended remedies for /s/ can be adapted as well for /z/.

Next try this verse:

> Star light,
> Star bright,
> First star I've seen tonight...

These drills will encourage the tongue to by-pass the teeth and reach instead toward the /t/ position.

Now test with this sentence: "Say something simple." Isn't the dental /s/ finally less apt to seek the teeth?

3. Remedy: The closed teeth approach (to the *protrusion lisp*). For the peeping tongue that insists upon thrusting itself between the teeth (even a little), practice all the /s/ words that come to mind with front teeth firmly closed. Careful, watch out for the bite!

4. Remedy: The /ē/ approach (to the *lateral lisp*). For the leaking /s/ that spills from the sides: whisper /ē/, holding tongue high in the mouth. Seal off the air with the sides of the tongue against the back teeth. Bring front teeth closer together and focus the breath over the top of the taut tongue-tip and out of the mouth at dead center. Read aloud anything at hand since this very common consonant can be found in all printed matter.

Fault: Over-aspirated /s/. Sibilant speech ("ssso what did you sssay?") comes from pushing excessive breath into this small consonant.

Remedy: Make this test: With teeth together imitate a soft noise like that of a leaking tire (sssssssssss). Keep at it until the "tire" is deflated. Observe that the original intake of air can readily stretch to thirty seconds at least and longer with practice. Therefore a minimum of air is required.

Never prolong /s/ into a hiss;* get off this sibilant with dispatch and on to the next vowel or consonant.

Fault: Whistling sibilants. Since sibilants are high frequency sounds, the /s/ and /sh/ should be sharp, but certainly not whistle. This embarrassing fault can be traced to excessive tension of the tongue at the sides and the tongue-tip forming a too-restricted channel.

Remedy: Practice this quick adjustment until routine. Just releasing the tongue slightly in both areas will aid in eliminating the whistle. Also, the tongue may be held too far back. If so, move it forward but away from front teeth. Remember, the tongue-tip should not touch anywhere in the mouth.

Attention: /s/ continued on pp. 226-228.

---

*There are no double sounds within English words, only double letters. Thus, only one /s/ is articulated in *kiss, mass,* etc.

sh [ʃ]

she, shame, sure, blush, washed, special, anxious, mission, nation, machine, conscience

Technical description: Voiceless tongue/palate *fricative*, also referred to as a *sibilant*.

Voiced counterpart: /zh/, p. 195.

OPERATION /sh/

Place: Tip and blade of tongue behind gum-ridge.

Action: Tongue somewhat farther back than for /s/ and held higher in mouth. Sides of tongue in close contact with back teeth and gums. Teeth occlude (or almost). Tip and blade of tongue point up behind gum-ridge but do not touch, forming broader channel than for /s/. Passing over tongue, voiceless breath is focused through wider channel and against barrier of upper teeth. Lips are softly pursed.

Acoustic Result: Characteristic voiceless "hushing" sibilant sound.

PRACTICE PERIOD

Test the Action. Articulate series of /sh/'s in sequence. Feel the unpressured, voiceless breath pass over tip and blade of the tongue. There should be no gust of air, but merely a gentle short "shush" through rounded lips.

Sample the Verse

The clouds were pure and white as flocks new shorn
And fresh from the clear brook...
For not the faintest motion could be seen
Of all the shades that slanted on the green.

Keats

Note: /s/'s as kindred sibilants are also indicated. Note also that both *cloud*s and *shade*s end with /z/.

Remedies for Faulty /sh/'s

Fault: A similarly malformed /sh/ afflicts those who lisp its sister sibilant, /s/. For either /sh/ or /s/, a flaccid tongue is the culprit.

Remedy: To discipline that unruly member, set about painstakingly to acquire correct tongue placement. Important: /sh/ uses both the tip *and* the blade (the tongue area right behind the tip) as a pointer toward the hard palate, back of the gum-ridge.

A /ch/ approach can be helpful, since many a chronically limp tongue has been known to bring its tip up for /ch/. Compare these pairs: *chin-shin, chew-shoe, chip-ship, cheese-she's, catch-cash.*

Fault: The leaking /sh/. When the tongue sides drop limply instead of adhering closely to the back teeth and gums, the result is a misbegotten /sh/ somewhat like the sound of a mushy /l/.

Remedy: To seal off the air flow and prevent its leaking over the sides, the tongue must be trained to remain high in the mouth, with its rim fastened to the inside of the back teeth. The teeth are approximately together.

Whisper the sound of the glide /y/ produced high in the mouth, then alternate with /sh/: yuh-shuh-yuh-shuh. (Remember, a whisper is voiceless.) Feel the sensation of /y/ gliding past the upper teeth. There is where the tongue properly belongs for /sh/. Then try these pairs: *use-shoes, year-sheer, yell-shell, yawl-shawl, yank-shank.*

Attention: /sh/ continued on p. 226.

f [f]

fly, few, leaf, laugh, coug**h**ed, **ph**antom, af**fl**ict, **ph**onetic
Technical description: Voiceless lip/teeth *fricative.*
Voiced counterpart: /v/, p. 196.

OPERATION /f/

Place: Lower lip and upper teeth.

Action: Tongue rests on floor of mouth. Cutting edge of upper teeth gently meets inside of lower lip. Unpressured, voiceless breath shapes the audible sound effect as it passes through barrier formed by lip and teeth, and through openings between teeth.

Acoustic Result: Characteristic voiceless, lip/teeth rustling sound effect.

PRACTICE PERIOD

Test the Action. Produce a long, continuing /f/, steady and controlled. Note how very little breath is required. *Feel* firm but light contact of teeth on lower lip as sound effect of /f/ flows forward without any sensation of blowing air.

Sample the Verse

> Fair is foul and foul is fair,
> Hover through fog and filthy air.
>
> > Shakespeare

> Swiftly, swiftly flew the ship
> Yet she sailed softly too.
>
> > Coleridge

Remedies for Faulty /f/'s

Fault: The slack /f/. Barely discernible /f/'s are a menace to clear speech. Once again, blame lazy lips.

Remedy: Review Action of /v/, /f/'s voiced counterpart (p. 196). Feel the buzz of /v/ inside lower lip, then unvoice the buzz and feel voiceless /f/. Try the following exercise with /v/ to /f/ action:

very ⟶ vf ⟶ ferry   save ⟶ vf ⟶ safe
vine ⟶ vf ⟶ fine   leave ⟶ vf ⟶ leaf

Another laxity is the omission of /f/ before /th/ in words like *fifth*. "Fith" and "twelth" are clearly substandard.

Attention: /f/ continued on p. 226.

th [θ]

thank, thought, throb, earth, wrath, giveth, width, pathetic

Technical description: Voiceless tongue/teeth *fricative*.

Voiced counterpart: /th̲/, p. 298.

Note: Unlike its voiced counterpart, voiceless /th/ is not underlined.*

Note also its specific IPA symbol [θ].

Does not appear in Italian, French, or German.

OPERATION /th/

Place: Tip of tongue and upper teeth.

Action: Tongue-tip securely placed behind upper teeth, very close to cutting edge. Unpressured voiceless breath shapes an audible sound effect as it passes through barrier formed by tongue and teeth, and through openings between teeth.

Note: /th/ can be produced with tongue held visibly between teeth. However, this intra-dental action is less efficient in speech context and certainly less attractive. (A glance in the mirror should prove revealing.)

Acoustic Result: Characteristic tongue/teeth voiceless, rustling sound effect.

PRACTICE PERIOD

Test the Action.   Produce a long, continuing /th/, keeping steady and controlled. Note how little breath is required. *Feel* firm but light contact of tongue behind upper teeth as sound effect of voiceless /th/ flows forward without any sensation of blowing air.

Sample the Verse

> I love **th**ee to **th**e dep**th** and bread**th** and height
> My soul can reach....
> > E. B. Browning

*This consonant, /th/, is found in Castilian Spanish and in Greek.

The wind blowe**th** where it liste**th**,
And **th**ou hearest the sound **th**ereof.

Gospel of St. John

Note: Compare voiced /<u>th</u>/ with voiceless /th/ in both verse excerpts.

Remedies for Faulty /th/'s

Fault: One, *two*, *tree*. This flagrant substitution of /t/ for /th/ requires no comment. But even a smidgen of /t/ for /th/ demands counteraction with a drill like the following:

Remedy: Compare these pairs. Feel the decisive difference between the tongue-tip on the teeth for /th/ and on the gum-ridge for /t/: *thigh-tie, thank-tank, thin-tin, oath-oat, death-debt, hearth-heart*.

Fault: Sank you. Speakers for whom English is not a native language frequently substitute /s/ for /th/. For them, the following drill is recommended.

Remedy: Compare these pairs. Feel the difference between tongue-tip on teeth for /th/ and tip not touching anywhere in the mouth for /s/: *sank-thank, sink-think, face-faith, truce-truth*.

HOW TO SING AND LINK /s/sh/f/th/

Effortless Transitions: Voiceless sound effects function admirably as bridges between notational pitch changes. Their tonelessness helps eliminate the hazards of scoop, hard attack, or glottal stroke in intervals between syllables.

No Breaks: To permit these voiceless sound effects to take over briefly, the tone, *not the breath*, ceases but there is no severing of the vocal line. All four ride on the breath along with the vowels in the flow of song.

Sufficient Duration: The voiceless sound effects of /s/sh/f/th/ must be heard long enough for their individual character to be recognized by the listener. The highly audible sibilants /s/ and /sh/ require a shorter time span, and acoustically weaker /f/ and /th/ a longer duration.

Muscle Memory: Kinesthetic sensation, the feel of the sound, operates importantly. Trying to project over piano accompaniment or orchestra, or performing in a hall with poor acoustics, singers need the reassurance of "muscle memory," especially with voiceless consonants. Reminder: You feel it ⟶ they hear it.

Freedom from Strain: Although the term *fricative* (friction sound) has been customarily associated with these four consonants and their voiced counterparts, the singer should not on that account attempt to project an abrasive effect. What happens instead, is the shaping of the voiceless breath, diverted around a specific barrier.

Therefore, allow no forcing of air, no throat involvement, and no muscular tension. Essential is the same low abdominal support which vowels receive. These deceptively "light" sounds produced with breath alone can never carry to the listener without big muscle support.

Whispering Drill: Slowly whisper:

> say something simple
> sea shells
> crushed feelings
> funny face
> birth and death

Do you feel a soft sensation produced by the articulatory actions? Now sing the same phrases carrying over the whispered sound effects. Note the necessary extended duration of /f/ and /th/.

ESPECIALLY FOR /s/

A Little Goes a Long Way: By far the most frequent voiceless continuant, super-abundant in song texts, /s/ demands exacting care and economy. A hiss, however slight in concert halls, picks up astonishingly. And every recording artist knows how microphones accentuate sibilants.

Have a Check-up: Whisper /s/ up and down a scale. Observe how a lower "pitched" /s/ sounds flat, and how the higher the "pitch," the sharper the sound (which eventually will turn into a whistle). Keep testing this way before settling on the correct individual /s/.

To retain desired sharpness: whisper sustained /ɛ̆/ vowel and feel the raised sides of the tongue adhering to back of teeth. This corresponds to the optimum /s/ position. Next lift the tongue-tip almost to the gum-ridge. Let a small amount of air pass over the tip as teeth come together. The sound emerging past the tip and through spaces between teeth at center is unmistakably a good /s/.

Joyce   Sessions: On The Beach At Fontana

A se-nile sea __ num-bers each sin-gle slime __ sil-

- vered __ stone, __

Prokosch   Barber: Nocturne

Andante, un poco mosso

Calm the lake of false-hood lies __ And the wind of

lust has passed

Remember, for a Singable /s/:

1. Sides of tongue seal off air at back teeth.
2. Teeth occlude, or almost.
3. Forepart of tongue is grooved.
4. Tongue-tip points up behind teeth, touching nowhere in mouth. (It may point down behind lower teeth.)
5. Thin stream of air flows evenly from unpressured throat.
6. Support with low abdominal muscles, same as for vowels.
7. Sound focused right through center of teeth.
8. Very short sound. (Move on quickly to the next sound.)
9. Words with double *s* spelling have a single /s/ sound. For two /s/'s *between* words, hold the first, execute the second.
10. All /z/ sounds spelled *s* should be voiced.

ESPECIALLY FOR /sh/

Lip Shape: Lip rounding helps considerably to project a more accurate /sh/ and to assist a succeeding vowel.

Agee — Barber: Sure On This Shining Night

Caution: Spelling: Extremely varied /sh/ spelling forms undoubtedly hinder prompt recognition and execution of this sibilant: precious, anxious, **chateau**, conscious, tissue, martial.

"Shun" Words: Problems arise from the plethora of "shun" words in song: pas**sion**, cu**shion**, o**cean**, na**tion**, and so on and on. More often than not, "shun" suffixes appear under notes too prominent or too long to correspond to the weak status of unstressed syllables.

What to do: With rapid tempo or fitting notation, no vowel is needed after /sh/ (*shn*)[ʃn], p. 47.

Dietz — Strauss: Die Fledermaus

But with slow tempo a vowel must be sung (shǝn). Shape a soft lip-rounded /sh/ which lip-rounds in turn the neutral vowel. (The effect is not unlike the German vowel in *schön*.) To keep the vowel weak, briefly prolong /n/.

ESPECIALLY FOR /f/

Floating /f/: *No gust.* Blowing air destroys the inherent quality of this lovely breath shape. Work for smooth and steady support of a *minimum* airflow. (See Test the Action, p. 224.)

Best location. Test for the best spot inside the lower lip upon which to rest teeth. Do not bear down or tighten lips. Keep contact light and lips soft.

Adequate length. With as scant duration in song as is usual in speech, /f/ will become lost to listeners. Let /f/ float effortlessly forward, held long enough to insure accurate reception at the listening end.

For identity. Followed by vowels (**fortune, future, fame**), initial /f/'s, when well produced, stand an excellent chance of recognition out front. In final position before a rest, and with nothing to link to, /f/'s tend to be tenuous (lau**gh**, enou**gh**, wi**fe**).

If the final word has been previously repeated in the text it ceases to be urgent. But when danger of losing a key word exists, then a minute, audible off-glide is permissible (*grief* ⟶ griefuh).

In the excerpt above the repeated word, *enough*, clearly does not require any off-glide as reinforcement.

ESPECIALLY FOR /th/

Like /f/: Resembling voiceless /f/ in acoustical quality, /th/ requires equally careful production and duration.

More Nouns: *Thought, thanks, earth, death*, with voiceless /th/, fill language and song.* Voiced cognate† /<u>th</u>/, however, most often

---

*Some nouns have voiceless /th/ in the singular, and voiced /<u>th</u>/ in the plural: youth-youths (youthz), mouth-mouths (mouthz).

†*Cognate:* A technical term for all voiced and voiceless counterparts.

appears in pronouns in constant use: **th**ese, **th**em, **th**eirs, **th**at, etc., and in the inevitable article, **th**e. Since both have the same spelling, there is no way to distinguish between voiced and voiceless *th*, save by familiarity. Of course, when in doubt, consult the dictionary.

Shakespeare   Freed: Sea-Change

Those are pearls   that_were his eyes: No th -ing of him that do th fade_

_ But suf-fer a sea - change _ in-to some-th ing rich and   strange

Not on TV!   Although an intradental position (the tongue-tip held visibly between the teeth) is often taught, it has proved less efficient than placing the tongue in back of the upper teeth to form /th/.
The peeping tongue approach, therefore, is not recommended.

On the Move: As with voiced /<u>th</u>/ which vibrates as it joins the next sound, the voiceless /th/ produces a soft rustling sound as the tongue pulls back from the teeth. (The ear**th** is round.)

Voiceless to Voiced: "Draw for*th* *th*y wounding darts."* For a slow tempo, move smoothly from voiceless /th/ in *forth* to voiced /<u>th</u>/ in *thy* simply by adding voice without change of position. For a moderate or rapid tempo, the second /<u>th</u>/ alone is heard.
    Review /f/ discussion opposite, *For Identity*, and apply to /th/.

    *From Purcell, *Dido and Aeneas.*

Testing with Text and Music /s/sh/f/th/

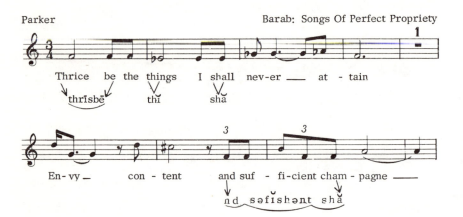

Parker

Barab: Songs Of Perfect Propriety

1

Thrice be the things I shall nev-er ___ at - tain
thrīsbē   thǐ   shā

En - vy ___ con - tent and suf - fi-cient cham - pagne ___
nd səfishənt shǎ

The Method (Removing and Replacing)   The target consonants /s/sh/f/th/ have been removed from the text of the music excerpt. Practice them as marked, in combinations with vowels and in clusters with other consonants between words. Apply the KEY below to follow the "shorthand" drawings on the next page which guide the movements of articulators. Continue until all sounds within the isolated segments are smoothly linked.

KEY:

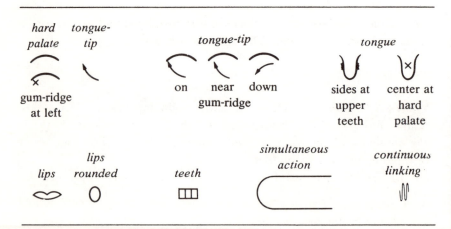

Target Consonant with Vowel:

thi (things) th ⟨symbol⟩ /ĭ/

sha (shall) sh ⟨symbol⟩ /ă/

Consonant Clusters Between Words:

thr...sb (thrice be) th ⟨symbol⟩ r ⟨symbol⟩ /ī/ s ⟨symbol⟩ b ⟨symbol⟩ /ē/

nds...f...sh...ntsh (and sufficient champagne)

nd ⟨symbol⟩ s ⟨symbol⟩ /ə/ f ⟨symbol⟩ /ĭ/ sh ⟨symbol⟩ /ə/
  nd

nt ⟨symbol⟩ sh ⟨symbol⟩ /ă/
  nt

For Legato: Replace within the phrase all the practiced combinations and clusters with /s/sh/f/th/. Now sing the entire excerpt. Take note of the improved level of lucid legato, which always includes correct stress on syllable and word as follows:

Thríce bĕ thĕ thíngs Ĭ shăll néver attáin...

Percussives Minus Pitch: /t/p/k/ch/

Here are sweet peas on tiptoe for a flight
With wings of gentle flush o'er delicate white,
And taper fingers catching at all things
To bind them all about with tiny rings.

Keats

THE GROUP

Fragmentary sound effects, the four voiceless plosives follow the voiceless fricatives on the Sonority Table. Included is the *affricate* /ch/, defined as plosive plus fricative, but articulated as a single entity. The IPA symbol [tʃ] makes clear this unique blend: the acoustic impression of /ch/ is mainly percussive /t/ mingled with sibilant /sh/.

Again, as with the voiced counterparts, it is necessary to reject the label *plosive* for /t/p/k/ch/, especially for singing. Specific hold-and-release muscular actions — *not* explosions of impounded air — give these consonants their distinctive acoustical impact. Conventional concepts encouraging typical breathy bursts may be held responsible for many a disjointed vocal line. Singers, fearful of such hazards, tend to bypass these consonants altogether. Diligent production of the pitchless percussives, however, endows speech and song with verbal clarity, implicit drumbeat, and forward impulse.

t [t]

to, tell, turn, what, tossed, slight, city, plenty, written, better, lately
Technical description: Voiceless tongue-tip and gum-ridge *stop-plosive*.
Voiced counterpart: /d/, p. 207.

OPERATION /t/

Place: Tongue-tip and gum-ridge.

Action: Sides of tongue in contact with upper back teeth. Action begins with tongue-tip securely held on gum-ridge behind upper teeth at center. Tip releases in spring-like movement to position behind and below lower teeth with slight escape of breath. Only in isolation or in final position in words before a pause does an abrupt stop occur. Within phrases, after bounce from gum-ridge, tongue adjusts to position of following vowel or consonant.

Acoustic Result: Characteristic voiceless, tongue-tip, percussive sound.
   Note: No build-up of air behind tongue-tip at start and no explosion as tongue descends.

PRACTICE PERIOD

Test the Action. Execute a series of percussive /t/ shapes. Hold the exhalation to a minimum, testing breath on back of hand.

Sample the Verse

> Night's candles are burnt out and jocund day
> Stands tiptoe on the misty mountain tops.
> > Shakespeare

Remedies for Faulty /t/'s

Fault: All those missing or dangling /t/'s. Daily drills are recommended to restore lost /t/'s to the language.

Remedy: A drastic cure begins with a handful of match books. Glue the very point of the tongue onto the ridge right above the teeth. Hold firm in that position. Now, light a match and hold in a direct line with the mouth, about five inches away. Take an easy breath. Then articulate /t/, and as the tip leads the tongue downward with a bounce, the action should blow out the match. Repeat process until several match books have been discarded.

Abandon the match part of the routine and repeat the exercise. It is important to reduce the amount of breath gradually to practically none at all. Discover that extinguishing all those matches has strengthened the tip, defined the action, and established the percussive feel of this most common English consonant.

Problems with first, middle, and last /t/'s. Native /t/'s found in all positions in words take a beating in careless speech. To raise the level of /t/ performance spoken and sung, an investigation of its main positions follows.

Fault in Initial /t/'s. The /t/ in its strongest position, beginning a word or a stressed syllable, (**tiptoe**, **attain**) can usually be heard. Simply to be heard does not suffice, however. If sluggish tongues miss the gumridge and flap instead against the teeth, a sound like /ts/ often takes over (*tiptoe* becomes tsiptsoe).

Remedy: Review specific directions under Action to produce a clear-cut initial /t/.

Faults in Medial /t/'s. City, battle, writing — all these /t/'s within words are especially vulnerable to inept articulation.

Wrong: city ⟶ ci-tee; *pretty* ⟶ prit-tee. (Over-corrected and prissy.)

Wrong: writing ⟶ wriding; *water* ⟶ wadder. (Common /d/ substitution.)

Wrong: battle ⟶ ba-uhl; *gentle* ⟶ gen-uhl. (Unpleasant glottal stop* instead of /t/.)

---

*Called variously *glottal stroke, stop, shock,* and *attack,* this forcing of air through closed vocal cords produces the familiar burplike sound. *Glottal* comes from the word *glottis* which is the space between the vocal cords.

235

Wrong also: Battle ⟶ batuhl; *gentle* ⟶ gentuhl. (Sounds overly precise and awkward with exaggerated vowel in weak second syllable.)

Remedies: Compare the /t/'s in *waiting* and *attend*. Use softer attack for *waiting*, since /t/ begins an *unstressed* syllable. Articulate /t/ with area directly behind tongue-tip in light contact, slightly back on gum-ridge.

Dispense with /d/ (*waiting* ⟶ wa-ding) by producing voiceless /t/ to blend with vowel (as above).

Fault in Final /t/'s. "What a stunning hat!" calls for three /t/'s delivered intact, even though frequently only the /t/ preceded by /s/, in "stunning," survives ("wha...uh *st*unning ha...!").

Remedy: Cultivate word completion as a daily discipline. The touch-tap of final /t/ contributes buoyancy and clarity in speech and song.

Compare These Pairs: Establish similarity as well as difference in the feel of /t/ and /d/ in three positions:

two-do	wetting-wedding	ate-aid
tip-dip	written-ridden	cart-card
tome-dome·	shutter-shudder	trite-tried

HOW TO SING AND LINK /t/

This most common of all English consonants demands detailed discussion, consistent practice, and skillful handling. It leads the top six in constant usage, *t d n s r l*.

Up Front: The tongue-tip tends to roll back behind the gum-ridge when /t/ precedes so-called back vowels (*t*old, *t*ool). Keep the tip on the ridge just above upper teeth regardless of which vowel follows. Try these pairs in this order: *tea-too, ten-ton, take-talk, tam-time, tell-toil, tear-tar.*

Same Breath Line: The seemingly airy elements /t/p/k/ require the identical strong support of the low abdominal muscles as do the vowels. The /t/'s form an integral part of the line, riding on the breath along with the vowels. Singers too often tack them on or propel them in "plosive" fashion. Sing as vocalises: *tee — tie — toe — too.* Feel the low muscular tug at each /t/. Make sure that while the tongue performs precisely and strongly, the jaw, facial and throat muscles remain uninvolved. Correctly produced /t/'s will cause no disruption of the legato line.

Dental /t/: Italian and French /t/'s differ from English in two important respects. Ours brings the tip of the tongue to the ridge just above the teeth; theirs are articulated directly against the teeth. Secondly, initial foreign /t/'s joining vowels are voiced instantaneously, with an effect more like /d/'s, whereas English /t/'s require a toneless instant as they join vowels. This does not imply any stop in the flow of air which supports the whole phrase. Performing in English means to sing English /t/'s and not imported /t/'s.

Vowels as Conveyers: Strictly speaking, any interruption of tone, as with voiceless consonants, does interrupt legato.* Skillful linking of voiceless percussive /t/, however, reduces any toneless time to a fraction. Though pitchless, /t/'s should be sung along with the pitch of vowels, and in the vowel shape.

Before a Rest: The only position in which /t/ does become a "stop" is at the end of a phrase. We find two extremes in performing these final /t/'s. Either singers tend to omit the /t/ altogether, or they emit it with a breathy blast. Instead, singers should master a skillful final /t/.

Try this experiment: Whisper "don't tell" several times. Note how though whispering, you can still distinguish the difference between voiced /d/ and voiceless /t/.

in   my   heart, —

Now sing "in my heart" followed by a rest as above. Begin final /t/, then convert immediately to whispered, unvoiced /d/. This helps check the air flow that might otherwise erupt breathily at the percussive release of /t/. Some more practice for /t/:

Allegro   Menotti: The Consul

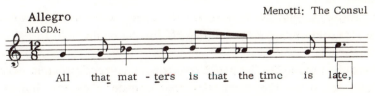

All   that mat - ters is that the time   is   late,

---

*The same pertains to all languages of the vocal repertoire.

237

PARTICULAR /t/'s

"Nigh-tiz": Final /t/ in a word (nigh*t* is) is always weaker than initial /t/. When carried over to the next word, /t/ should still be reduced in intensity and never stressed.

Special Case of /ts/: Hearts, meets, lights, etc. Singers stumble over endings such as these, which actually function much like the so-called affricates /ch/ and /j/. To articulate /ts/ as one blended sound begin with tip on gum-ridge for /t/, then rapidly lower it for /s/ just below ridge, producing simultaneous /ts/ as in a single, unified, voiceless sound.

That "Little" Word: Found profusely in song, *little* has given rise to a variety of sung pronunciations, *littŭhl, litĭll, littōōl,* and even *lĭ'l.*
 Depending on tempo:
 In *slow tempo:* The second unstressed syllable, lit**tle,** must be sung with a vowel like /ə/ or short /ŏŏ/ (lit-əl, lit-ŏol). Note: To keep the second syllable inconspicuous, sustain the vowel briefly and prolong the final /l/, that lyrical sound.

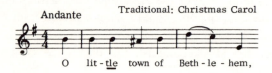

In *moderate tempo:* The vowel sound between /t/ and /l/ becomes the shortest distance between those two consonants.

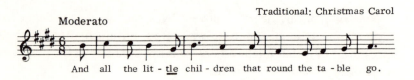

In *rapid tempo:* As in speech, /tl/ is sung without any vowel. Produce /t/ in the shape of /l/, holding /l/ for the count.

"Gentuhly, Latuhly": To avoid an intrusive vowel slipping in between /t/ and /l/, speak the word *atlas,* then transfer the same linked /tl/ into *lately, gently, softly,* etc.

238

Natyure, etc.: The artificial "singerish" spelling pronunciation of words like *nature* continues to turn up; "na-chər" or "nachŏŏr" is correct.

Soft Touch: Double /t/'s between words follow the rule of preparing the first /t/, holding it briefly, and executing the second, depending of course on the tempo of the music. At *lento*, two /t/'s may be required.

Soft Drink: Here we use the same approach as for two /t/'s: When /t/ meets its voiced counterpart /d/ between words, the /t/ is held and the /d/ executed.

"I Love You Tuhruly": Watch for a vowel interpolated between /t/ and /r/. Produce /t/ in the lip-rounded /r/ shape which glides to the lip-rounded vowel /ōō/ in *truly*.

Ast?: Very common in song, the word *asked* receives much maltreatment. Approach as follows: After the vowel /ă/, a short /s/, then /kt/ delivered like a double drumbeat and practically airless (ă͜skt).

Between Two Vowels: In these excerpts the /t/ as in *waiting* and *pretty* beginning an unaccented syllable, must be softened. In song, when such /t/'s are stressed the effect is unnatural. Place tongue back of gum-ridge but articulate with the area just behind the tip to reduce the sharp impact of percussive /t/. Keep the accented syllable strong and bright.

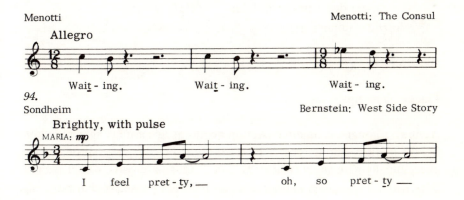

Menotti   Menotti: The Consul

Allegro

Wait - ing.   Wait - ing.   Wait - ing.

94.

Sondheim   Bernstein: West Side Story

Brightly, with pulse

MARIA: *mp*

I   feel   pret - ty, —   oh,   so   pret - ty —

239

T Clusters:

Stepped quietly, limped painfully, wrenched free.
  pt kw   mptp   ncht fr

Between words is the point at which a breakdown in legato is most likely to occur, particularly where such clusters appear in sequence. There can be no consonant dropouts, since each works to promote meaning and beauty of song. (See the musical excerpt, p. 250, for consonant legato.)

Summary Rules for a Singable /t/:

1. Sing pitchless /t/ together with ensuing vowel pitch and in vowel shape.
2. Support with low abdominal muscles as for vowels.
3. Keep tongue-tip sharp, jaw disengaged, throat muscles relaxed.
4. Do not blow or explode air, (/t/ rides on breath along with vowels). Remember: Muscular hold-and-release action in the main produces the percussive sound effect.
5. Avoid Italian or French dental /t/.
6. Make certain of momentary voicelessness before /t/ joins vowel.

p [p]

peace, **p**ray, sto**p**, ha**pp**en, **p**assion, a**pp**lause, sli**pp**ing
Technical description: Bi-labial voiceless *stop-plosive*.
Voiced counterpart: /b/, p. 204.

OPERATION /p/

Place: The lips.

Action: Tongue is inactive. Action begins as lips are brought together lightly in firm but untensed closure. Held briefly, they spring apart energetically with slight, voiceless "pop." This percussive sound occurs only when /p/ appears in final position before a pause. Within phrases, lips adjust without pause to position of following vowel or consonant.

240

Acoustic Result: Characteristic two-lip, voiceless, percussive sound.

Note: No compressed air should be held behind lips to erupt explosively. Specific muscular lip action produces shape of /p/ which rides on the breath along with vowels and other consonants.

PRACTICE PERIOD

Test the Action. Develop sensation of lip closure with energy and without push. Repeat p-p-p-p. With back of hand close to mouth, feel how slight is the puff of air. With practice, the amount of breath can even be reduced.

Sample the Verse

> Into the street the **p**i**p**er ste**pp**ed
> Smiling first a little smile,
> As if he know what magic slept
> In the quiet **p**i**p**e the while.
>
> Robert Browning

Remedies for Faulty /p/'s

Fault: Proverbially immobile mouth. Since they are not complicated sounds to produce, most /p/ and /b/ problems can be attributed to that American prototype, the tight-mouthed and laconic speaker.

Remedy: Needed nationally are a firm, flexible lip posture and a quick muscular let-go. This nursery rhyme makes a good drill:

> Hi**pp**ity-ho**p** to the **b**ar**b**er sho**p**
> To **b**uy a stick of candy.

or a brisk /b/ can lead to a proper /p/ (see Remedies for Faulty /b/'s, p. 210).

Fault: Puleeze! Watch those vowels inserted between /p/ and /l/, and /p/ and /r/ (puhrize), which add a touch of caricature to conversation.

Remedy: For words like *please*, *plan*, or *prize*, *prim*, place the tongue-tip on the gum-ridge for /l/ or directly below the gum-ridge for /r/ *before articulating* /p/. This economical co-ordination yields two concise, linked consonants.

HOW TO SING AND LINK /p/

Save Your Breath: Because /p/ blends with the oncoming sound, any spilling of air blurs this consonant's clean outline. Aspirated /p/'s, not only unnecessary, are harmful to the vocal line. Once learned, correct hold-and-release patterns for percussives /t/p/k/ become a source of security in song delivery.

Foreign and Domestic /p/'s: Note the important difference between the English /t/p/k/ and the Italian and French equivalents. For example, in a word like *pay*, Italians and French voice the /ā/ vowel immediately, even before the lips open for release action. The sound they produce resembles /b/ and the word is more *bay* than *pay*.

English /p/ calls for a very quick voiceless interval before joining the vowel /ā/. Actually, the acoustic effect gives the illusion of simultaneous action, but it is that voiceless fragment of time which identifies the English character of /t/p/k/.

Attention: The voiced counterparts, /d/b/g/, when directly fused with vowels are produced without this voiceless interval. Immediate voicing does not alter the English character of these consonants. Therefore, in the interest of seamless legato, continue to voice /d/b/g/ promptly.

Britten: In Freezing Winter Night (a Ceremony of Carols)

The beasts are par-cel of his pomp,_ The wood - en dish his plate.

Problem /p/ Before a Rest: Even a most vigorous "pop" (incidentally, undesirable) can scarcely be heard out front. Of course, with a good view of the singer, an audience can see lips part for /p/, or the context of the phrase may supply the meaning. But these, at best, are tenuous means of communication.

Recommended action: Sustain the vowel in the exclamation "Stop!" Then produce /p/, but immediately convert to /b/ (a mere onset of *uñaspirate* /b/), and come to a halt. A fleeting audible off-glide released by /b/, when essential, makes "stop" intelligible out front.

Recording note: Air blown through popping lips is especially shattering over a microphone. Instead, use the /p/-/b/ approach just described (or /t/-/d/, /k/-/g/), but use the technique sparingly.

When Two Meet: "Help please," "hate tyranny," "knock quietly."

At average or fast tempo: Follow the rule for speaking: hold the first consonant briefly and execute the second clearly. The acoustic impression of this slightly delayed action creates the illusion, for the listener, of two sounds. Besides, in song, the single, combined action makes possible unbroken linking.

At slow musical tempo: Pronounce both consonants, holding down explosive action. For interpretive emphasis, too, both may be desirable.

Adjacent Partners: "Keep busy," "put down," "look grim." Handle these cognates between words as if both were identical. Hold the first, execute the second subject to the tempo as explained in the previous paragraphs.

Double Drumbeats:

pt: stoppéd, wept.

pch: capture, rapture.

pk, tp, pd, etc.: stop coming, start pushing, jump down.

Combine both percussive consonants: the air-free action of the first links with the hold-release action of the second. There must be no vowel sound between the two.

k [k]

key, coo, come, talk, kick, fix, quiet, chorus, accuse, action, echo
Technical description: Voiceless tongue and velar *stop-plosive*.
Voiced Counterpart: /g/, p. 210.

OPERATION /k/

Place: Middle of tongue and *hard palate*.

Action: Mouth is open. Tip of tongue rests behind bottom teeth. Middle of tongue makes contact with hard palate* just back of center. Tongue springs away from this position and adjusts to oncoming sound.

---

* Although /k/ is conventionally described as a soft palate sound, it is recommended, especially for singing, that /k/ be produced at the hard palate.

Acoustic Result: Characteristic voiceless, palatal clicking sound effect.

Note: As with other *plosives*, there need be neither a build up of air behind the tongue at start, nor an "explosion" as the tongue releases. The energetic hold-and-release pattern creates the percussive sound.

PRACTICE PERIOD

Test the Action. Execute a series of clear-cut, percussive /k/'s. Feel the air held down to minimum, testing with back of hand.

Sample the Verse

> By the pricking of my thumbs,
> Something wicked this way comes.
>> Open locks
>> Whoever knocks
>> * * * * * * * * * * * * * * *
>
> Nice customs curtsy to great kings.
>> Shakespeare

Remedies for Faulty /k/'s

Fault: Croaking /k/'s. The habit of hitting the back of the tongue against the soft palate with hammer strokes accounts for typical k-induced throaty speech.

Remedy: Stay away from the soft palate, which traps /k/ and /g/ deep in recesses.

Important: Locate area just back of the center of hard palate and place tongue there. Now practice with phrases for non-throaty /k/'s. Feel the /k/ kick on the hard palate: **cute kitten, keep calm, Kris Kringle, quiet contented cows.**

Fault: Dijuh astim? The /k/ in *ask* has long been a casualty in careless speech. Even a touch of substandard *ast* calls for instant correction.

Remedy: Begin by isolating *sk* action: the short /s/ brings the tongue up front, then with a quick movement bring the middle of the tongue to the hard palate and release the click of /k/. Repeat.

244

Now practice on words: **ski, skip, sky, sc**orn, **sc**ope, etc. Next: ba**sk**, ta**sk**, a**sk**! And this, all told, should eliminate *ast*.

HOW TO SING AND LINK /k/

Singers often shy away from /k/'s in fear that the percussive consonant will endanger the tonal line. With correct action mastered, however, /k/ becomes an asset lending firmness and precision to text and voice.

It is one of four potentially throaty consonants, /k/g/ng/h/, calling for very careful handling in song. For each there is a recommended technique. To repeat, for /k/ the middle of the tongue (*not* the back) and the hard palate (*not* the soft) are involved in the characteristic hold-release action.

Match Placement: Words with so-called front vowels guide the tongue forward onto the hard palate. With these as models, follow suit with other vowels, keeping the kick of /k/ on the hard palate. Sing on a comfortable pitch:

keep——➤ cap ——➤ cope   *leak*——➤ lack——➤ luck
keen——➤ can——➤ coon   *lick*——➤ look——➤ lock

Borrow from French (Partly): Repeating *qui-que-quoi-quand* makes a fine drill for the most effective placement of English /k/. With this difference: French /k/ is a tighter clicking sound. English /k/ requires fleeting voicelessness as it merges into the following vowel or consonant. Borrowing the French forward placement and keeping our touch of toneless sound effect add up to a well-sung English /k/.

Feel the Bounce: Try this experiment: Breathe out first, then when practically airless articulate /k/ (proof that the explosive emission of air is not necessary for this so-called plosive consonant).

And now, to establish the feel of the percussive pattern, whisper *crack, quick, echo, ache*. Kinesthetic result: A continuing sensation of pulsation against the surface of the *hard palate*; a more vigorous bounce than for the voiced counterpart /g/.

Thus as always, do not press or push air. Instead, use the firm support of the abdominal muscles, without which /k/'s have no carrying power.

Double /k/'s:

$$1\ \ 2\ \ 3\ \ 4$$
The black cock crowed.

A moderate to fast tempo calls for two /k/'s (black cock crowed). The final /k/ is held and the initial /k/ in the next word is articulated.

With a slow tempo, all four /k/'s should be heard distinctly.

Always scan a phrase for proper English stress to offset the danger of *black cat* coming through as *black hat*, or *like king* as *liking*. In both cases the strong word-types the nouns *cat* and *king*, have primary stress in which the /k/ sounds share.

Double Percussives: Past participles like *tricked*, *thanked*, exemplify the rule that final voiceless consonants are followed by voiceless /t/ not /d/. We find this combination also in effe*ct*, a*ct*, infli*ct*, etc. Too often singers side-step the dynamic /kt/ double drumbeat.

Action /kt/: After hold-release for /k/, the tongue does not drop but remains high in the mouth, shifting forward as the tip hits the gum-ridge for /t/, and rebounding.

No Sparkuhling: Sing two, *not* three, syllables in words like *sparkling*, *buckling*, *crinkling*. Action /kl/: The middle of the tongue springs forward *not down* from hard palate as the tongue-tip makes contact at the gum-ridge for /l/.

Hidden /k/'s: Spelling hides the presence of /k/ in many sung words. *Qu* is always pronounced /kw/: *quick* (kwĭk), *quench* (kwĕnch).

Action /kw/: /k/ is produced in shape of lip-rounded /o͞o/, which begins the /w/ glide, and is carried along with /w/ to join the oncoming vowel.

Final *x* is always pronounced /ks/: *fix* (fiks), *sex* (seks).

Action /ks/: Airless /k/ clings to brief /s/ in simultaneous drumbeat-sibilant sound effect.

Before a Rest: Final /k/, like other voiceless percussives, runs the risk of a breathy blast. The antidote is the same. Action: For the word *black* sustain the vowel /ă/. As the middle of the tongue articulates /k/, convert instantly to unvoiced /g/. The result is reduced aspiration and minimum off-glide.

Practice these /k/'s in the various positions in which they appear along with /t/ and /p/ in both excerpts.

Auden

Rorem: Stop All The Clocks

Mozart: Marriage Of Figaro

ch [tʃ]

chant, church, each, match, Christian, question, nature, touched

Technical description: Voiceless tongue-tip/gum-ridge/palate *affricate.**

Note: IPA symbol [tʃ] makes clear two blended components, /t/ plosive plus /sh/ fricative.

Voiced counterpart: /j/, p. 212.

Appears in Italian and German, not in French.

*Affricate: Combined plosive-fricative forming a single sound.

OPERATION /ch/

Place: Tongue-tip, gum-ridge, and palate.

Action: Sides of tongue in close contact with upper back teeth. Action begins with flattened tongue-tip including blade, placed securely on gum-ridge and front section of hard palate. Lips round slightly as for /sh/. Tip and blade release in springlike movement as /t/ and /sh/ simultaneously blend into single entity /ch/. Because of sibilant /sh/ component, release for /ch/ is not as rapid as for percussive /t/ alone. Tongue adjusts to position of oncoming sound.

Acoustic Result: Characteristic voiceless, percussive sound with sibilant overtone.

Note: There is no explosive release of compressed air. Specific muscular action produces /ch/ shape and sound.

PRACTICE PERIOD

Test the Action.   Articulate a series of staccato /ch/'s (ch-ch-ch-ch), something like the sound of a chugging train. Feel the sensation of percussive, tongue-tipped /t/ blend with lip-rounding /sh/.

Sample the Verse

> Oh peal upon our wedding,
> And we will hear the **chi**me,
> And come to **church** in time.

A. E. Housman

Remedies for Faulty /ch/'s

Fault: Inert /ch/'s. This consonant suffers along with other incisive ones from the lazy tongue which lolls about apparently unable to negotiate the rise to the ridge. As a consequence, many ordinary words (*which, such,* etc.) hit the ear as thick and even lisped.

Remedy: Simply to remember the phonetic composition of /ch/, IPA [tʃ], is remedial. Think /t/ and the tongue will respond upwards. Once the tip reaches the ridge, the rest of the action readily adjusts. The tip flattens to include the blade; the sides of the tongue make

248

firm contact with the back teeth. Now all is set for a crisp hold-and-release action of welded /t+sh/, or /ch/. Compare these pairs: *too-chew, tin-chin*; *sheep-cheap, shoes-choose.*

Fault: Can'choo, wha'choo, aren'choo, won'choo? All too prevalent are these "choo" blends with /ch/ substituted for /t/ linked to /y/ (can't *you*, etc.). The penalty for these contagious /ch/'s is sibilant daily speech.

Remedy: Practice linking /t/ and /y/ using these word combinations: *eat yeast, late yesterday, don't yell, hot yellow, eight yen, mate young, wet yacht.* With /t/ and /y/ co-ordination clear, return with confidence to *can't you, what you, aren't you.*

HOW TO SING AND LINK /ch/

Predominant Percussive Character: Sharing with /t/p/k/ the basic hold-and-release operation, /ch/ bears all the earmarks of percussive quality. The /sh/ sibilant influence, however, slightly slows the release of /ch/ from the hard palate. A too delayed release develops a "shushy" off-glide; a too rapid one sounds close to a sneeze. Action should be just long enough to establish the individual identity of /ch/.

Warlock: Chopcherry

When as   the rye   reach _ to the chin,   And

chop cher-ry, chop cher-ry   ripe _   with - in.

Lip Reinforcement: One of a handful of consonants fortified by lip-rounding, /ch/ is especially effective in song. (Others: /j/sh/zh/w/hw/-r/.) For /ch/ execution, lips purse gently and adjust promptly to the shape of the oncoming vowel.

When Two /ch/'s Meet: *Such charm, each child.* Articulate *both* /ch/'s always. The blends of /j/ and /ch/ are exceptions to the general rule applying to identical or related consonants meeting between words. These affricates, /j/ and /ch/, demand double exposure.

Same and Different: In all other respects, /ch/ adheres to the same rules for optimum production as do the percussives /t/p/k/:

Non-explosive, energetic hold-and-release action

Close union with vowels on supported breath and pitch

Relaxation of facial and throat muscles

Conversion, prior to a rest, of final /ch/ to unvoiced /j/.

Testing with Text and Music /t/p/k/ch/

Frost   Reif: Birches

The Method (Removing and Replacing)   The target consonants /t/p/k/ch/ have been removed from the text of the music excerpt. Practice them as marked, in combinations with vowels and in clusters with other consonants between words. Apply the KEY on next page to follow the "shorthand" drawings below which guide the movements of articulators. Continue until all sounds within the isolated segments are smoothly linked.

250

KEY:

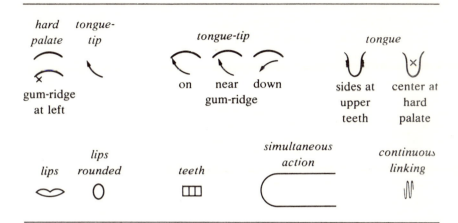

Target Consonant with Vowel:

kli (**cli**mbing)   **kare** (**care**fully)

kl ⌒ᵥ⌒ ∭ /ī/   k ⌒ᵥ â ∭ /ər/

kup up (**cup up to**) k ⌒ᵥ /ŭ/ ∭ p ⌣ /ŭ/ ∭ p ⌣ ∭ t ⌒ /o͞o/

Consonant Clusters Between Words:

zk...pth...zp...z (always **k**ept **h**is **p**oise)

z ⌒ᵕ ∭ k ⌒ᵥ /ĕ/ ∭ p ⌣ ∭ t ⌒ ∭ (h/ĭ/ ∭ z ⌒ᵕ ∭

p ⌣ /oi/ ∭ z ⌒ᵕ

t...pbr...nch...z (**t**op **br**anches)

t ⌒ /ä/ ∭ pbr ⌣⌒ O ∭ /ă/ ∭ n ⌒ ∭ ch ⌒ᵕ O /ĭ/ ∭ z ⌒ᵕ

mp (same pains) m ⌣ ∭ p ⌣ /ā/

251

For Legato: Replace within the phrase all the practiced combinations and clusters with /t/p/k/ch/. Now sing the entire excerpt. Take note of improved level of lucid legato, which always includes correct stress in syllable and word as follows:

He always kept his poise...

The Breath Shapes: /hw/h/

Happy thou are not
For what thou hast not...

Shakespeare

The eye marvelled — marvelled at the dazzling whiteness;
The ear hearkened to the stillness of the solemn air...

Robert Bridges

THE GROUP

Breath shapes /hw/ and /h/ appear at the end of the consonant sonority table. The /h/ is merely a breath sound, functioning exclusively as an adjunct to the English vowels and is also that voiceless feature in /hw/ which distinguishes that consonant from /w/. Frequent in the language, /h/ compensates with uniqueness for its lack of sharpness.

While the /hw/ glide can be replaced by /w/ without linguistic loss, /h/ is indispensable to English. Because of its indissoluble link to all sixteen vowels, it can be said that there are as many /h/'s as vowel shapes. Thus, when correctly produced, /h/ can become an interpretive asset in song, rather than a breathy handicap.

hw [hw]*

where, when, why, whelp, whisper, whistle, meanwhile

Exceptions: who, its related forms and whole (/w/'s are silent)

Technical description: Voiceless, bi-labial semi-vowel glide.

Voiced counterpart: /w/, p. 173.

Does not appear in Italian, French, or German.

*The dictionary and IPA symbols for *wh* are both /hw/ which makes clear that *h* is articulated before *w*.

252

OPERATION /hw/

Place: Lips.

Action: Lips rounded closely as for /o͞o/. Tongue-tip behind lower teeth. Back of tongue raised. Articulate /h/ simultaneously with brief /o͞o/ lip shape. Lips move back in gliding action to assume shape of instantly following vowel.

Acoustic Result: Characteristic blend of voiceless /h/ with /w/ glide.
Note: The glide is voiced as it joins oncoming vowel.

PRACTICE PERIOD

Test the Action. Execute a series of /hw/ glides linked to vowel /ē/ (hwee, hwee, hwee). Feel the sensation of brief /h/ merging instantaneously into /o͞o/ position for /w/ glide, as lips move back slightly to encompass /ē/. The whole action is rapid.

Sample the Verse

> Why,* **wh**at make you here?
> **Why** are you virtuous? **Why** do people love you?
> O, **wh**at a world is this, **wh**en **wh**at is comely
> Envenoms him that bears it.
> Shakespeare

Remedies for Faulty /hw/'s

Fault: Going, going, gone? Throughout the land *w* has pretty much taken over *wh*. Pockets of resistance, however, persist, and the voiceless /hw/ glide survives, most often in good speech patterns.

Remedy: For song, usage of the /hw/ glide is enthusiastically recommended. For those who wish to retain the distinctive quality and color of *wh* in speaking and to avoid confusing *witch* with *which*, *weather* with *whether*, etc., study *Action* above and practice /hw/. Compare these pairs: *while-wile, whine-wine, whet-wet, whale-wail.*

HOW TO SING AND LINK /hw/

Why One Less? For its unique quality poets select this breathed sound effect by design, not accident. In words like **wh**isper, **wh**imper, /hw/

---

*The interjection "why" is often pronounced with /w/ instead of /hw/: (wī). Yet interrogative "why" is pronounced /hwī/.

is notably onomatopoetic (imitating in sound what is expressed in words). All in all, it seems a pity to rob the listener of these hushed fragments of time in music.

Caution: Look out for affected overblown /h/'s that spread excessive breathiness through the entire phrase "*huh-why* do I love you?" Important: /h/ before /w/ is the merest breath — a puff, not a huff.

Be consistent. Learn to make use of all *wh*'s in words, **wh**erever they appear in song, **wh**ether weak word-types (when, where, which) or strong (whip, wheel, overwhelm). Refrain from inconsistently singing such effects as "**w**en you hair is **wh**ite," or "**wh**y is the baby **wh**ailing?"

Review pp. 173-76 for discussion of /w/ that applies as well to /hw/.

h [h]

he, who, whole, holy, hear, behave, somehow, inhuman, prohibit, happiness

Exceptions: honest, hour, heir, exhaust, etc. (/h/ is silent)

Technical Description: Voiceless glottal *fricative*

No voiced counterpart

Appears in German, not in Italian or French

OPERATION /h/

Place: Any vowel position.

Action: No specific tongue or lip action for /h/, other than that of vowel that invariably follows. Before /h/ is heard, articulators take position for vowel. No change occurs in articulators from /h/ to vowels. The glottis (space between vocal cords) is open as breath of /h/ passes through; cords close with phonation of oncoming vowel. Thus /h/ is produced in single, unified pattern with vowels. (There are as many /h/'s as vowels — sixteen in all.)

Acoustic Result: Characteristic voiceless breath sound.

Note: The conventional description of /h/ as *glottal fricative* is misleading and often mischievous in its effect on the voice. The term *glottal* suggests constricted back placement: actually /h/ is as open-throated and frictionless as the vowels it precedes.

PRACTICE PERIOD

Test the Action. Chant he-hay-ho-hi-hoy-how. Place /h/ directly on vowels and out of the throat. Feel the sensation /h/ as an integral part of the vowels.

Sample the Verse

> Here he lies where he longed to be;
> Home is the sailor, home from the sea,
> And the hunter home from the hill.
> > R. L. Stevenson

Note: Make certain to articulate /hw/ in *where*.

Remedies for Faulty /h/'s

Fault: Too far back. Our daily /h/'s are apt to be too aggressive (*h*hijah, *h*hello, *h*hurry, etc.). Pressured from tense throats (an American syndrome), the proliferation of harsh /h/'s is hard on the ear. By attracting words and phrases back into glottal recesses, guttural /h/'s obstruct good speech patterns.

Fault: Too much air. Excessively aspirate /h/'s spilling over into neighboring sounds causes breathiness.

Remedy: Pre-hear the vowel to come and then shape /h/ in its mold to weld the two together in a forward, non-throaty, resonant pattern. Apply this technique of anticipating the vowel to the following pairs: *add-had, is-his, ear-hear, and-hand, ate-hate, ill-hill.*

HOW TO SING AND LINK /h/

Toneless Vowel Shape. Always think of /h/ as a softly whispered, transitory, unvocalized vowel, which the approaching vowel has pre-fashioned in its own image. Singers should no more place /h/ back in the throat than they would place a vowel there.

255

Unforced and Unpressured. Defective /h/'s flow from speaking into singing with dire results to the vocal line. Therefore, only the merest breath should pass relaxedly from throat to oral cavity, then through the lips to communicate as English /h/. Never sever /h/ from its vowel in a separate action.

Agee   Barber: Sure On This Shining Night

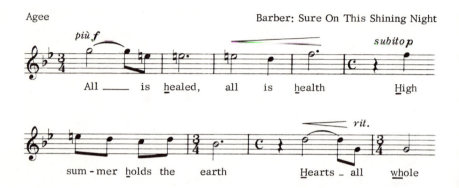

Either-Or. Some /h/'s are optional in words like *humble, vehement, annihilate, exhibition.* Forehead is pronounced *forrid*, although admittedly *fore-head* is gaining adherents.

Coloring with a Soft Brush. Soft /h/ enhances many a text. For the word "*h*asten," the breath sound can express urgency, for "*h*appy," a sigh, for "*h*ate," suppressed feeling, for "*h*eart," deep fervor, and so on.

Testing with Text and Music /hw/h/

Vaughan Williams: Whither Must I Wander

Berg: Wozzeck

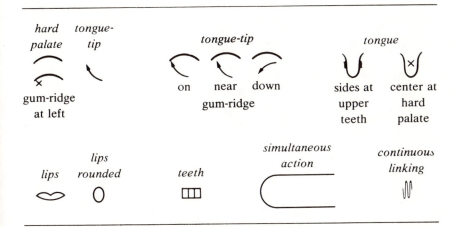

The Method (Removing and Replacing)   The target consonants /hw/h/ have been removed from the text of the music excerpt. Practice them as marked, in combinations with vowels and in clusters with other consonants between words. Apply the KEY below to follow the "short-hand" drawings on the next page which guide the movements of articulators. Continue until all sounds within the isolated segments are smoothly linked.

KEY:

hard palate	tongue-tip	tongue-tip			tongue	
(gum-ridge at left)		on	near	down	sides at upper teeth	center at hard palate
			gum-ridge			

lips	lips rounded	teeth	simultaneous action	continuous linking

257

Target Consonant with Vowel:

ho (home)   h /ō/

hwi (whither)   hw ⟅O⟆ /ĭ/

wa (wander)   w ⟅O⟆ /ä/

Linked Phrase

hw...h...ngzy (Why hangs your)

hw ⟅O/ī/⟆ ⟅h /ă/⟆ ng ⟅⟆ z ⟅U⟆ y ⟅U⟆

Consonant Clusters Between Words:

kh (black hair)   k ⟅⟆ ⟅h /â/⟆ /ər/

rhe (your head)   r ⟅O⟆ hĕ ⟅h /ĕ/⟆ d ⟅

For Legato: Replace within the phrase all the practiced combinations and clusters with /hw/h/. Now sing the entire excerpt. Take note of the improved level of lucid legato, which always includes correct stress in syllable and word as follows:

Hóme nó mófe hóme tŏ mĕ...

Whý hángs yŏur fíne bláck háir...

Comparative Summary
of Vowels and Consonants

The dividing line between vowels and consonants is not as sharply drawn as some would imagine. For example, *y*, *w*, and *r* have vowel-like qualities; other consonants, such as *m*, *n*, *ng*, and *l*, are all tone. Following are final particulars:

SIMILARITIES

Both vowels and consonants:

1. Shape sound waves produced by outgoing breath.
2. Require the same conditions of intrinsic body support and relaxation of extrinsic muscles of the face, throat, and chest.
3. Benefit mutually by forward articulation.
4. Need each other for mutual support and identification in a firm partnership (vowels would sag without their partners, consonants would splutter without theirs).
5. Form an integral part of words in time and space for listeners' comprehension.

DIFFERENCES

Vowels	Consonants
contribute most to tone	contribute most to meaning
are produced in resonant shapes, molded by size and shape of cavities	are produced by muscular interaction of tongue, lips, teeth, and palate
are all voiced	are sometimes voiceless
include *ah*, most open sound	include *s*, most closed sound
demand unobstructed free passage: mouth open, tongue-tip behind lower teeth	demand precise shaping of articulators in active contact
depend for identification largely on placement and duration	depend for identification largely on their characteristic sounds

259

are shaped by comparatively little variation in articulators or resonance	are greatly varied in execution and quality
require sustained length for tonal continuity	require accurate and quick execution
are sung with greater intensity than consonants	need greater energy to match vowels
develop feedback responses from over-all sensation of pitch, resonance, and breath support	develop feedback responses from exact muscle movement and vibrating, humming, or voiceless sensation
must be one per syllable (**a**-lone)	may be one or more (or none) per syllable (a-**l**one)
should follow consonants whenever possible in enunciation of syllables	should begin syllables whenever possible
function as prime carriers of vocal line	function as prime movers of vocal line

CHAPTER SIX

INVITATION TO

A DICTION CLASS

TO PREPARE A TEXT

There can be no more appropriate way of concluding these chapters than by presenting a working method, step by step, for the study of the words of a song. The essential features of well-sung English previously explored are now integrated into an effective "how to." Page references indicate additional study material.

The discussion takes place in an open session of a diction class to which professional guests from related fields of music have been invited: a voice teacher, vocal coach, conductor, choral director, composer, and professional performers. While the cast of characters may be partially imaginary, the classroom demonstration by the students is wholly realistic.

"To Music, to Becalm his Fever"* by Paul Hindemith has been selected as the demonstration song. Everyone has a copy, the first two verses of which provide the basis for the discussion. (An outline of the working method follows this informal class setting. See p. 277.)

*The Robert Herrick poem, set to music by Paul Hindemith. Robert Herrick (1591-1674), English poet often called greatest of Cavalier Poets, wrote "Upon Julia's Clothes," "Gather Ye Rosebuds," and "Cherry Ripe" among other famous titles. Paul Hindemith (1895-1963) German-American composer, teacher (Yale and Harvard), conductor, theorist, who composed operas, orchestral works, chamber works, and songs including a collection *Nine English Songs,* of which the above selection is one.

Robert Herrick
(1591-1674)

Paul Hindemith
(1944)

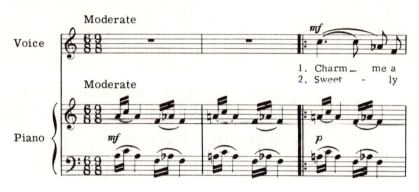

1. Charm _ me a
2. Sweet - ly

sleep, _____ and melt me so With _ thy de-
canst _____ con - vert the same From _ a con -

li - - cious num - bers,
sum - - ing fire _____

262

That   be - ing rav - ish'd, hence I
In   to   a   gen - tle lick - ing

go   A - way   in eas   -   y
flame, And make   it   thus   ex -

slum   -   bers.   Ease   my sick
pire.   Then   make me

head, And make   my bed,   Thou pow -
weep My pains   a - sleep;   And give   me

- er that canst sev - er From me _____ this ill, And
such re - pos - es That I, _____ poor I, May

quick-ly _____ still, Though thou not kill, ____ My fe - -
think ____ there-by I live and die ____'Mongst ros - -

1.

ver.

2.

2. Thou - es.

1. BEGINNING WITH THE POEM

Each student has a copy of the text without music and in turn speaks the poem as an entity by itself apart from the score. They are instructed to read with good speech tone and without dropping the ends of lines. They aim for an American standard of pronunciation, free from regionalism and affectation.

Professional Performer: *Why bother copying the poem separately when it is already there in the song?*

Class Teacher: *By disassociating the words from the notation, the singer can more readily grasp and absorb the meaning of the poem. In the beginning the score tends to act as a distraction.*

2. MARKING OVER-ALL STRESS PATTERNS

The Class Teacher writes the first verse on the blackboard with special markings to indicate the contrasting words and syllables within the lines. She explains that the encircled words, the strong word-types carry the main meaning and that those outside the circles, the weak word-types have mainly a connective function. The strong and weak syllables are marked: / for strong, ∪ for weak.

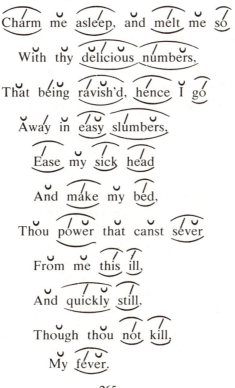

Professional Performer: *It's perfectly obvious which are the strong and weak words, and everybody knows which syllable to accent. Why all the fuss?*

Class Teacher: *It's true that in speaking we automatically stress and unstress. But in song, music interposes its own accents, and unless the performer has a keen perception of the built-in beat within words he is in danger of losing the implicit stress patterns of English. When English is deprived of the natural rhythms, its sense stress, the audience cannot understand the song. (See pp. 20-21.)*

The students re-read the verse* aloud, carefully following the indicated strong and weak stresses, highlighting one and subduing the other. As a result, the natural word values conveying the basic meaning of the poem are heightened.

Vocal Coach: *The interpretation of the song determines what words should be emphasized. This is what the performer and the coach work out together.*

Class Teacher: *Of course, that is understood. Stress analysis, however, is* not *interpretation. The strong and weak contrasts, which are much stronger in English than in other languages, give the sense of the text, and nothing more.* Emphasis *underscores thought and emotion that belong to interpretation. Natural grammatical stress merely lays the diction groundwork of the text. The structure of English is unchanging, whereas interpretation takes many forms. (See Chapter II.)*

Voice Teacher: *The performer delivers a song, not a poem.*

Class Teacher: *Whether song or poem, the indispensable words function like the ones used in a telegram. A performer should likewise*

*The first three pages and two verses of the song are covered in the discussion. For those interested in the complete Herrick poem, the third verse is included:

Fall on me like the silent dew,
   Or like those maiden showers
Which, by the peep of day, do strew
   A baptism o'er the flowers.
     Melt, melt my pains
     With thy soft strains:

That, having ease me given,
   With full delight
   I leave this light,
   And take my flight
     For Heaven.

deliver the messages of song to the listener with the strong word-types standing out in relief.

3. SPEAKING TO THE MELODIC LINE

Everyone listens as the accompanist at the piano plays just the melodic line through twice.

The students, together, speak the verse, this time to the metrics of the music. As they hold a word or syllable for the allotted time in the notation, problems of adjustment begin to reveal themselves.

Two examples of inflated weak word-types:

with on tied eighth notes on a rise.

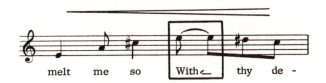

that on a dotted quarter note.

The students now beat out the rhythm to the melodic line, exaggerating the vowels with matching consonants until the word and syllable accents seem to become part of bodily sensation.

Voice Teacher: *This form of declamation may be interesting, but when do these people begin to sing?*

Class Teacher: *That is the next step, from speech to song (See pp. 18-19).*

4. SINGING TO THE MELODIC LINE

The students individually sing the verse to the melodic line while they attempt to hold on to the inherent stress patterns of the language. As they adjust from speech to song and the predominant patterns of the music, the text continues to come through more clearly.*

Various guests comment — a few are impressed by the retention of word meaning, others remain skeptical. After all there has been no accompaniment, merely single notes on a piano sung in a classroom. How would this work with an orchestra, or in a recital hall?

Class Teacher: *The job is only half done. More distinctness will come with specific matching of words sung to music, especially with accurate use of vowels and consonants.*

5. MATCHING TO MUSIC

The words are now weighed specifically in relation to the score, and stress conflicts are resolved. The opening phrase of the song:

When a student sings the phrase, the word *asleep* descending to the low note seems in danger of being lost.

Composer: *Unless the singer carefully sustains the word* asleep *it can be obscured on the drop to* d. *But the setting with the accented syllable on the downbeat should prevent this. The first phrase, like the whole piece is extremely well set. Hindemith employs a descending line achieving an effect of dropping off to sleep.*
　Everyone agrees that the point is valid.

Class Teacher: *The song* is *beautifully composed, but just the same diction problems occur as we can see.*

The student tries again, this time sustaining the *l* and the long vowel *ē* for the full count. She goes to the next phrase.

*The students use, as most suitable for singing, an American standard pronunciation adapted to the needs of both sides of the footlights. This recommended diction is described in Chapter I.

Professional Performer: *Why has the important word* melt *been lost? The quarter note should take care of that.*

He sings the phrase, skillfully underscoring the verb *melt*.

Class Teacher: *By starting the* m *in* melt *ahead of time our guest has performed intuitively what is always recommended. Intuition, however, cannot always be counted on to respond when needed. Sonorous consonants, like* m *and* n, *particularly in important stressed words, should always be given full value and whenever possible begun beforehand.*

The demonstration continues as a student sings.

That be-ing rav-ish'd, hence I   go   A-way in | eas - y | slum-bers,

The word *easy* ascends on a crescendo, and thus its weak second syllable (ea*sy*) becomes magnified.

Composer: *That elevated note, the last in the measure, is the composer's device leading to the next downbeat.*

Class Teacher: *But the weak syllable nonetheless must be subdued in relation to the strong one and to the on-coming strong word* slumbers.

She tells the student to make sure to sing sy (sē) in easy with reduced intensity as well as produce a short *z* buzz for the *s*. She points out that the word *numbers*, set to two equal dotted quarter notes tended to sound evenly stressed (| |) rather than with intrinsic strong and weak beats (/ ◡).

Conductor: *In order to satisfy the word rhythms would a diction teacher really want to alter the score to accommodate the words!*

Class Teacher: *Of course not, the score is primary and never violated. But the singers must make use of flexible techniques to retain the illusion of correct word rhythms.*

A student sings the word *numbers*.

num -| bers.

He accents the first syllable and reduces the second dynamically as the notation helps with a descent.

Class Teacher: *By shortening the vowel in* -bers *(numbers) and starting the z (spelled s) ahead of time to lengthen it slightly, the illusion is created of a shorter syllable.* (See pp. 45-46.)

Choral Director: *That technique seems to work for a soloist, but what would happen if a group were to sing it?*

The students oblige by trying to deliver the phrase in unison, but the result is ragged and the text begins to blur.

The Choral Director steps in to cue the students so that they all keep together. On the word *numbers* he counts to five and on the sixth count as he raises his hands, everyone simultaneously voices a short, clear *z.*

Class Teacher: *Thank you. That counting technique is most instructive and should be used by soloists to make sure of voicing final consonants. The dropping of the last sounds always cuts down intelligibility.*

Voice Teacher: *Let us discuss the vowels. For example, the vowel* ih *in* delicious *on the* f *sharp lacked true clarity of tone. That vowel should be stable in all ranges, why not here?*

Class Teacher: *The problem might well be the student's insecure production.*

Voice Teacher: *Vocalises with the vowel on various pitches would help to achieve a more stable sound. Other vowels in the text, even though within confortable reaches of the voice, also require stability of production. For instance, the long* ē *occurring in* easy, ease, *and* fever, *and the* ā *in* make.

Professional Performer: *But how can anyone sing an accurate vowel on notes above the staff?*

Class Teacher: *Voice teachers will agree that all vowels, with some few exceptions, must be modified in extreme ranges, whether high or low. The illusion of a recognizable sound can be achieved if the modified*

270

vowel is produced in an area comparatively near that of the original vowel. (See Vowel Ladder III.)

Vocal Coach: *Words like* power *and* flower *are often troublesome. Often set to a single note, they can be matched to the note only with difficulty.*

Class Teacher: *The practical way to handle these two-syllable words is to divide the single note.* (p. 175)
    She goes to the blackboard, draws a quarter note, and then divides the note as follows:

power   pow- er

She explains that *pow-* would be sung on the first, longer note and *-er* on the second.

Voice Teacher: *But the setting here (m. 15-16) is very long.* Power *in the song is set* not *on one, but on six notes! The performer should hold on to* ah *for four counts until the very last instant of the last note, then attach quickly a brief* o͞o *before* er, *which is pronounced* uh, *without the* r*!*

Class Teacher: *The distortion of* ow *to* ah-ah-ah-o͞o *makes an artificial sound of a common compound English vowel. This traditional approach to diphthongs needs reappraising. (See Vowel Ladder II.)*

Voice Teacher: *We certainly cannot have sliding, gliding inflection between notes.*

Thou pow   -   er   that canst   sev - er

    A student performs *ow* as a long vowel blend, not as two sounds. Carefully avoiding a *w* glide after the prolongated diphthong, she links it deftly to the weak syllable *-er.*

Class Teacher: *my students use not* uh *but* er *with a mere touch of* r *which is more color than consonant. (See pp. 124-27.)*

Professional Performer: *If I sang the word* canst *I would pronounce the vowel more like the Italian* ah *than the flat* a *sound.*

271

Class Teacher: *The maltreated ă needs only good voice production to be a thoroughly singable sound. Besides, it is the correct American vowel, and therefore much better than* ah, *which sounds affected. (See pp. 99-103.)*

Vocal Coach: *Let us talk about consonants; what about double ones between words? Should both be sung?*

A student demonstrates the two *m's* in *Charm me asleep* to be sung as one prolonged sound of *m*. The first *m* is prepared and the second executed.

Char(m)   me   a - sleep, —

Class Teacher: *In English we have double consonant sounds occurring only between words, and double letters (as spelling forms) within words. For example, in the song,* ill, still, *and* kill *have just one* l *sound each.*

Composer: *What the composer creates is diminished in meaning by the slurring of consonants.*

Vocal Coach: *Though necessary to the meaning, consonants should be gotten out of the way as quickly as possible so as to preserve an unbroken vocal line.*

Class Teacher: *No sound in English need break the vocal line. The language doesn't, singers do. The problem is not over-done but under-done consonants. If not sung larger than life these vital and often beautiful sounds become lost to the text. (See Consonant Guidelines.)*

Conductor: *Without clear consonants the text can never surmount the big sound of an orchestra.*

Composer: *American singers who downgrade our English sounds will often lavish tender care on the more numerous sibilants and percussive consonants found in German lieder.*

Professional Performer: *Which English ones, for example, are so beautiful and vital in the song we have been discussing?*

Class Teacher: *Let us begin with the* l's. *This sonorous consonant, without a shred of friction, occurs in all positions in English words. In the copy of the song, note* asleep, melt, delicious, slumbers, quickly, gentle, flame live, *etc. Note also the* m, *whose content is all hum:*

charm, **me,** **m**elt, *numbers,* **m**ake, *consuming, the* ng *with its unique humming quality, and the vitalizing sound of* z, *spelled* s, *in ease, pains,* reposes *and* roses. *Taken together, all these and other sounds of varied color, equip the performer with expressive tools for interpreting vocal literature.*

6. DEVELOPING A LUCID LEGATO

The Class Teacher writes on the blackboard the following cryptic letters: /ntll/ /ngfl/ /ngstr/.

Class Teacher: *These are clusters of consonants found between words of the song. The white space between words should be regarded as an optical illusion. This area where legato tends to sag particularly requires propping. To guard against breaking the legato, we have a useful method of extracting the clusters, practicing them separately for smooth linking, and then replacing them in the phrase. Let us analyze these few examples on the blackboard which the students will demonstrate, from the second verse (m. 9, 10, 20, 21). (See pp. 176-77.)*

/ntll/ linked in sequence:

The *n* takes the tongue-tip to the gum-ridge, then merely shifts for *t*, next to the first *l* to be held, and the second *l* stressed.

/ngfl/ linked in sequence:

For *ng* the tongue-tip remains below lower teeth, the teeth meet the lower lip for voiceless *f*, then the tongue-tip rises to the gum-ridge for *l*.

/ngstr/ linked in sequence:

The tongue-tip is down for *ng* hum, moves up to stop short of

273

the gum-ridge for brief *s*, then continues up to make contact with the ridge for percussive *t*, lowering again for rounded *r*.

All the clusters when isolated sound like foreign words, especially Slavic as the students drill them, then replace them in the words and text.

Class Teacher: *These demonstrations make clear that this practice technique brings an improved level of legato with no sounds slighted. All sounds should eventually emerge coherently in economical co-ordination, clarifying the text.*

Professional Performer: *What about punctuation? Does a comma mean a stop? In the phrase,* ease my sick head, and make my bed, *should there be a pause at the comma after* head?

Class Teacher: *The marks of punctuation are designed primarily for silent reading and serve merely as a rough guide to meaning. An unmotivated mechanical halt as at a red light, however, contributes nothing but a break in the line.*

She suggests that the performer try singing the line without a pause at the comma after *head*.

The performer delivers the whole phrase non-stop in lovely legato style.

Ease —— my sick head, And make —— my bed

Composer: *The uninterrupted line with its smooth somnolent quality works better and carries out the intention of the composer.*

Vocal Coach: *When the printed words of poetry become song, the true artist seeks deeper meaning with his own punctuation through holds, retards, and other effects.*

7. ADDING ACCOMPANIMENT

As the accompaniment is joined to the text, the students adjust to the music, which differs substantially from the melodic line.

Conductor: *The accompaniment, whether for song, oratorio, or opera, often puts considerable strain on the text. It is a constant problem in performing in any language.*

Class Teacher: *We have been gradually integrating text with notation. Without such prior working through of English text and music, singers might well flounder as they undertake the full score. This grounding builds a secure foundation for whatever musical challenge might arise.*

Incorporating all the previously practiced segments into a lucid legato, the students take turns singing the final phrase of the second verse of the song.

Class Teacher: *These excerpts will sum up main aspects of the method already discussed, from English stress to legato.*

The stress patterns are strictly adhered to, with the weak word-types (*that*, repetitive *I*'s, *and*, *may*) receiving weak accent, while the strong word-types stand out clearly in contrast.

For legato all words are smoothly linked without pause.

Linking consonant to vowel between the words *That I, poor I*: thus the *t* in tha*t* is articulated lightly avoiding "tha-tie," the *r* in *poor*, untrilled, joins I.

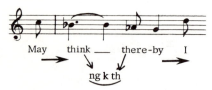

Linking consonant to consonant, *nkth*, the cluster between words, *think thereby*: the *n* (really an *ng* before *k*) is produced with tongue-tip down behind lower teeth for *ng* hum, and middle of tongue in position on hard palate for *k* click. Then tongue-tip moves forward to back of upper teeth for th buzz.

For seamless legato, in the phrase *and die* only one *d* is articulated; the first one, in *and*, is held on the gum-ridge and the second, in the verb *die*, is executed and stressed. Also, this *d* is produced in one action in shape of vowel ī, held stable for the tied notes.

'Mongst   ros -   -   es.

Then finally the students take a quick breath after *die* and finish with the last two words *'Mongst roses* closely joined. They deliver the final weak syllable *ses* with the muted vowel ə and two *z*'s. (See pp. 193-94.)

Conductor: *When all falls into place with distinct text matched to music in the flow of song, then diction as a discipline and an art fulfills its purpose.*

Class Teacher: *Now diction signs off and interpretation takes over. With the process of studying this text, the performer has absorbed its basic sense stress patterns and its sounds of English vowels and consonants. He also added legato-linkage to all words and syllables. The rest lies in his creative hands and with his mentors who, like our expert visitors, bring to fruition the art of song.*

The guests depart stimulated by the professional exchange of ideas in a master class devoted to raising English as a sung language to a high level of performance.

How to Study a Text — An Outline

All the steps in preparing an English text discussed in *Invitation to a Diction Class* are here presented in concise form for easy reference. For this short outline, only the final page of the song *Walking* by Charles Ives*will be the model. To serve as a guide a few selected examples of problems in the text will be analyzed.

*Charles Edward Ives (1874-1954), American, won in 1947 the Pulitzer Prize for his third symphony. He wrote prolifically, in a modern idiom advanced for his time, four symphonies and other works for orchestra, chamber music and piano works, choral music and song.

on - ward, to - day we do __ not choose __ to

die __ or to dance __ but __ to live and

walk. __

più decresc. non rallen.

1. BEGIN WITH THE TEXT

Copy the text so it can be seen apart from the score and read it aloud. The words should be delivered with good speech tone and articulation.

2. MARK OVER-ALL STRESS PATTERNS

Mark all stresses and encircle strong word-types of the text* in this manner:

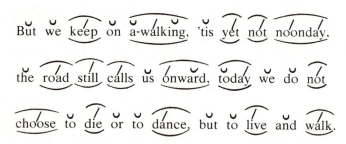

In sending a telegram we omit small words and feature the key words as in the stress markings. For example, the first phrase if sent by wire would read like this:

Keep walking — yet not noonday — road still calls onward...

Now re-read the text, faithfully following the indicated strong and weak stresses, highlighting one and subduing the other so that the basic meaning of sense-stress of the text comes through clearly.

3. SPEAK TO THE MELODIC LINE

Speak the text this time to the metrics of the music. Hold word or syllable for the time allotted in the notation. Carefully keep as far as possible to the word rhythms as spoken without music. Beat out the rhythm to the melodic line, exaggerating the vowels and matching consonants, until the word and syllable beat becomes part of bodily sensation.

* Complete text of *walking* up to the last page:

   A big October morning, the village church bells, the road along the ridge, the chestnut burr and sumach, the hills above the bridge with autumn colors glow. Now we strike a steady gait, walking towards the future, letting past and present wait, we push on in the sun. Now hark! Something bids us pause

   (down the valley, — a church, — a funeral going on)

   (up the valley, — a roadhouse, a dance going on).

4. SING TO THE MELODIC LINE

Adjust from speech to song, trying to hold on to the implicit stress patterns within the text. Feel the carry-over of the words into the singing voice in preparation for the next step.

5. MATCH TO MUSIC

Weigh the words specifically in relation to the score, working to resolve the stress conflicts.

Weak syllable on half-note rise (m. 8)

walk - ing,

Solution: Accent first syllable, *walk-*, especially the vowel, on down-beat. Subdue the *-ing* on half-note: shorten vowel, begin *ng* ahead of time, holding the hum softly for the count.

Even stresses on uneven notes (m. 10) (nóon-dáy)

noon - day,

Solution: Brighten long /o͞o/ vowel in *noon*, intensifying the hum on both *n's* to give illusion of even stress.

Important negative on weak position and descent (m. 13)

we   do — not

Solution: Use initial *n* hum and accent open *ah* vowel in *not*.

281

But we keep on a - walk - ing,

The text on the whole is well set, the key words appearing on downbeats. The matching problem in this song, however, is one of rhythm. The melodic line, which keeps to a forceful walking beat, often with even note values, tends to ride over the stress patterns, particularly of the weak word-types.

Re-read, if necessary, the marked text to help keep the correct rhythm going beneath the words.

6. DEVELOP A LUCID LEGATO

Compare vowels, notation, and pitches.

Analyze consonants for quality and duration.

Link consonant and vowel combinations smoothly.

Isolate consonant clusters between words, practice them separately, and replace in the phrase.

Examples: Sustain all vowels especially those in the active verbs *choose*, *die*, *dance* set to varying intervals (m. 14, 15, 16). Use clear-cut *ch* and *d* produced in the shape of these vowels.

choose _ to die ___ or to dance, ___ but ___

Make the most of all the *z*'s, spelled *s* ('ti*s*, call*s*, choo*s*e) and other voiced consonants to offset the strong beat of the accompaniment.

Isolate, practice, and replace consonant clusters between words: *zy* ('tis yet), *dst* (roa**d st**ill).

Link the final phrase in seamless legato.

but ___ to live and walk. _____

282

In *but to* articulate only one *t* by holding the first with tongue-tip on gum-ridge and executing the second in release action to the vowel. Subdue the vowel /o͞o/ for the unobtrusive preposition *to*.

In *live* lean on *l* for bright resonance and join to vowel. Buzz a good *v* sound and join to *and*, also subdued.

Then link smoothly the cluster *ndw* (*and walk*). Make sure of a firm lip-rounded *w* sound for the last word *walk*.

Strongly support the long vowel (twelve counts) in *walk* to keep the sound from distorting. Use a very brief off-glide after *k* (kə), otherwise the final consonant might be lost and thus the key word, *walk*, as well.

7. ADD ACCOMPANIMENT

Now adjust carefully all phrases to the accompaniment, which in this case differs considerably from the melodic line.

Pull together all the steps of the method, from stress contrasts to lucid legato. Adhere to all previously practiced stress patterns in order to prevent the incisive forward walking beat of the score from obscuring the text.

The diction has prepared the groundwork for interpretation.

Interpretation deepens the content of our selection *Walking*. The personal responses of the artist will elevate the words. He will transmit to the audience the spirit of optimism and its American beat in this Ives song, which ends with the ringing affirmation "we...choose... to live and walk" — or to live and *sing*!

to   live   and

SING!

283

APPENDICES

List of Symbols Used

for Vowels and Consonants

Note: IPA symbols for consonants appear only when they differ from the dictionary symbols.

The Sixteen Vowels

Dictionary	IPA	Key Word	Other Forms
ē	[i]	beat	
ĭ	[ɪ]	bit	ih
ā	[eɪ]	bait	
ĕ	[ɛ]	bet	eh
ă	[æ]	bat	
ī	[aɪ]	bite	
ä	[ɑ]	bard	ah
ŭ	[ʌ]	butt	uh
ə	[ə]	about	
ûr	[ɜ]	bird	
ər	[ə]	bother	
ōo	[u]	fool	
ū	[ju]	fuel	
ŏo	[ʊ]	full	
ō	[ou]	foal	
ô	[ɔ]	fall	
oi	[ɔɪ]	foil	
ou	[ɑu]	foul	

Note: The vowel symbol /â/ always followed by *r* in words like *fair, care, there* applies only to these and similarly pronounced words and syllables. [ɛɚ]

287

The Twenty-Five Consonants

Dictionary	IPA	Key Word
r		red
w		wet
y	[j]	yet
m		met
n		net
ng	[ŋ]	sing
l		let
z		zeal
zh	[ʒ]	beige
v		vim
th	[ð]	then
d		debt
b		bet
g		get
j	[dʒ]	jet
s		set
sh	[ʃ]	shin
f		fit
th	[θ]	thin
t		ten
p		pet
k		kin
ch	[tʃ]	chin
hw	[hw]	when
h		hen

Note: IPA symbols for consonants appear only when they differ from the dictionary symbols.

The Diction of Dialects

By adding color and character to delivery, dialectal touches deepen the content of song. Performers who use the same variety of English for all vocal materials lose a valuable interpretive aid. The problem is to use dialect without permitting it to become labored or obtrusive.

A dominant feature of a national dialect is characteristic inflection, the relative pitch patterns of its speech melody. The inflection of the musical design within the score, however, precludes the use by singers of dialectal intonation. Singers, therefore, do not require the same in-depth study of regional vowels and consonants to do actors, whose speech must include intonation to communicate the play's whole dialogue.

The recommended method for singing a dialect consists of selecting a limited number of authentic touches, based on some key variants from standard American English pronunciation.* For references to vowels specific pages in Chapter IV are indicated. The following musical excerpts exemplify the most frequent dialects in English vocal literature.

*The following books are available for those interested in more detailed instruction in these dialects and others: Lewis Herman, *Foreign Dialects*, Ziff-Davis, 1943; Lewis Herman, *American Dialects*, Ziff Davis, 1947; Jerry Blunt, *Stage Dialects*, Chandler Publishing Co., 1967, with three tapes available following the text.

BRITISH DIALECT

Since First I Saw Your Face

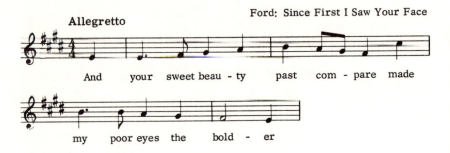

Allegretto

Ford: Since First I Saw Your Face

And your sweet beau - ty past com - pare made

my poor eyes the bold - er

Modify these words:

your	the vowel is /ô/ (pp. 142-43), dark, closely lip-rounded. Final *r* is omitted.
sweet	crisp /t/ joined deftly to /b/ in beauty.
beauty	the vowel /ū/ more tense than in American English. The weak syllable *-ty* becomes *tĭh*.
past	the vowel broad and open (pahst). Crisp /t/.
compare	the vowel in second syllable is short *eh*, with an *uh* /ə/ substituted for *r*.
poor eyes	the *r* in *poor*, linked to *eyes*, should be a single tap resembling a /d/, since it occurs between two vowels as in *very* (veddy).
bolder	the /ō/ becomes what might be called a triphthong uh-oh-oo (bŭ-ōŏ-ōld); uh without /r/ substitutes for *er*, a weak syllable.

Additional selected sounds for British dialect: *r* dropped before consonants, laʃk, poʃt, and biʃd, with vowels lengthened.

IRISH DIALECT

Oh! 'tis Sweet to Think

Allegretto

Irish Song: Oh! 'Tis Sweet To Think

Oh! 'tis sweet to think that wher - e'er we rove, We are

sure to find some - thing bliss - ful and dear;

290

For an Irish dialect all vowels in the song excerpt are typically elongated and more sustained than in American English. Irish is thus well suited to the prolonged vowels of song. The following sounds are variants:

oh	very rich in tone with lips well rounded; an alternate pronunciation also often used is *ah-oo*. The same pertains to vowel in rove.
that	the *a* becomes middle *à* between *ă* as in *cat* and *ä* as in *father*.
something	the *o* is the same as the vowel in *that*; the *ng* is dropped and last syllable becomes -*thin'*.
find	this extra long vowel becomes *fuhihnd*, not as extreme as *foynd*.
blissful	second syllable -*ful* becomes more like -*fool*.
where'er	the *r* in this word, and all other words with *r* in this excerpt, is the most distinctive of all Irish sounds. A lovely trill, the *r* begins at the throat and moves from the back to the front of the mouth. Like this:

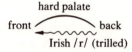

hard palate

front   back

Irish /r/ (trilled)

There are many additional Irish variants, but those indicated will suffice. Since the score obviates its use, singers must forego the infectious lilt, probably the most characteristic of all Irish features.

SCOTTISH DIALECT

Charlie Is My Darling

Scottish Song: Charlie Is My Darling

Allegro marziale

As   he   cam' march - ing   up   the   street. The

pipes play'd loud   and   clear.

Modify these words:

As	the vowel is *ah*, open sound (ahs)
came	the vowel *a* as in *cat* (pp. 97-101) (kăihm).
marching	the vowel *ah* moves toward *uh* followed by the strong *r* like an extra syllable; *ng* in *-ing* is dropped (mahurchin').
street	the vowel *e* is elongated.
pipes	vowel sometimes (very Scottish) becomes /ĕ/ (peeps).
play'd	vowel elongated (playeed) — almost like two vowels
loud	vowel becomes /ōō/ (lood)
and	pronounced *'n'*
clear	the characteristically Scottish *r* begins in the front of the mouth and ends at the soft palate. Like this:

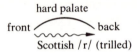

hard palate

front ⌒ back

Scottish /r/ (trilled)

Note: the *r* in *marching* and in *street* are the same front to back action.

Additional selected sounds for Scottish dialect: the *ih* in *minute* becomes *eh*, producing *mehnite*, and *six*, *seks*, etc. The vowel in *earth* becomes *ehrth*, in *girl,* *gehrl* incorporating Scottish /r/ etc. Final consonants are omitted in many common words: *cannot* abbreviated to *canna*, and *small* to *sma'*.

SOUTHERN DIALECT

Despite regional differences between types of speech below the Mason-Dixon line, characteristics common to all Southern dialect provide a broad, truthful basis for singers' diction. For example:

Sometimes I Feel Like a Motherless Child

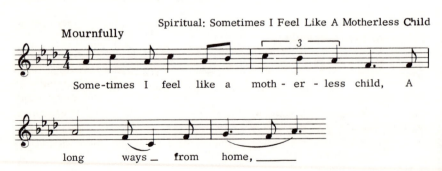

Spiritual: Sometimes I Feel Like A Motherless Child

Mournfully

Some-times I feel like a moth - er - less child, A

long ways — from home, ———

292

Sometimes	the vowel /ī/ of *times*, is the midway sound between /ă/ in *cat* and *ah* in *park*, and not *ah*, an exaggeration.The same applies to the other words with /ī/: *I, like, child*.
feel	typical Southern diphthongized vowel, *feeuhl* or *feeyuhl*.
motherless	/d/ could be substituted for *th*; the vowel in *-less* becomes *lihss*; the *r* is omitted (*mothuhliss* or *moduhliss*).
long	again elongated, adding an extra vowel, *law-uhng*.
home	resembles *o* as in standard American (pp. 138-39), but more like *hawm*.

Additional selected sounds for Southern dialect: the *r* is omitted in final positions and before consonants, and pronounced very softly before vowels. The *ng* is dropped in *-ing* endings so they become *in'*. Final sounds are often softened or lost altogether; *d* in *child*, for example, is dropped and the word becomes *chile*.

Other word examples from the spiritual *Swing Low Sweet Chariot:*

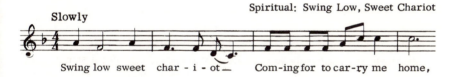

Spiritual: Swing Low, Sweet Chariot

Slowly

Swing low sweet char - i - ot — Com-ing for to car-ry me home,

sweet	vowel is diphthongized to *sweeiht*
coming	becomes *cuhuhmin'*, final *ng* dropped
for	becomes *fawuh*
to	becomes *tuh*
carry	*a* is diphthongized to *ca-uhrih*, final *-ry* becomes *rih*

In addition, in Southern dialect the *ô* sound in *dog, thought, shawl* sounds like *aw-wuh*, as in *daw-wuhg*. The *r* in *bird* is dropped, and the vowel sounds more like *buh-ihd*.

COLLOQUIAL AMERICAN

For the large number of colloquial American songs from musical theater, the pronunciation, while clear, should sound somewhat careless. For example, in songs from *Carousel, Kiss Me Kate, Paint Your Wagon*, etc., *and* always shortens to *'n*, or *'nd; around* loses the *d; for* becomes *fer; of course* is *uh course; all right, awright; got to, gotta; can, kin;* and *how to, howta*. Despite this slipshod articulation the dialect, while contributing authentic color, should not negate standards of good voice production.

Suggested Recordings

This list, by no means complete, includes a selection of available examples of American English mostly sung and some spoken along with a sampling of British made recordings. Since comparatively few recordings of art songs, opera, and oratorio are produced in this country, their listing is necessarily limited. (Apparently, the greater expense of production in the United States acts as a deterrent.) The American selection, however, from opera to musical theater including popular songs and folk material does offer some fine examples of clear pronunciation in song regardless of content. Despite the heterogeneous mixture, the over-all impression of a developing native standard of quality emerges unmistakably.

The diction, not all of one caliber, even within a single disc, does not always represent the pronunciation standards recommended here for song and study. The uneven performance of the language in these recordings can be instructive by encouraging singers to develop listening discrimination as an aid in the study of well-sung English.

Opera

MENOTTI, Gian Carlo.

The Consul. Powers; Neway; MacNeill; Lane; Jongeyans; McKinley; Summers: Andreassi; Marlo; Lishner; Monachino. (2 LP set — Decca DX 101)

The Medium & The Telephone. Keller; Powers; Dame; Mastice; Cotlow; Rogier; Balaban. (2 LP set — Columbia OSL 154)

MOORE, Douglas.
The Ballad of Baby Doe. Sills; Bible; Cassel; New York City Opera Orchestra
and Chorus. (3 LP set — Heliodor 25035)

Oratorios, Choral Work

BRITTEN, Benjamin.
Ceremony of Carols & Rejoice in The Lamb. Saramae Endich; Florence Kopleff.
(RCA Victor LSC 2759)
HANDEL, George Frederick.
L'Allegro ed Il Penseroso. Adele Addison; John McCollum; John Reardon.
(2 LP set — Decca DXS 7165)
Messiah. Adele Addison; Russell Oberlin; David Lloyd; William Warfield.
(2 LP set — Columbia M2S 603)
Messiah. Heather Harper; Helen Watts; John Wakefield; John Shirley-Quick.
(3 LP set — Philips PHS 3-992)
HAYDN, Joseph.
The Creation. Judith Raskin; John McCollum; Chester Watson. (2 LP set —
Decca DXSA 7191)
The Seasons. Heather Harper; Ryaland Davies; John Shirley-Quick. (3 LP set —
Philips PHS 3-911)
MENDELSSOHN, Felix.
Elijah. Dietrich Fischer-Dieskau; Gwyneth Jones; Janet Baker; Nicolai Gedda.
(3 LP set — Angel SC 3738)

Songs and Arias

BARBER, Samuel.
Knoxville: Summer of 1915. Eleanor Steber. (Odyssey 32 16 0230)
BRITTEN, Benjamin.
Serenade for Tenor, Horn & Strings, op. 31. Charles Bressler. (Decca DL 10 132)
CHANLER, Theodore.
Epitaphs. Phyllis Curtin. Also contains Lester Trimble's *Four
Fragments From Canterbury Tales.* Adele Addison. (Columbia CMS 6198)
IVES, Charles.
Songs. Marni Nixon. (Nonesuch 71209)
ROREM, Ned.
Songs. Phyllis Curtin; Charles Bressler; Donald Gramm. (Odyssey 32 16 0274)

Recital Discs

Marian Anderson: Songs at Eventide. (RCA Victor LSC 2769)
Janet Baker: Treasury of English Songs, 1597-1961. (Angel 36456)

Eileen Farrell: Songs America Loves. (London 25920)
Robert Merrill: Americana. (London SP 44065)
Jan Peerce: Sings Handel Arias. (Westminster 17028)
John Reardon: Songs. (Seraphim 12019)

Musical Theater

Carousel. (Richard Rodgers & Oscar Hammerstein II). Alfred Drake; Roberta Peters; Norman Treigle; Claramae Turner; Lee Venora; Jon Crain (Command RS 33-843 SD)
Lady in The Dark. (Kurt Weill & Ira Gershwin). Rise Stevens; John Reardon; Adolph Green (Columbia OS 2390)
The Popular Music Of Leonard Bernstein, Alfred Drake and Roberta Peters sing the . . . (Command RS 33-855)
Showboat. (Jerome Kern & Oscar Hammerstein II). John Raitt; Barbara Cook; William Warfield; Anita Darian (Columbia OL 5820)
The Student Prince (Sigmund Romberg & Dorothy Donnelly). Gordon MacRae; Dorothy Kirsten (Capitol SW 1841)

Folk, Dialect

Leon Bibb: Foment, Ferment, Free. (RCA Victor LSP 4202)
Kathleen Ferrier: English Folk Songs. (London 5411)
John McCormack: Memories. (Avoca 156)
Odetta: At the Gate of Horn. (Tradition Records TLP 1025)
Paul Robeson: Favorite Songs. (Monitor MPS 580)

Spoken Word

Best Loved Poems of Longfellow. Hal Holbrook. (Caedmon 1107)
Caedmon Treasury of Modern Poets Reading. (2 LP-set — Caedmon 2206)
Carl Sandburg Reads the Poems of Carl Sandburg. (Decca 9039)
Dramatic Readings from Eugene O'Neill. Jason Robards, Jr. (Columbia OL 5900)
Emily Dickinson; A SELF PORTRAIT: POEMS & LETTERS. Julie Harris. (2 LP set — Caedmon 2026)
John Brown's Body (Benet). Tyrone Power; Judith Anderson; Raymond Massey (2 LP set — Columbia OSL 181)
No Man Is An Island. Orson Welles. (Decca 9060)
Readings From Hamlet. Robert Vaughn; Diana Maddox; Joel Michaels (MGM S-4488)
The Rubaiyat of Omar Khayyam. Alfred Drake. (Caedmon TC 1023)
Treasury of Walt Whitman. 2 volumes. Alexander Scourby. (2 LP set — Spoken Arts 907/946)

Selected Bibliography

English diction as sung proved to be an unusually elusive subject for research; few works on the subject as such exist, and those mainly from the early part of the century. The broad range of titles reflects the author's search in related territory for material relevant to singing the language. Since how to sing sense in English (the major thrust of the book) requires more than a presentation, however detailed and explicit, of vowels and consonants, it became necessary to consult a variety of sources in preparation for this comprehensive study.

The selection includes works on linguistics with special emphasis on the structure of English; speech books and materials on phonetics (particularly of American English), on comparative sounds of languages, and on general voice and speech development including oral interpretation; books and articles on singing both contemporary and of historical interest, including vocal production and techniques, English diction, and choral singing.

This bibliography, of course, is not a complete list of writings which have contributed through the years to teaching the spoken and sung word. Nor should it be regarded as a listing which represents ideas espoused by the author. It is rather a personal selection of materials, whether in whole or in part, in a few pages or a chapter, which were useful and germane to the content of *To Sing in English* and which served at times to sharpen areas of disagreement as well as to affirm and define ideas.

Though not intended as a "guide to further study," these assembled books and pieces may well stimulate the reader to further exploration of an ever-rewarding subject.

From the Field of Linguistics:

Allen, Harold B., compiler. *Linguistics and English Linguistics.* (Goldentree Bibliographies.) New York, Appleton-Century-Crofts, Inc., 1966.

Brooks, Nelson. *Language and Language Learning: Theory and Practice.* 2nd ed. New York, Harcourt, Brace & World, 1964.

Fries, Charles Carpenter. *The Structure of English.* New York, Harcourt, Brace & World, 1952.

Hall, Robert A. *Linguistics and Your Language.* 2nd ed. New York, Doubleday & Company, 1960.

Harsh, Wayne. *Grammar Instruction Today.* (Davis Publications in English No. 1.) Davis, California, University of California, Department of English, 1965.

Hudspeth, Robert N., and Donald F. Sturtevant. *The World of Language: A Reader in Linguistics.* New York, American Book Company, 1967.

Joos, Martin *Acoustic Phonetics.* Language Monographic No. 23. Supplement to *Language,* Journal of the Linguistic Society of America, XXIV, 2. suppl. (April-June 1948).

Kerr, Elizabeth M., and Ralph M. Aderman. *Aspects of American English.* New York, Harcourt, Brace & World, 1963.

Mencken, H.L. *The American Language: An Inquiry into the Development of English in the United States.* 3rd ed. New York, Alfred A. Knopf, 1926.

Moulton, William G. *A Linguistic Guide to Language Learning.* New York, Modern Language Association of America, 1966.

Potter, Simeon. *Modern Linguistics.* New York, W.W. Norton & Company, 1964.

Searles, John R. *Structural and Traditional Grammar: Some Uses and Limitations.* Madison, Wisconsin, University of Wisconsin, 1965.

From the Field of Speech:

Agard, Frederick B., and Robert J. DiPietro. *The Sounds of English and Italian.* (Contrastive Structure Series.) Chicago, University of Chicago Press, 1965.

Avery, Elizabeth, Jane Dorsey, and Vera A. Sickels. *First Principles of Speech Training.* New York, D. Appleton-Century Company, 1928.

Bronstein, Arthur J. *The Pronunciation of American English.* New York, Appleton-Century-Crofts, Inc. 1960.

Carrell, James, and William R. Tiffany. *Phonetics: Theory and Application to Speech Improvement.* (McGraw-Hill Series in Speech.) New York, McGraw-Hill Book Company, 1960.

Eisenson, Jon. *The Improvement of Voice and Diction.* 2nd ed. New York, Macmillan Company, 1965.

Jones, Daniel. *An Outline of English Phonetics.* 7th ed. New York, E.P. Dutton & Company, 1948.

Kantner, Claude E., and Robert West. *Phonetics.* Rev. ed. New York, Harper & Brothers, 1960.

Lynch, Gladys E., and Harold C. Crain. *Projects in Oral Interpretation.* New York, Henry Holt & Company, 1959.

Moulton, William G. *The Sounds of English and German.* (Contrastive Structure Series.) Chicago, University of Chicago Press, 1962.

Parrish, Wayland Maxfield. *Reading Aloud.* 3rd ed. New York, Ronald Press Company, 1953.

Stanislavski, Constantin. *Building a Character*, trans. Elizabeth Reynolds Hapgood. New York, Theatre Arts Books, 1949. Chap. VII.

Thomas, Charles Kenneth. *An Introduction to the Phonetics of American English.* 2nd ed. New York, Ronald Press Company, 1958.

Turner, J. Clifford. *Voice and Speech in the Theatre.* 2nd ed. London, Sir Isaac Pitman & Sons, 1962.

Uris, Dorothy. *Everybody's Book of Better Speaking.* New York, David McKay Company, 1960.

From the Field of Vocal Production and Diction for Singing:

Appelman, D. Ralph. *The Science of Vocal Pedagogy; Theory and Application.* Bloomington, University of Indiana Press, 1967.

Arnold, William H. *French Diction for Singers and Speakers.* Boston, Oliver Ditson Company, 1912.

Christy, Van A. *Foundations in Singing: A Basic Textbook in the Fundamentals of Technic and Song Interpretation.* Dubuque, Iowa, Wm. C. Brown Company, 1965.

Coffin, Berton, et al. *Phonetic Readings of Songs and Arias.* Boulder, Colorado, Pruett Press, 1964.

Davies, David Ffrangcon. *The Singing of the Future.* London, John Land, 1905.

Drew, W.S. *Notes on the Technique of Song-Interpretation.* (Oxford Musical Essays.) London, Oxford University Press, 1926.
      "The Sounds of Words in Speech and Song." *Musical Times,* LXXXVIII, (July 1947) 219-22.

Garretson, Robert L. *Conducting Choral Music.* 2nd ed. Boston, Allyn and Bacon, 1965.

Greene, Harry Plunket. *Interpretation in Song.* London, Macmillan and Company, 1956.

Hawn, Henry Gaines. *Diction for Singers and Composers.* London, Publication Department of Hawn School, 1900.

Henderson, Charles, and Charles Palmer. *How to Sing for Money.* New York, Harcourt, Brace & Company, 1940.

Henderson, W.J. *The Art of the Singer.* New York, Charles Scribner's Sons, 1906.

Henschel, Sir George. *Articulation in Singing.* New York and London, The John Church Company, 1926.

Jacques, Reginald. *Voice-Training and Conducting in Schools.* 3rd ed. London, Oxford University Press, 1963.

Johnson, Edward. "Diction as an Aid to Interpretation." *Singing* (New York), IV, (1929), 23, 29-30.

Jones, Dora Duty. *Lyric Diction for Singers, Actors and Public Speakers.* New York, Harper & Brothers, 1913.

Kagen, Sergius. *On Studying Singing.* New York, Dover Publications, 1960.

Lawrence, T.B. "Music and Words." *Royal Musical Association Proceedings.* 70th Session (1944), pp. 75-84.

Lehmann, Lilli. *How to Sing.* New York, The Macmillan Company, 1902.

McClosky, David Blair. *Your Voice at Its Best.* Boston, Little, Brown and Company, 1959.

Marshall, Madeline. *The Singers' Manual of English Diction.* New York, G. Schirmer, 1947.

Rogers, Clara Kathleen. *English Diction: Part I: The Voice in Speech.* Philadelphia, Oliver Ditson Company, 1915.
   English Diction for Singers and Speakers. Published by the author, 309 Beacon St. Boston, 1912.

Strauss, Richard. *Recollections and Reflections,* ed. Willi Schuh, trans. L.J. Lawrence. London, Boosey & Hawkes, 1953.

Vennard, William. *Singing: The Mechanism and the Technique.* Rev. ed. New York, Carl Fischer, 1967.

Waring, Fred. *Tone Syllables.* Delaware Water Gap, Pennsylvania, Shawnee Press, 1951.

Wilcke, Eva. *German Diction in Singing,* trans. Arthur Edward Smith. Rev. Ed. New York, E.P. Dutton & Company, 1930.

Wragg, Gerald. "The Singers' Language." *Musical Opinion,* LXXIX, 945 (June 1956), 529-31.

GENERAL INDEX

two-way process of, 55-56
vowels as main vehicle of, 58
Length of consonants, legato and,
60-61
Liaison, defined, 57; *see also*
Legato
Lincoln Center for the Performing
Arts, 4
Linkage
defined, 15
purpose of, 54
See also Legato
Longfellow, William Wadsworth,
180, 210
Lowell, Amy, 207

Marlowe, Christopher, 218
Melba, Nellie, 11
Melodic line, speaking and singing
to, 267-68, 280-81
Mendelssohn, Felix, *Elijah,* 230
Menotti, Giancarlo
"The Black Swan," 116
The Consul, 237, 239
Merging, defined, 56: *see also*
Legato
Metropolitan Opera House, 4
Modification
for extreme registers, 77
sense stress and, 25-26
Modifiers
oversized, 29
overwhelming, 26
vital connection with, 25-26, 29
Moore, Douglas
Carry Nation, 46
The Devil and Daniel Webster,
27
Mozart, Wolfgang Amedeus
Don Giovanni, 67
Marriage of Figaro, 63, 132, 247
Music, choral, 9
My Fair Lady (musical), 18*n*

Negatives, accentuating, 27
Neutral sounds, 43, 47; *see also*
ŭ and ǝ *in* Index of Vowels
and Consonants
Neutralized vowels, 46, 118-20
Notation
syllable stress and, 47-49, 51
time value in, 162
weak word-types and, 37-39
Nouns
function of, 23
as strong word-types, 22, 29
Noyes, Alfred, 108, 114

Opera, English language
production of, 4-5
Opera Workshop of University of
Texas, 4*n*
O'Shaughnessy, Arthur William,
180

Passive audiences, effects of, 5
Pauses, adjustments in, 28
Percussive consonants, 59-60
adjacent, 64
percussives minus pitch
characteristics of, 233-34
See also t; p; k; ch; *in* Index
of Vowels and Consonants
percussives plus pitch
characteristics of, 206-7
See also d; b; g; j; *in* Index of
Vowels and Consonants
Personal pronouns, unstressing,
35, 40
Phoneme, 80
Pitch changes, consonants
between, 61-62
Poe, Edgar Allen, 95, 180
Poetry, best renderings of, 13
Porter, Cole, "Why Can't You
Behave?", 36, 136
Prepositions, unstressing, 33, 40

INDEX OF VOWELS AND CONSONANTS

THE SIXTEEN VOWELS

THE TWENTY–FIVE CONSONANTS

how to sing and link, 253-54
loss of, in American speech,
    173*n*, 253-54
o͞o related to, 253
recommended for song, 253
testing with text and music,
    257-58
voiced counterpart (w), 173
in word "while," 174*n*

See also w *above*
h [h], 254-58

on articulation chart, 164
how to sing and link, 255-56
as least sonorous consonant, 18
shaped as each vowel, 254
testing with text and music,
    257-58